Verbivore's
FEAST
Second Course

MORE
WORD & PHRASE
ORIGINS

ISBN-13: 978-1-56037-404-6 (hardcover)
ISBN-10: 1-56037-404-7 (hardcover)

ISBN-13: 978-1-56037-402-2 (softcover)
ISBN-10: 1-56037-402-0 (softcover)

For more information on our books write Farcountry Press,
P.O. Box 5630, Helena, MT 59604; call (800) 821-3874;
or visit www.farcountrypress.com.

Created, produced, and designed in the United States.
Printed in Canada.

10 09 08 07 06   1 2 3 4 5

Library of Congress Cataloging-in-Publication Data

Chrysti, the Wordsmith.
  Verbivore's feast : second course : more word & phrase origins/from
Chrysti the Wordsmith.
      p. cm.
  Includes bibliographical references and index.
  ISBN-13: 978-1-56037-404-6 (hardcover)
  ISBN-10: 1-56037-404-7 (hardcover)
  ISBN-13: 978-1-56037-402-2 (softcover)
  ISBN-10: 1-56037-402-0 (softcover)
  1. English language--Etymology. 2. English language--Terms and
phrases. I. Title.
  PE1571.C484 2006
  422--dc22
                                                2006025385

Verbivore's
FEAST
Second Course

Preface

We can both nibble and feast at dictionaries. Nibbling satisfies our need for proper word spelling, pronunciation, and definition. But the feasting begins when we open the dictionary and fall face first into the trough of words for the delight of it.

I love a good word gorging and see to it that I indulge in one almost every day. I have the good fortune to collect and read dictionaries for a living. My dictionary feastings eventually turn into two-minute word studies for "Chrysti the Wordsmith," a radio series recorded at KGLT-FM on the campus of Montana State University in Bozeman. This book is a collection of 338 radio scripts generated for the series between 2004 and 2006.

When you read a lot of dictionaries and specialized wordbooks, stories begin to emerge from their pages—the tales that flesh out our vocabulary and the events and lives behind it. If you trace the history of the word *bedlam,* for example, you'll find that it begins in a sleepy Judean village and winds up in the lunatic asylums of 15th century London. Any good standard dictionary will tell you that the word cereal comes from the name of the Roman goddess of the harvest, Ceres. Page through a dictionary of English language clichés, and you'll find that the expression *raising Cain* was inspired by the dysfunctions of an ancient family.

Anyone with an appetite for words and a bit of patience can uncover hundreds of stories just like these. If dictionary reading appeals to you, look in the bibliography for lexical works you might not be able to put down once you've cracked their covers. A nice handful of websites hosted by erudite cyberspace verbivores is included in the bibliography too.

On the other hand, if you'd rather just read this collection of word histories, then pull on up to the table for *Verbivore's Feast, Second Course*. If you listen to "Chrysti the Wordsmith" on the radio, you've probably heard these stories before.

And if you like this book, there's more to be had in an earlier work, *Verbivore's Feast: A Banquet of Word & Phrase Origins*.

Acknowledgments

Tim Crawford, Brian and Sally Barker, Brodie Cates, Phil Charles and KGLT-FM, Craig "Nous" Clark, Phil Gaines, Karen Gaulke, Barrett Golding, Marvin Grainger and staff at Yellowstone Public Radio, John Thomas, Farcountry Press, Stuart Weber, and all who have contributed word suggestions over the years.

Acro-

Someone with an abnormal fear of heights suffers from acrophobia. This term is a member of a small family of Greek-based words with the prefix *acro-* as the common element. *Acro* means top, summit, tip, or extremity. *Acrophobia* is etymologically the "fear of the summit," or, as we say in everyday English, "fear of heights."

The Greek morpheme *acro* also shows up in *acrobat,* another word for gymnast or one skilled in feats of balance. An acrophobe would never consider acrobatics, because this type of athletic activity is frequently performed aloft. *Acrobat* literally means "one who walks on tiptoe," probably referring to the distinctive deportment of such an athlete.

Acronym also belongs in this etymological family portrait. The word means "name from the tip" and refers to a word formed from the first or topmost letters of the words in a phrase. A poem or puzzle in which the first letters of each line form a word or a phrase is called an *acrostic,* another Greek word in the *acro* family meaning "top of the row or line" of poetry.

An *acropolis* was the fortified citadel of an ancient Greek city. *Acropolis* means "city at the top" or "on the heights." If the element *polis* for "city," sounds familiar, it's probably because you've heard it in names like Indianapolis and Minneapolis.

ADAM'S APPLE

The visible projection of the thyroid cartilage of the larynx is the laryngeal prominence, more commonly known as the *Adam's apple*. This feature, more visible in human males than females, is associated with the traditional biblical tale of humankind's fall from grace.

When Eve, the first woman, was induced by the serpent to eat the forbidden fruit of the tree of the knowledge of good and evil, she immediately invited her mate Adam to partake as well. This he did, and legend says that the bite lodged in his throat forever as a visible reminder of that original sin.

The story is remarkable for a couple of reasons. First, the account of the fruit lodging in Adam's throat is not mentioned in the Bible's book of Genesis, nor was the fruit ever identified as an apple. The Adam's apple story is clearly a folk accounting of the laryngeal prominence.

Attempts have been made to identify the fruit responsible for the "original sin," some scholars claiming it was a pomegranate and others, an apricot. But in our culture, Adam's disobedience will forever be associated with the apple. In fact, 18th century anatomists put an academic spin on the ancient biblical tale by calling the laryngeal prominence *pomum Adami*—Latin for *Adam's apple*.

ALLITERATIVE CLICHÉS

The cliché is one of the most characteristic aspects of American English. Clichés are expressions used so much they're often dismissed as throwaway verbal shorthand: *piece of cake, sick as a dog, calm before the storm, fish out of water* are common examples.

A generous percentage of our clichés owe their popularity—and some would say overuse—to alliteration, the repetition of sounds or syllables within a phrase.

Consider *bolt from the blue,* an expression that repeats the initial *b* sound. This cliché refers to an unexpected event that seems to strike like lightning from a cloudless sky. *Bolt from the blue* was first seen in print in 1857.

The *lap* in the alliterative cliché *lap of luxury* is a metaphor for an environment of nurture and comfort. Those cradled in the lap of luxury were raised in affluent circumstances.

Doing something *to beat the band* is an alliterative way of saying "to perform with gusto." When you beat the band, you metaphorically drown out the noisiest ensemble.

The expression *the more the merrier* is an abbreviated version of *the more the merrier, the fewer, the better fare.* The entire expression was published as early as 1530. Today only the alliterative truncation remains, and it means that the greater the number of participants, the more the fun increases.

The word *Amazon* does triple duty as the name of a race of mythical warrior women, a South American river, and an e-commerce leviathon, amazon.com. What's the connection here?

The Amazons, a legendary tribe of women living in the Caucausus Mountains, were admired throughout the ancient world for their skill in battle. Talented archers and fearless in combat, the Amazons fought on the side of Troy in the Trojan War.

The myth persists to this day that the Amazons were so dedicated to warfare that they cut or burned off their right breasts in order to draw a bowstring more skillfully. This account is reinforced by a theory that Amazon comes from a Greek word meaning "without a breast." But most word scholars dismiss the idea, convinced instead that *Amazon* derives from an Iranian term that means "fighting together."

In 1541, Spanish voyager Francisco de Orellana ascended an enormous South American river, which he named *Rio Amazones* after a tribe of warrior women he claimed to have encountered on his journey.

This ancient word entered the digital age in 1994 when entrepreneur Jeff Bezos applied it to his fledgling e-business, amazon.com. The December 1999 edition of *Time* magazine put it this way: "As far as names go, Amazon is a perfect choice. The wild Amazon River, with it's limitless branches, remains an ideal metaphor for a company that now sells everything from power tools to CDs."

Anthropos

The Greek word *anthropos* is the matriarch of a large family of modern English terms, including *anthropology, anthropomorphic, anthropocentric, anthropophagy,* and *misanthrope.*

Anthropos means "man, humankind, or human being." This Greek-based root is best showcased in the term *anthropology,* the science of human beings, specifically the study of their customs, languages, beliefs, and physical characteristics.

To assign human attributes to animals or inanimate objects is to *anthropomorphize* them—an activity common among animal lovers, who often attribute human emotions to their pets or create human language dialogues for them. We rely on *anthropomorphic simile* when we speak of, for example, the hands of time, the eye of a needle, or the teeth of a storm.

Anthropocentric literally means "centering on human beings." The doctrine of anthropocentrism asserts that the universe revolves around humankind, and that all things must be interpreted in terms of human values.

The unusual word *anthropophagy* is simply a Greek-based synonym for cannabalism. The word literally means "the eating of humans."

Finally, we come to *misanthrope,* which is also a member in good standing of the *anthropos,* or "mankind," family. Borrowing a form of the Greek word for hate, *miseo,* a misanthrope is a jaundiced, unfortunate "hater of human beings."

The expression *apple of my eye* is a linguistic marker of something cherished with the greatest regard. Sons and daughters are often the apples of their parent's eyes. Sweethearts, too, may use this fond phrase. Literally interpreted, of course, the idiom seems to make no sense. But a brief look at the history of anatomy reveals the logic behind the apple of the eye.

The phrase is an ancient one, appearing in print as early as A.D. 885. It reflects the ancient belief that the eye's pupil was not just circular but spherical, like any type of round fruit...say, an apple.

The pupil, or the "apple" of the eye, the essential seat of vision, is precious and fragile and must be cherished and protected. We shield our faces and close our eyes when physically threatened, reflexively guarding our vision. So, whoever is as precious to us as our eyesight is metaphorically the apple of our eye.

This expression occurs several times in the Bible's Old Testament, most notably in a verse of Deuteronomy that describes God's love for Israel.

Incidentally, the word *apple,* which has cognates in all the Germanic languages, was once the generic word for all manner of fruits—plums, peaches, apricots, as well as the fruit we now exclusively call the apple.

APTRONYMS

A *pseudonym* is a "false name," a *homonym* is a "same name," and a *patronym* is a "father's name." *Synonym, antonym,* and *acronym* are others in this etymological family.

One of the most entertaining of the *-onyms* is *aptronym,* or, as some prefer, *aptonym.* This word literally means "apt name" and refers to a moniker especially suited to the profession, character, or behavior of its owner.

Aptronyms have a long history in English literature. In the 17th century Christian allegory *Pilgrim's Progress,* author John Bunyan "aptronymed" two of his characters Mr. Worldly Wiseman and Mr. Talkative. Shakespeare's character Hotspur in *King Henry IV* is quick-tempered and impatient. We can find "apt" titles in contemporary popular culture as well. Snidely Whiplash is the aptronym of the black-caped, moustache-twirling nemisis of Dudley Do-Right. Sweet Polly Purebred is a dog who is always rescued from peril by her hero in the 1960s cartoon series *Underdog.*

Aptronyms exist in the real world as well. Consider these famous examples: Larry Speaks, former White House spokesperson; Sally Ride, astronaut; poet William Wordsworth; tennis player Anna Smashnova. Lorena Bobbitt is without a doubt the past century's most infamous aptronym.

Local examples from around the country illustrate the serendipitious aspect of real-life aptronyms: the barber named Dan Druff, or James Bugg, the exterminator. And somewhere in this great land of ours is a cardiologist with the aptronym Dr. Valentine, and a Sharpei dog named B Flat.

Zeus, the king of the Greek gods, was a notorious philanderer. His wife, Hera, ever suspicious of her husband's illicit activities, tried to foil his many affairs. After Zeus seduced a beautiful princess named Io, he turned her into a white heifer to hide her identity from his jealous wife. But wily Hera discovered Zeus's deception and demanded that he give her the heifer as a present.

Hera tied the heifer to a tree and appointed one of her servants, Argus, to stand guard so that Zeus could not seduce the princess again. Argus was a powerful giant, and especially well-suited to Hera's task since his body was covered with a hundred eyes looking in every direction.

In a strategic repartee, the god Mercury, disguised as a shepherd, was sent by Zeus to distract Argus and reclaim the princess. Hour after hour, Mercury recited tedious stories until every one of Argus's hundred watchful eyes surrendered to sleep.

The modern English adjective *Argus-eyed* is a linguistic reminder of this Olympian drama. Though the giant ultimately drifted off to sleep when lulled by Mercury's boring tales, his reputation for vigilance remains intact in his name: *Argus-eyed* means keen-sighted, attentive, alert.

At the Drop of a Hat

To do something *at the drop of a hat* is to respond without hesitation. Interesting, considering that our contemporary signals for quick action might be, say, a referee's whistle or a starting gun. Though the notion of a dropped hat might lack the pizazz of these more modern symbols, the cliché persists. What custom underlies this saying *at the drop of a hat?*

Brewer's Dictionary of Phrase and Fable suggests that the expression was hatched and reared in the American West of the mid-19th century: "The expression alludes to the American frontier practice of dropping a hat as a signal for a fight to begin, usually the only formality observed."

Christine Ammer, in her cliché dictionary *Have a Nice Day, No Problem!* concurs, adding that the saying "is thought to come from the practice of dropping or waving a hat as a starting signal for a race, fight, or other event."

The *Oxford English Dictionary*, normally so helpful, doesn't offer any biographies of our expression, but it does include historical citations like this one, a playful excerpt from a 1944 novel by Mae Sharp: "Miss Cream's visit coincided with a week of superb weather. At the drop of a hat she stripped and sunbathed, or rather, a hat was the only thing she didn't drop."

Auto-

Behold the prefix. It may be small but it's mighty, like the tiny bit in a horse's mouth that subtly commands the direction of the whole beast. Consider how the prefix *auto-* steers a whole corral of words: *automobile, autograph, autonomy, autocrat, autopsy, automatic, autobiography.*

Auto- is a Greek-based prefix that means "self." An automobile is a self-powered vehicle; it does not rely on an animal to pull it.

An *autograph* is a signature written by a celebrity for an admirer. At its heart, the word means "self-written," or "written by one's own hand."

An *autobiography* is a memoir of one's life, or "bio,"— "graphically" produced by the self. A self-taught person is an *autodidact. Autonomy* is the right of self-government—*nomo* meaning law. An *autocrat,* etymologically, is a "self-ruler," or one who is guided by his own rules.

Autopsy and *autism* are also members of this linguistic family, guided as they are by the prefix *auto-.* An autopsy is a post-mortem examination, but literally the word means "seeing for one's self."

Autism is the word for a mental disorder characterized by the experience of being imprisoned in one's interior world. *Autism* simply means "self-ism."

Avocado

The avocado tree is native to Mexico and Central America, and its fruit has been a vital constituent of the local diet there for thousands of years. When the Spanish penetrated the heart of the Aztec empire in the early 1500s, they found this unfamiliar fruit both palatable and nutritious. An early Spanish historian noted that the flesh of the avocado tasted like butter. Later, English-speaking sailors who voyaged with avocados aboard called the fruit "subaltern's butter" and "midshipman's butter."

The Aztecs, in their native language Nahuatl, called this delicacy *ahuacatl;* it was this word that the Spanish were trying to pronounce when they came up with *avocado,* which, oddly enough, is also an early Spanish word for a lawyer or barrister. In some records, the Spanish word is rendered *aguacate.*

When the Aztecs pounded the ahuacatl into a sauce and flavored it with the tomatoes they grew, they called the concoction *ahuacamolli,* from which the Spanish-Mexican word *guacamole* derives.

But let's take a look at the etymology behind the original Aztec word. *Ahuacatl* not only refers to the food of the avocado tree, it also means "testicle," because of the suggestive shape of the fruit. Possibly because of its resemblance to this part of the male anatomy, the Aztecs considered the avocado an aphrodisiac as well as a nutritious mainstay of their diet.

Baby Boom

Between the years 1946 and 1964, a staggering number of Americans were born—about 76 million. This post-World War II natal bonanza is commonly known as the *baby boom;* Americans from that generation currently account for about one-third of the U.S. population.

Though it's unclear who coined the alliterative expression *baby boom* (which suggests an explosion of infants), its first use occurred in the December 1941 issue of *Life* magazine—five years before the beginning of the era it would later identify. Then, in July 1971, *Scientific American* magazine used the term in quotes to refer specifically to the dramatic postwar increase in births.

Soon after came the term *baby boomer,* for a member of the postwar kid cohort. This expression showed up in the January 21, 1974, issue of *Time* magazine. Close on the heels of *baby boomer* came its clipped version, *boomer,* in 1982, followed in 1984 by *boomer generation.*

The phrase continues to morph. When the adult children of boomers return to live with their parents, they are dubbed *boomerangs.* Today, aging boomers with expanding family trees are designated *grandboomers* as they dote on their children's children.

BABY RUTH

Americans have been carrying on a love affair with the candy bar for over a century. In 1903, Milton Hershey introduced the all-chocolate Hershey bar and sold it for a nickel. The Goo Goo Cluster came next in 1912, followed in 1920 by the Oh Henry! The Milky Way and the Butterfinger showed up in 1923.

Another perennial confectionary favorite is the Baby Ruth bar, introduced by the Curtiss Candy Company in 1920. Was there a real Baby Ruth who inspired the name of this sweet treat?

Possibly. In 1891, Francis Cleveland, wife of President Grover Cleveland, gave birth to their daughter Ruth, who was affectionately known to the American public as "Baby Ruth." She died of diphtheria at age 12 in 1904, but the Curtiss Company maintained that their candy bar was named in Baby Ruth's honor, even though she was sixteen years in the grave when this candy was introduced in 1920.

Skeptics, however, claim that the name was taken from baseball legend Babe Ruth. That the candy was named *Baby Ruth* when the home-run king was at the height of his fame does seem to be more than coincidence. Some say that the Curtiss Candy Company unfairly exploited Ruth's celebrity, since they paid him no royalties for the use of his name.

BACKRONYMS

English speakers use acronyms every day: NASA, SARS, ZIP code, and NAFTA are examples of acronyms, words made up of the first letters of a phrase.

Everyone knows about acronyms, but have you ever heard of a *backronym?* This is the result of taking an existing word and making up a phrase based on its letters. For the lexically frolicsome, bacronyming can be great sport. An example: "Stupid Pointless Annoying Messages" comes from backronyming *spam*.

Backronymese seems to be popular among opinionated automobile enthusiasts. Most know what the backronym of Ford is: "Fix Or Repair Daily." For Jeep: "Just Empty Every Pocket." "Drips Oil, Drops Grease Everywhere" is the backronym of Dodge, and Fiat is cynically spelled out as "Fix It Again Tomorrow." The Saturn's backronym is "Sorry About That Unusual Rattling Noise," and Mazda becomes "Made At Zoo by Demented Apes."

Fans of Arthur Conan Doyle have a society called Sherlock Holmes Enthusiastic Readers League of Criminal Knowledge, or SHERLOCK, a creative, if strained, backronym. In 1982, admirers of comedian Jackie Gleason organized the Royal Association for the Longevity and Preservation of the Honeymooners, or RALPH, which happens to be the first name of Gleason's TV character, Ralph Cramden.

Our word *backronym* started showing up in print in the early 1980s and is a blending of the words *back* and the Greek suffix *-nym,* meaning "name."

The common expression *look before you leap* was inspired by one of the fables of Aesop. Shakespeare was the first to record the phrase *at one fell swoop,* and from the Old Testament comes the idiom *handwriting on the wall.*

These are just three examples of the hundreds of English clichés that have come to us from literature, fable, and history. But one of our most beloved expressions comes from a wartime cartoon caption published in 1941.

The cartoon, submitted by an artist named Peter Arno, shows a crashed plane with its nose buried in the ground. The pilot is seen parachuting to safety in the background, while military personnel and ambulances race to the crash site. In the center of the scene an aircraft designer, rolled-up blueprints under his arm, strides away from the demolished plane, saying, "Well, back to the old drawing board."

This caption became a permanent American cliché in very short order. We all use it when we are convinced that a scheme has gone awry and needs redesigning. We can find it quoted almost daily in the print media, like this example from the *New York Times* in 1987: "The story of the W-4 is not over yet. The IRS is back at the drawing board...thinking about...a redesign of the employee tax withholding form."

Have you ever noticed the many magnificent words in the English language that refer to nonsense? *Claptrap, poppycock, hooey, horsefeathers, gobbledygook, bunkum, hogwash, baloney, hokum, balderdash*. Let's shine the eytmological spotlight on the last of the list: *balderdash*.

Some may recognize this as the name of a word bluffing game that was introduced in 1986. But the term *balderdash* is of considerable antiquity. In the early 1600s it referred to a jumbled mixture of liquids such as milk and beer, beer and wine, or ale and mineral waters. In 1629, playwright Ben Jonson wrote, "Beer or butter-milk, mingled together....It is against my free-hold...To drink such balder-dash."

Some sources express uncertainty about the origin of the *balderdash* that means piffle or nonsense. But others think it reasonable to assume that the word arose from the notion of an incongruous mixture of beer and buttermilk or wine and beer. For my money, such a commingling provides a perfect metaphor for the balderdash that is a sensless jumble of verbosity.

BALL BOUNCES, COOKIE CRUMBLES

When we need to convey resignation to a life circumstance verbally, we often rely on the well-worn expressions *that's the way the ball bounces* or *that's the way the cookie crumbles.*

As familiar as these American idioms are, their origins are elusive. This is surprising since both are of recent vintage; they didn't begin showing up in print until the mid-1950s.

In 1957, for example, singer Pat Boone said, "Maybe some year someone will say I was big, and the person he's talking to will have to be told why I was big and who I was. Guess that's the way the ball bounces." A character in Edward Albee's 1960 play *Zoo Story* voices his disappointment and resignation about not having an heir when he says, "Well, naturally, every man wants a son but...that's the way the cookie crumbles."

What is the logic of the bouncing ball and crumbling cookie in these clichés? There are no reliable explanations, only these educated guesses. A ball bouncing on an irregular surface can certainly be unpredictable. Ultimately, the erratic motion of the ball, and not human skill, may determine the result of a game—and *that's the way the ball bounces.* A cookie disintegrates into random bits, and the crumbs, although still desirable, cannot be neatly consumed—and *that's the way the cookie crumbles.*

BALONEY

In a campaign speech in 1936, New York governor Alfred E. Smith is supposed to have said, "No matter how thin you slice it, it's still baloney." Governor Smith was not, as any slang-slinging American would know, literally referring to sausage. This *baloney* meant foolishness, lies, pretentious nonsense. In a 1929 film called *Great Gabbo,* one character complains about another for "bowing down, clicking his heels, and all that sort of imported baloney."

Though bologna sausage was developed in its namesake Italian city Bologna, it's not too clear where the *baloney,* meaning "bunk, prevarication," comes from. One suggestion is that sausage of any variety, including bologna, is so full of scrap meat and unidentifiable parts that it's really a type of "junk" food, thus providing a metaphor for verbal garbage.

Others claim there is no connection to the sausage. Some think the word is an alternate pronounciation of the Gypsy term *pelone,* slang for "testicles," making *baloney* analagous to *bollocks,* a Britishism that means "nonsense."

The word is sometimes pronounced "bull-oney," making it a euphemism for *bullshit.* It's also been fashioned into a handy reduplication: *phony-baloney,* along with its mock-Latin sibling, *phonus-balonus.*

It's a universal custom to shroud unpleasant or sensitive topics with indirect terminology. Americans consider it good form to put linguistic fig leaves over such uncomfortable notions as death or military force. These less-offensive terms are called *euphemisms.*

Over the decades, English speakers have devised an array of euphemisms to mask our anxiety surrounding certain bodily functions and where they take place: *restroom, bathroom, commode, toilet, lavatory.* Let's take a look at the pedigree of some of these euphemistic terms.

Commode was originally the name of a style of chest of drawers. French for "convenient" or "suitable," the commode became a 19th century designation for a piece of furniture containing a concealed chamber pot. *Commode* is now a euphemistic synonym for a toilet.

The word *toilet* is also French in origin, from *toilette,* originally meaning "dressing room." The word was expanded in the 19th and 20th centuries to include a room with "facilities" (yet another euphemism).

A lavatory, prior to the 1800s, was a place for washing, or a room containing the implements for cleaning hands and face. This is reflected in the source of the word *lavatory,* which is the Latin verb *lavare,* "to wash."

Public toilets are commonly called *restrooms,* although visitors to such places don't exactly "rest" in them. This euphemisim was coined in early 20th century America.

BEAT AROUND THE BUSH

To beat around the bush is to approach an objective indirectly, to equivocate, engage in circumlocution, be vague. With all these concise synonyms available to us, why do we still use the rather odd but remarkably persistent English idiom *beat around the bush?*

The custom and technology that inspired this expression are more than eight hundred years old. "Beating the bushes" was a traditional European method of flushing wild animals from cover. Beaters were employed to drive game across the fields by flailing the underbrush with sticks. A company of archers or netters waited opposite to dispatch the animals.

The hunters, skilled marksmen, brought down the game, while the beaters were involved in the secondary, less demanding task of driving the animals from cover. Those who beat around the bush rushed the game but never dispatched the target.

Likewise, someone who circles an issue without engaging it directly is said, like the ancient game drivers, to *beat around the bush,* but never to actually bag the quarry.

Have you ever been curious about the origins of common English phrases like this one? Check any library or bookstore for cliché dictionaries that outline the biographies of everyday expressions such as *beat around the bush,* or *rule of thumb,* or *live high on the hog.*

BEDLAM

The ancient city of Bethlehem, just south of Jerusalem, has for centuries been revered by Christians as the birthplace of Christ. According to tradition, Mary and Joseph found shelter in a manger in a cave in Bethlehem, where Mary gave birth to her divine son. In the Hebrew language, *Bethlehem* means "house of bread."

This ancient name was given to a hospital established a continent away, in London, in the 14th century. Originally intended for the sick and indigent, Bethlehem Hospital provided shelter and succor to all.

Then, in the 16th century, Bethlehem Hospital, its name telescoped to Bedlam Hospital, became a lunatic asylum. As the decades passed, it gained an unsavory reputation for inhumane treatment of its inmates. Members of London's leisure class, seeking novel forms of amusement, were admitted to the asylum to watch and mock the behavior of the patients.

Gradually, the name of this hospital became inextricably associated with the confusion exhibited by the mentally ill. *Bedlam,* contracted from *Bethlehem,* is now a synonym for disorder, uproar, and panic.

Did you know that when you *go berserk* you are, etymologically, behaving like an ancient Norse warrior?

The berserkers were a cult of Norsemen renowned for their ferocity on the battlefield. In some traditions, berserkers prepared for war by inducing hallucinogenic trances. Then, clad only in bruin pelts, these warriors rushed into battle, roaring and howling like their totem animal, the bear. In ancient sagas, the berserkers claimed to be invincible in combat, with iron blades said to glance off their flesh. The berserkers savagely slashed and grappled with their enemies until they were victorious, slain, or overcome with exhaustion.

While these warriors were certainly a battlefield asset, they were also terrifying to their own people. A berserker, while in a trance, might slay his kinsman or destroy his own property. Berserking became associated with paganism, witchcraft, and animal worship, and by the 12th century the cult was banned.

Berserk is an Old Norse word meaning "bear shirt," a reference to the warrior's battle attire. But in modern English the word means "frenzied, destructive, or wildly emotional," the disposition of the ancient berserkers, the "bear shirt wearers."

THE BEST LAID PLANS

When our most carefully fashioned strategies are ruined by unforeseen events, a familiar response is to repeat this philosphical cliché: "Well, the best laid plans of mice and men..."

This expression of resignation is another common saying extracted from the canon of English poetry. Scots bard Robert Burns penned the verses that inspired this phrase in the late 1700s. Burns, sometimes called the "Ploughman Poet," was born to a farm family in 1759. With an early talent for writing, Robert began composing verses celebrating Scottish country life and romance while he was still a teenager.

One windy autumn day, while he and his brother were plowing a piece of land, Robert spied a field mouse scurrying from a freshly turned furrow. The small incident inspired him to compose *To A Mouse, On Turning Up Her Nest with the Plough*. In the poem, Burns apologizes to the mouse for disturbing her home, forcing her to build another in the face of the coming wind and frost of winter. But, he adds philosophically, mice are not alone in experiencing such tragedies and frustrated plans, because, as he writes, "The best laid schemes o' mice an' men/Gang aft a-gley."

Though in popular speech the famous line has been altered to "the best laid plans of mice and men often go awry," the meaning remains true to Burns's original sentiments.

America's Corn Belt is most commonly identified with the Midwestern states where corn is the predominant cash crop. The southern states from Florida to California make up the Sun Belt. And with Utah declaring jello the official state snack food, it and portions of the surrounding states have been nicknamed the Jello Belt. But where exactly is America's Bible Belt? Is it a geographically delineated region, like the belts mentioned above?

The man responsible for coining this term is H. L. Mencken, social critic and journalist for the *Baltimore Sun*. Also a critic of religion, Mencken, in the early 1920s, began searching for a term that described, in his words, "parts of the Republic where Beelzebub is still as real as Babe Ruth...and men drink raw fusel oil hot from the still—for example, in the rural sections of the Middle West and everywhere in the South save a few walled towns." Mencken went on to say that his Bible Belt existed anywhere that "Baptist and Methodist barbarism reigned."

Today, nearly a century after Mencken coined this term, the boundaries of a so-called Bible Belt are extrememly elastic. Yet the region is perceived by most to exist roughly in the South, from the Carolinas to New Mexico, where there are concentrated communities of religious conservatives whose beliefs are Bible-based.

BIGWIG

In 1624, France's King Louis XIII covered his prematurely balding head with a wig. With this one act of vanity, the 23-year-old monarch ignited a fashion trend that raged throughout Europe for the next century and a half.

Imitating King Louis' whim, French courtiers and nobles began sporting wigs. By the 1660s, wealthy, fashionable English aristocrats took up the trend, and throughout the 1700s no respectable European male would be seen in public without his custom-designed hairpiece.

Fashioned from locks of human hair and sewn, curled, and powdered by wigmakers, a man's *peruke* (as it was sometimes called) was an indicator his socioeconomic status. The more important the man, the more elaborate the headgear. The wealthy owned several hairpieces and could afford to finish them with ribbons and scented powders.

Clergymen, barristers, judges, shopkeepers, and even common soldiers paid handsomely for the wigs appropriate to their stations. Certain perukes were so valuable that thieves made handsome profits by stealing them from the heads of their owners and reselling them to wig makers.

This mania for elaborate hairpieces began to wane near the close of the 1700s, but the custom left a permanent linguistic reminder—the term *bigwig,* referring to an important, powerful or wealthy person, one who, in an earlier century, could afford a peruke of notable proportions.

Humans have long admired birds for their beauty and envied them for their freedom of flight. Paradoxically, we've also included certain bird names in our arsenal of verbal insults.

For example, *dodo,* a Portuguese slang term, was the common name given to a now-extinct bird of the Mauritius Islands. Having no natural enemies, the creature was both flightless and guileless, and as such it was easily captured. In the 15th century, Portuguese mariners called it *dodo,* meaning "fool, idiot." The notion of the bird as intellectually inferior is found in the expression *dumb as a dodo.*

Popular perceptions of the turkey, likewise, have not been so favorable. Since it's often an easy target, the turkey is not considered cunning. To call someone a *turkey* is to imply that he is bumbling or incompetent. A failed, flopped theatrical performance is often branded a *turkey.*

Though the parrot is both beautiful and intelligent, its name, when applied to people, is not complimentary. The parrot cannot understand human language, but it has the capacity to mimic the sound of words. So, to *parrot* someone is to merely memorize and repeat words and phrases mechanically.

Incidentally, from the 14th through the 18th century, parrots were called *popinjays,* and this term appears in both Chaucer's and Shakespeare's works as a contemptuous term for a vain person who repeats words without comprehending their meaning.

BLACKGUARD

We American English speakers don't use the term *blackguard* much any more, and that's unfortunate because it is eminently serviceable. Today's word, pronounced "blaggard," is synonymous with *scoundrel, ruffian,* and *rogue,* terms that are likewise associated with villains of bygone ages.

The *Oxford English Dictionary* admits that the origin of *blackguard* is unclear but offers several etymological possibilities. When the word began appearing in print in the 1530s, it referred to a kitchen servant in charge of the pans and pots in a royal household. Such a scullion allegedly became as filthy as the vessels he cleaned and was known sardonically as the "black guard" of the kitchen utensils.

Another possibility offered by the *OED* associates the word with elite palace guards in black uniform, or, more darkly, with a cadre of evil or black-hearted attendants to an important official.

The *Dictionary of the Vulgar Tongue,* published in England in 1785, calls *blackguard* "a term said to be derived from a number of dirty tattered and roguish boys, who attended at the horse guards...to black the boots and shoes of the soldiers, or to do any other dirty offices; these...were nicknamed the black guards."

In any case, the moniker *blackguard* was a "term of the utmost opprobrium" between the 15th and 18th centuries. It's lately lost its sting; in fact, it's nearly impossible to find the word in any 21st century conversation.

BLARNEY

A word we associate with the legendary Irish gift of gab, the facility of smooth speech, loquacious eloquence, is *blarney*.

Blarney is the name of a village a few miles to the north of Cork in Ireland, dominated by an imposing stone castle built there in 1446. In 1602, the castle at Blarney came under siege by the English under the rule of Queen Elizabeth I.

Elizabeth sent her emissary to Blarney castle to demand the surrender of its ruler, Dermot McCarthy. McCarthy promised absolute compliance but asked the queen's emissary to return another day to discuss terms of surrender.

Days turned into weeks, then into months, as McCarthy devised sweet and eloquent reasons to postpone surrender of Blarney castle. The emissary became a local laughingstock as he repeatedly caved in to McCarthy's cajolery.

Blarney became synonymous with flattery and loquacious prevarication. A legend emerged that whoever kissed the distinctive triangular stone imbedded in the castle wall—the famous Blarney Stone—would be blessed with the powers of persuasive eloquence. Or, as *Slanguage: A Dictionary of Irish Slang* so delicately puts it, the stone "is supposed to give to whoever kisses it the peculiar privilege of deviating from veracity with unblushing countenance whenever it may be convenient."

One of the ways new words enter the English language is by the blending of two existing words. Some classic examples of well-established blended words are *brunch,* from *breakfast* and *lunch; smog,* from *smoke* and *fog;* and *motel,* from *motor* and *hotel.*

Though these examples are decades old, new blend words appear on the wordscape every year. Consider the recent coinages *Japlish, Spanglish,* and *Germlish*—blends of *English* with the names of other languages to describe a hybrid of the two.

Television has spawned a host of blends such as *infomercial, infotainment,* and *televangelist.* A rock documentary has become a *rockumentary,* and a "scripted documentary" as entertainment is a *mockumentary.*

Technically, a blend consists of the beginning of one word and the tail end of another, with the second word controlling the meaning of the whole. Reflecting this logic, says linguist David Crystal, author of the *Cambridge Encyclopedia of the English Language,* "brunch is a kind of lunch, not a kind of breakfast—which is why the [word] is brunch, and not, say, lunkfast." Similarly, *Jazzercise* is exercise based on jazz moves rather than an aerobic form of jazz dance.

Writer Lewis Carroll imaginatively called these types of terms *portmanteau words.* In Carroll's day, a portmanteau was a suitcase with two separate compartments. When snapped together, the compartments made a complete carrying case, just as two separate words, blended, form one.

An Internet search for the expression *blessing in disguise* indicates that this sentiment is extremely popular. Online articles innumerate scores of circumstances that writers consider blessings in disguise, from high oil prices that stimulate alternative energy technologies to the basketball player whose knee injuries force him to pursue a new and unanticipated career.

A blessing in disguise is, of course, an apparent misfortune that turns into something beneficial. This joins the roster of optimistic catchphrases such as *every cloud has a silver lining, April showers bring May flowers,* and *when one door closes, another opens.*

As is the case with so many of our bright lines, this one has its genesis in literature. The expression first appeared in a poem by 18th century English poet James Hervey, who wrote, "E'en crosses from his sov'reign hand are blessings in disguise." When Hervey wrote "crosses," in this poem, he meant burdens or trials. The phrase was common in the 1800s and has been considered a cliché now for about a century.

Blood Is Thicker than Water

When we use the expression *blood is thicker than water,* we're not literally comparing the viscosity of the two fluids. *Blood is thicker than water* is an English-language idiom, shorthand for the notion that family relationships are more enduring than, say, friendships or business associations.

The sentiment appeared in print in a collection of English proverbs in 1670. So the properties of blood and water have, for centuries, provided metaphor for the nature of relationships. That blood leaves a stain when spilled suggests permanence, whereas water can evaporate without leaving a mark.

We've also traditionally cherished the belief that blood is literally the substance shared among family members. This is reflected in statements like "she's my blood relative," or "he's got the blood of aristocrats flowing in his veins." Recent scientific investigations, however, suggest that DNA, not blood, is the stuff that relatives have in common.

Does that mean we'll soon be saying "DNA is thicker than water," or "He's my DNA relative"? Not likely. As linguistically playful as we American English speakers are, we're extremely reluctant to alter our beloved idiomatic formulas.

BOGART

In 1999, the American Film Institute named Humphrey Bogart the top male movie star of the 20th century. Bogart, with seventy-five feature films to his credit, made quite an imprint on American popular culture. Through his roles in such film classics as *The Maltese Falcon, Casablanca,* and *The African Queen,* Bogart helped define the reckless yet courageous hero type in American cinema. Though his characters snarled and menaced, they often revealed a kind heart and a strong moral code.

Humphrey Bogart is probably the only actor to have his surname turned into a verb—twice. His brash, tough-guy onscreen persona inspired a phrase that means to bully, coerce, intimidate; that is, to *pull a Bogart,* or simply *to bogart.* These expressions began appearing in print early in the 1950s.

Then, in the late '60s, *bogart* acquired a strange new verbal personality. The actor's name showed up in the counterculture song "Don't Bogart That Joint," by Elliot Ingber, a tune featured in the 1969 film *Easy Rider.* To *bogart a joint* meant to suspend a marijuana cigarette between the lips for an inordinate amount of time, in the manner of the actor who habitually squinted through the smoke of his dangling cigarette. Bogart, who died in 1959 of throat cancer, was a real-life chain smoker who incorporated the habit into every character he created.

Boob, Booby

A boob is someone you don't want to be seen with, much less be seen as. A boob is a dolt, a buffoon, a clod. How did this epithet arrive in the English vocabulary?

Boob is the clipped variant of the original moniker *booby*, which is thought to have come from the Spanish *bobo*, meaning "fool." *Bobo*, in turn, is a derivative of the older Latin word *balbus*, which means "stammering." *Balbus* comes from the same source as our modern word *babble*. Our disparaging words *boob* and *booby* are heir to the ancient Latin belief that stammering was evidence of mental deficiency.

Booby, meaning a fool or dupe, was first cited in English text around 1600. The epithet inspired an imaginative taxonomy of *booby* words over the centuries. There's *booby-trap*, originally a practical joke for an unsuspecting victim; *booby prize*, one awarded to the loser of the game; *booby hatch*, insane asylum; and *boob tube*, television.

American journalist and critic H. L. Mencken fashioned a suite of *boob* words in cynical reference to members of the American middle class. One was *booboisie*, or the general public, consisting, in Mencken's view, of nothing but boobs. Another was *boobocracy*, a political force of the middle class ruled by *boobocrats*.

The plural form, *boobs*, slang for "breasts," cannot be traced to a Latin source. This word might be connected to a dialectal German word *Bübbi*, which means "teat."

Born with a Silver Spoon

Some are born into poverty, some are born into modest circumstances, and others are born with silver spoons in their mouths. These fortunate ones have inherited wealth, status, and privilege.

Though we've retained the phrase *born with a silver spoon in his mouth,* we've forgotten the custom behind the expression. How does a silver spoon symbolize wealth and privilege? Why not gold, or property?

The spoon in the phrase probably refers to apostle spoons, made of silver or pewter, with images of a Christian apostle stamped on the end of the handle. It was a tradition in 16th and 17th century Europe for godparents to present a newborn with apostle spoons in sets of thirteen, consisting of the twelve apostles and one of Christ.

Only the wealthy could afford to purchase a set of thirteen silver spoons for a baptismal or christening gift. While poor children ate from wooden utensils, children of wealthy families were given silver spoons at birth.

Born with a silver spoon in his mouth turned up in a 1712 English translation of Cervantes's *Don Quixote,* so the expression is at least four hundred years old, and probably older. A coin appeared in place of the spoon in an English expression cited in 1639: "He was born with a penny in his mouth."

BOUSTROPHEDON

Written text in both Hebrew and Arabic is read from right to left—while most other languages, including English, go from left to right. But some ancient languages of the Mediterranean region actually read in both directions.

The lines of these early inscriptions, incised in clay or stone tablets, were composed with alternating lines running in opposite directions. When the scribe began a line of text on the left, for example, he continued until he reached the right margin. But instead of returning his hand to the left margin (as we would, in writing an English text), the scribe simply dropped directly below to the next line, then continued the script in the opposite direction.

The name of this style of composition is *boustrophedon*— a word of Greek heritage meaning "turning like an ox in plowing"; *bous* means "ox" and *strophien* is the Greek verb for "turn." The combination is an imaginative reference to the path of an ox furrowing a field, turning at the end of each row to draw the plow in the opposite direction.

This magnificent word has been brought into a modern context—used to describe the print head motion of line printers, which print text not only from left to right in the conventional manner but also from right to left to save the time of a carriage return.

It's traditionally been considered bad luck to wish an actor good luck, especially on the opening night of a performance. Instead, the proper sentiment for the occasion is *break a leg.* The origin of this traditional well-wishing is unclear, but there are plenty of folk explanations.

One has the expression coming from the 1865 assassination of Abraham Lincoln. The perpetrator, sometime actor John Wilkes Booth, broke his leg when he leapt to the stage of Ford's Theatre while trying to escape the building. In this scenario, good fortune is somehow thought to be conjured by wishing a performer the same fate that befell the assassin.

In another speculation, actors who performed with great skill were said to "break a leg" (actually, "bend" a leg) in a deep bow as the audience applauded enthusiastically. To *break a leg* in this context, then, would be to wish an actor a performance worthy of positive audience response.

But most word watchers seem to agree that the expression arose from the ancient superstition that wishing luck invites calamity, and that wishing calamity brings luck. *Break a leg* may be a translation of the German expression *hals und beinbruch,* or "break your neck and leg." Some historians believe this phrase was transported to the American theatre by Yiddish- or German-speaking immigrant actors.

She was identified sometime in the mid-1990s—the fanatical fiancée who destroys everything in her path in a quest to achieve the perfect nuptial experience: *Bridezilla*. Paul McFedries, in *Wordspy,* www.wordspy.com, a website devoted to new words and phrases, says a bridezilla is "a bride-to-be who, while planning her wedding, becomes exceptionally selfish, greedy, and obnoxious."

Today's word got a lot of press back in 2002 with the publication of *Bridezilla, True Tales From Etiquette Hell,* authored by etiquette experts Gail Dunson and Jeanne Hamilton. The book, packed with anecdotes about hostile, high-strung brides, also advises readers how to defuse—or better—avoid the *Bridezilla syndrome.*

Though this handbook was published in '02, the title word made its initial printed appearance in 1995 in an article by Diane White of the *Boston Globe*. Ms. White suggested the term *bridezilla* was coined by wedding consultants dealing with "brides who are particularly difficult and obnoxious."

The term, of course, is based on the name of the perpetually enraged dinosaur of the *Godzilla* film series, launched in 1954. Breathing his atomic death ray, Godzilla strides through various centers of civilization, annihilating everything that does and doesn't move.

The *-zilla* suffix has recently become quite productive, lending itself to such constructions as *momzilla* (mother of bridezilla), *Dogzilla* (the title of a children's book), and *Mozilla* (the name of a web browser).

A person suffering from *brontophobia* may spend his days obsessively watching the skies or listening to the weather report. If dark clouds accumulate on the horizon, he becomes anxious, growing increasingly fearful of any impending storm. The brontophobe may even hide under a bed or in a closet as the threatening weather approaches, refusing to move until the tempest is long past.

People with brontophobia have an abnormal, persistent fear of thunder. The *bronto* in *brontophobia* comes from *bronte,* the Greek word for thunder.

This word shares etymological kinship with the name of the ponderous Jurassic behemoth *brontosaurus.* At 70 feet in length with enormous, pillar-like legs, the beast was named *brontosaurus,* or "thunder lizard," in 1879, the year its first gigantic fossil was discovered in Wyoming. Paleontologists re-christened the dinosaur *apatosaurus* in 1978, but its more evocative original moniker was given to suggest the booming sound of its locomotion: like thunder.

Another prehistoric creature in the same etymological family but less known than the brontosaurus is the *brontotherium,* an Oligocene mammal that lived in North America about 35 million years ago. Fossil remains suggest a stocky, rhino-like herbivore. Weighing 5 tons and standing 8 feet at the shoulder, the creature was given the name *brontotherium,* "thunder beast."

Everyone knows how to rack up brownie points. With your boss, it could be accomplished by doing an unexpected task. With a partner, it might be a surprise gift. Wikipedia, the online dictionary, cleverly defines brownie points as "hypothetical currency, which can be accrued by doing good deeds." What can we find by tracing the etymological path of the quirky expression *brownie points?*

The merit system of the Brownies, the junior division of the Girl Scouts, is likely responsible for this phrase. Lady Baden Powell, the founder of this originally British organization for girls, named the Brownies after the benevolent elves who were said to be especially helpful with household chores. Girls who joined up earned Brownie points for their helpfulness and good deeds. The phrase seems to have jumped to the vocabulary of American slang in the 1950s.

A rival theory associates *brownie points* with the obliquely scatological expression *brown-noser,* one who hopes to curry favor by "kissing the ass" of a teacher, professor, or boss.

If you type this phrase into your search engine, you'll find www.browniepointsinc.com, where you can order gourmet brownies to be sent as corporate or family gifts. Or you might find Scorebrowniepoints.com, an online delivery service where men shop for romantic gifts for wives and girlfriends. The site motto is "making men happy by making women happy." Powerful stuff, that "hypothetical currency" of brownie points!

The word *buff* is a hard-working member of the American English lexicon. *Buff* is a color. As an adjective, it's also a synonym for "naked," or alternatively for "muscular" and "well-toned." To *buff up* is to clean or polish. And a *buff* is an ardent fan or enthusiast, as in *sports buff* or *camera buff.*

Though the word appears to glance off at schizophrenic angles, all the American English senses of *buff* have the same source—the mighty North American bison. During the mid- to late 1800s, thousands of buffalo hides were shipped from the American plains to the urban East, where they were converted to items of apparel such as coats, shirts, and robes. Fashionable city dwellers sported bison clothing throughout the last decades of the 19th century.

The light tan we call *buff* comes from the color of a tanned buffalo hide. The soft leather "buff" skins were also used to polish or *buff up* brass and copper. To be nude or, as we say, *in the buff,* is an early 20th century phrase derived from the comparison of the color of naked human skin to the light tan of a buffalo hide.

BUFF II

If you love football, baseball, or basketball, you've likely been called a *sports buff*. And if you've been labeled a *camera buff*, it's probably for all the photographic equipment you own. But why do we call an enthusiast or amateur expert a *buff*?

This sense of the word began appearing in American English in the early 20th century. In America's larger cities at that time, anyone who showed up at a fire to help fight it or just gawk was labeled a *fire buff*. It's well documented that enthusiastic pyromaniacs of various sorts were the original *buffs*, but the tales behind the origin of this meaning are unverified.

Some say the waterproof buffalo skins worn by both amateur and professional firefighters were behind the nickname. Another account suggests that organized urban firefighters wore buffalo hide or buff shirts as uniforms.

Other sources suggest this moniker comes from cold-weather spectators who huddled under buffalo robes while watching fires blaze. These fascinated bystanders who rushed to every conflagration but didn't participate may very well have been the first buffs.

Leave it to American English speakers to tease out a word that means "ardent fan" from the name of the North American bison.

BUICK

The English language owes its teeming vocabulary in part to eponyms—personal names that have become common nouns. An example of a famous eponym is George Washington Gale Ferris, inventor of the ferris wheel. Many automobile brand names are eponymous: Dodge, Chrysler, Chevrolet. Today we'll look at Buick, a name stamped on millions of American automobiles.

This brand is the namesake of David Dunbar Buick, a Scot who immigrated to the United States in 1856. Buick apprenticed in the plumbing trade in Detroit at age 15. A productive innovator, Buick devised improvements for bathtubs and flushing devices and patented a new lawn sprinkler.

David's passion, however, was the internal combustion engine. In 1902, he and a partner organized the Buick Manufacturing Company, which, several owners and incarnations later, would become General Motors. Under the aegis of his company, Buick patented a carburetor and designed the first Buick automobile, but business debts and failed investments prevented him from realizing profits on his inventions. He died, impoverished, in 1929, but eight years later General Motors saluted his ingenuity when it adopted the Buick name and family crest for its new line of automobiles.

BUNK

In 1820, the 16th Congress of the United States was engaged in a contentious debate about statehood for the territory of Missouri. Pro-slavery representatives from the South emphatically insisted Missouri be admitted as a slave state, while Northern abolitionists demanded that it be free.

In the midst of this rancorous deliberation, Congressman Felix Walker requested permission to speak. Walker, who happened to represent a district that included Buncombe County, North Carolina, stood before the House and delivered a long, rambling oration entirely unrelated to the topic of slavery.

Despite protests from his colleagues, Congressman Walker droned on. Finishing his bombast, Walker explained that his Buncombe County constituents had sent him to Washington to deliver a speech, and that he had simply completed what was expected of him. Felix Walker claimed he was not speaking so much for Congress, he was "talking for Buncombe."

The story became a joke in Washington. Very soon, the name Buncombe became synonymous with political insincerity and nonsense. *Buncombe* became the phonetically rendered *bunkum* and finally was distilled to the monosyllabic *bunk,* which today still means malarky, hogwash, and drivel.

It's easy to grasp the simple, folksy observation behind the expression *busy as a bee*. Bees, famous for their industry, work endlessly gathering pollen, tending to the queen, and cooling and cleaning the hive.

What is astounding about this phrase is its antiquity. English speakers in the 1300s used it; we know this because *busy as a bee* shows up in Chaucer's *Canterbury Tales,* written in 1380.

One of Chaucer's characters is a man suspicious of women's motives. He says: "Now such a wife I pray God keep from me! Behold what tricks, and lo, what subtleties in women are. For always busy as bees are they, us simple men thus to deceive."

So, throughout the 14th century into the 21st, a 700-year span, the simple phrase *busy as a bee* has aged well. Its alliterative quality—the repetition of the *b* sound—has no doubt ensured its popularity.

The efficiency of the bee is also featured in the expression *bee line,* the shortest distance from point A to point B, and usually traced at high speed in the tradition of bees traveling between hive and pollen source. Some etymologists believe the cooperative nature of these insects is represented in the quilting, spinning, building, and spelling *bees* common in the earliest years of America.

BUTTERFLY

For all its familiarity, the word *butterfly* is an etymological mystery. No one has plumbed the origin of the common name of this insect of the order Lepidoptera, meaning "scaly-winged creatures."

Several theories have been suggested over the centuries. The simplest explanation is that *butterfly* is simply an inversion or metathesis of *flutter-by*. This notion, though charming, is thought to be a product of folk etymology, the linguistic equivalent of an old wife's tale.

The earliest form of the word appears in the vocabulary of Old English, spoken from the 400s to the 1100s. In a document from the year 1000, the word was spelled *buttor-fleoe*. In 1386, poet Geoffrey Chaucer spelled it *boterflye*.

The insect has long been associated with butter, at least in the minds of English speakers. One suggestion is that many butterflies are literally butter colored. Others, claiming to have seen it, report that the excrement of these insects is the color and consistency of butter.

Finally, a European folk tale asserts that witches often assumed the form of butterflies. Disguised as colorful insects, the hags would fly into cottages and steal butter, which according to legend was their favorite food.

CALLOW

The popular song "Try to Remember" from the Broadway musical *The Fantastiks* has been recorded by dozens of crooners from Perry Como and Harry Belafonte to the Kingston Trio and Patty Page. One of the lines included in songwriter Tom Jones's ballad contains an evocative but rarely used word. "Try to remember the kind of September/When you were a tender and callow fellow."

Bless Tom Jones for including the sadly neglected word *callow* in this lovely lyric. In the context of the song, *callow* means inexperienced, naïve, young. If we follow *callow's* path backwards to its origin, we travel through some interesting etymological territory.

The word's earliest ancestor is probably the Latin *calvus,* which means "bald." One of *callow's* earliest citations comes from 1388, when it was recorded that "a man of whos heed heeris fleten awei, is calu" (a man whose head hair is gone is callow). By the early 1600s, the word was expanded to include young unfledged or downy birds. *Callow* as an adjective also referred to soft hairs, as in the callow down of a boy's cheeks and chin.

Then the word was extended to the world of metaphor, where by the mid-1600s it came into its modern meaning of "young, inexperienced, lacking adult perception." In essence, the word is applied to anyone too young to have grown significant amounts of hair, one who is still callow, or bald.

CAMEO

People have been wearing cameos for brooches, clasps, rings, and pendants for thousands of years. Archaeological sites from Sumeria, dated from 3100 B.C., have yielded hundreds of cameos carved from onyx and agate. Ancient Greek and Roman cameos were fashioned into portraits and images from classical mythology.

Archaeological discoveries in Italy and Egypt sparked a cameo revival during the Renaissance, and again in the Victorian period, when specialized carvers fashioned elaborate cameos for European royalty.

Cameos are traditionally made of stone or shell of stratified hues. Artisans carve a design into the top layer to produce a color contrast with the background layer.

Although the history of the cameo itself is well documented, no one is certain of the derivation of the word. Latin, French, Italian, Portuguese, and Spanish versions of *cameo* have been in print since the 1200s. The term appeared in English manuscripts in the 1600s. The *Dictionary of Word Origins* suggests *cameo* may derive ultimately from an Arabic term meaning "flower buds." In the early 1800s, writers began producing short sketches or portraits known as literary cameos, so called because, like the jewelry, they were small but striking. Motion picture producers adopted the term in creating brief appearances of notable actors, politicians, and movie directors; consider the many cameo appearances of Alfred Hitchcock. Like cameo reliefs, these roles "stand out" in the film.

CAT GOT YOUR TONGUE?

Has anyone ever asked, in response to your silence, "What's the matter? Cat got your tongue?" Here is another English idiom that not only defies logic but also appears to have suffered etymological abandonment, since no one agrees on its origin.

Several theories have surfaced over the years to explain *cat got your tongue.* The most popular points not to the household pet but rather to the cat that is a whip, the cat-o-nine-tails, used to flail lawbreakers and malcontents, especially in maritime settings. The anticipation of laceration by this instrument might render a man speechless with fear, prompting the comment "Cat's got his tongue."

Sound improbable? Well, another theory suggests that the expression is topsy-turvy and might be better rendered *do you have a cat's tongue?*—a question reflecting the creature's relative silence as she sits for hours on end, observing the world with little comment.

Although this cliché seems to have the ring of antiquity about it, the *Oxford English Dictionary* dates its first citation at 1911. Respected British lexicographer Eric Partridge, author of many books on etymology, is silent about the origin of the phrase. In his *Dictionary of Catchphrases,* Partridge offers only this on *cat got your tongue:* "It forms one of the small group of domestic phrases often used in speaking to a child that, after some mischief, refuses to…answer questions."

A Cat Has Nine Lives

Cats have always been admired for their grace, agility, and stealth. But the centuries-old English proverb *a cat has nine lives* reveals something else about the nature of these animals: they are remarkably resilient. Cats are famous for surviving fire, flood, deprivation of food and water, and a host of other dire circumstances. A person with a knack for cheating death is said, like the cat, to have nine lives.

This expression was first recorded in a book of proverbs compiled by British playwright John Heywood in 1546, but Heywood's version reads "a woman hath nine lives, like the cat." This expression, or a variant of it, was well established by Shakespeare's time. In *Romeo and Juliet,* written in 1591, a character named Mercutio provokes a fight with his enemy, Tybalt. When Tybalt asks, "What would thou have of me?" Mercutio replies, "Good King of Cats, nothing but one of your nine lives," adding that he would soundly thrash the other eight.

The expression *a cat has nine lives* has been a wonderfully serviceable proverb in both literature and the media. In 1993, Bob Thaves, in his cartoon strip *Frank and Ernest,* drew a guilty-looking cat standing before a judge. "You have been a bad kitty," says the judge. "I hereby sentence you to life, life, life, life, life, life, life, life, and life."

CATCHPHRASES

We Americans are addicted to catchphrases—expressions or even single words which, for one reason or another, become fashionable. Examples abound: *get a life, yabba dabba doo, Elvis has left the building.*

Catchphrases are generated from a variety of sources, including cinematic dialogue, popular novels, television serials, political speech, advertising, and sports talk. A *catchphrase* is an expression so appealing that it "catches" the people's attention, and that's exactly how the word was coined in the middle of the 19th century.

Members of each generation cherish the catchphrases of their youth. The chronologically gifted among us will remember Jimmy Durante's wistful *Goodnight Mrs. Calabash, wherever you are,* while *melts in your mouth, not in your hand* resonates with the baby boom crowd. Younger Americans are well acquainted with *Crikey,* the signature catchword of Steve Irwin, the Crocodile Hunter.

Though the popularity of most catchphrases fades as the years pass, a few have endured for decades. Almost everyone recognizes *Play it again, Sam; Meanwhile, back at the ranch...;* and *Me Tarzan, you Jane.*

CAUGHT RED-HANDED

To catch someone red-handed is to apprehend him in the commission of a crime, and as the *Oxford English Dictionary* puts it, with "all the evidences of guilt still upon" him. The *red* in *caught red-handed* refers to the blood of a victim on the hands of a killer. But whose blood it was depends on the etymological story you prefer.

One generic history of this phrase explains that game animals in medieval England were the sole property of the king. When royal game wardens apprehended poachers, it was most likely when they were cleaning and dressing the kill, with their arms and hands stained with blood. Here's where medieval poachers were captured in the act of a crime, or *caught red-handed.*

Theory number two is better documented and is preferred by most etymological experts. Our modern phrase *caught red-handed* almost certainly comes from a 16th century Scottish legal term, *taken red-hand,* which refers to being caught in the commission of a murder, not in the act of taking a game animal. Sir George MacKenzie wrote in *A Discourse upon the Laws and Customs of Scotland in Matters Criminal,* "If he be not taken red-hand the sheriff cannot proceed against him."

Today the expression *caught red-handed* refers to being seized in the act of any violation, from shoplifting to kidnapping.

CEREAL

When you hear the word *cereal,* what comes to mind? Cornflakes? Oatmeal? Count Chocula? Well, it's likely that this word for one of America's favorite breakfast foods doesn't make you think of a revered goddess from ancient Rome. But that's exactly where the word cereal comes from.

The Romans made supplications to the divine Ceres for a bountiful harvest because she was the goddess of agriculture. The ancients respected her so much that they held games, called Cerealia, in her honor.

The Roman Ceres is directly identified with the Greek goddess Demeter. The seasonal cycle of summer and winter was explained in both mythological traditions through a legend of this powerful patron of earth and agriculture. When Ceres' daughter, Persephone, was abducted by the king of the underworld, the goddess was miserable. As she searched for her daughter, the disconsolate Ceres abandoned her duties, causing every plant on earth to wither and die.

Moved by this crisis, the god of the underworld agreed to allow Ceres to spend half the year in Hades with Persephone, so long as she would return to provide the earth with summer and the harvest.

Generally regarded as the protectress of the edible grains wheat, rye, barley, oats, and millet, the goddess was enshrined in 19th century English in the word *cereal,* literally, "of Ceres."

CHAD

Hanging, swinging, tri, dimpled, and pregnant, chad got a lot of air time during the 2000 presidential election. When Florida voters' ballots were manually recounted, the fate of the U.S. presidency pivoted around that little ballot hangnail, the chad.

As the manual recounts of votes progressed throughout November, this previously obscure little term became a linguistic celebrity. Everyone wanted to know if it was somehow connected with the African country, maybe linked eponymously with some obscure inventor named Chad, or perhaps simply an acronym, like NATO or NASA.

Investigation ensued. One story that emerged out of the etymological inquiry involved a certain Mr. Chadless, who invented a teletype machine that eliminated the little bits of loose paper generated by the keypunch process. When his machine, called the "Chadless Keypunch," was patented, those unaware of the eponymy assumed the name meant "without chad." So, the reasoning went, the bits of paper generated by other teletype machines must be called *chads*.

This makes a satisfying but, unfortunately, unfounded story. So does the acronym theory, which claims that *chad* stands for Card Hole After Denting. The *Oxford English Dictionary* and most other reputable word sources indicate that the origin of the term is unknown. Though is appears to be a lexical orphan, *chad* should be proud that it was voted by the linguistic panel of www.yourDictionary.com as word of the year for 2000.

CHARLEY HORSE

There are some good stories attached to the origin of the term *charley horse;* unfortunately, none of them is all that believable as an authentic etymology.

Charley horse is a slangy Americanism for a painful muscle cramp or spasm in a limb. In the early decades of the 20th century, the term was almost always attached to athletes who suffered stiffness and muscle cramps during a game.

This takes us to the baseball stadium, where, according to a couple of stories, the phrase was born. One account has it that the term arose in Boston in the late 1880s. Ballplayer Charley Radbourn, nicknamed "Old Hoss," was rounding third base during a game when he was suddenly seized by a leg cramp. Limping painfully to home plate, he was met by his concerned teammates. "What happened, Charley Hoss?" they asked. "My leg is tied up in knots," was the reply. After that, a baseball player's cramp was called a *charley hoss* or *horse.*

Story number two alleges Charley was the name of an actual equine, a lame draft horse used for grounds maintenance at Chicago's White Sox ballpark around the turn of the 20th century. Cramped-up ballplayers were said to limp like Charley the horse.

These are two stories, but you can find other explanations of this term in any good slang dictionary.

CHEESECAKE

An article in the September 17, 1934, issue of *Time* magazine defined the slang term *cheesecake* as "leg-pictures of sporty females." This was one of the first times *cheesecake* was seen in print in this context.

Popular throughout the 1930s, '40s, and '50s, "cheesecake" illustrations of sparsely clad women were printed on calendars, pulp novel covers, playing cards, and the like. Numerous writers and word watchers have attempted to identify the source of *cheesecake* used in this sense. But because no etymological consensus has been reached, we are left with several interesting possibilities.

Evan Morris, in his book *Making Whoopie, Words of Love for Lovers of Words,* theorizes that during the Depression of the 1930s cheesecake—the dessert variety made of cream cheese, butter, and sugar—was a prohibitively expensive confection. The leggy, "sporty" females depicted on magazines and calendars of the day were also "cheesecake," as unattainable to the average male as the dessert was to the average American.

Another theory simply associates the color of cheesecake with the creamy skin of these mid-20th century models.

Yet a third possibility comes from the classic plea of the photographer—"say cheese"—in an attempt to solicit a smile from his subject. Or, perhaps cheesecake is a variation on *cupcake,* another culinary term of endearment for an attractive woman.

According to Kennedy family lore, Joseph, father of John and Robert, repeatedly encouraged his sons with the proverb, "When the going gets tough, the tough get going."

Joseph Kennedy's motto is a classic example of a *chiasmus:* an expression in which the key words in a phrase are immediately repeated, but in the opposite order. It seems John F. Kennedy inherited his father's penchant for this type of expression. In his 1963 inaugural address, he uttered what has become one of the classics of chiasmus: "Ask not what your country can do for you, ask what you can do for your country." Kennedy also said, "Mankind must put an end to war, or war will put an end to mankind."

A century before Kennedy gave us his classic phrase, another president, Abraham Lincoln, declared words of chiastic wisdom as the Civil War raged: "We trust that God is on our side. It is more important to know that we are on God's side." This expression was reiterated by democratic presidential candidate John Kerry during his nomination acceptance address in July 2004.

Other politicians have used chiasmus to provoke and inspire. Theodore Roosevelt said, "The Constitution was made for the people, and not the people for the Constitution." Will Rogers, in a criticism of politicians, quipped chiastically, "With Congress—every time they make a joke it's a law. And every time they make a law it's a joke."

We also find chiasmus in the sports world. Earl Woods, father of Tiger, once said, "You learn very little about golf from life, but you learn a lot about life from golf." Professional British golfer Harry Vardon once said, "Golfers find it a very trying matter to turn at the waist, more particularly if they have a lot of waist to turn." And then there's "It's not the size of the man [or dog] in the fight, it's the size of the fight in the man [or dog]."

The word *chiasmus* is based on the Greek term *chi,* which we call the letter X. The letter is a symbol for the crossing or switching of relevant words in two otherwise identical statements. For more information about this charming quirk of speech, visit www.chiasmus.com.

CHINOOK JARGON

The indigenous people who lived along the coast of southern Alaska to Oregon are thought to have been among the most linguistically diverse in the world. Coastal native peoples such as the Nootka, Chehalis, Kwakiutl, and Tillamook lived in close proximity to one another yet spoke mutually unintelligible languages.

These many groups, interdependent for trade goods and food specialties, crossed the language barrier by developing a common tongue consisting of a few hundred words to describe basic ideas. This trade language, named *Chinook Jargon,* incorporated vocabulary from several languages in the region but with the heaviest borrowing coming from the tribal language of the Chinook, a group living on the lower Columbia River.

Chinook Jargon consisted of words for food, animals, topographical features, greetings, and trade goods. It was inadequate, however, to express the nuanced cultural distinctives of government, spirituality, and technology.

This "business" language may have developed among the coastal groups long before European contact, but as Europeans traded and settled in the area, many English, French, and even Scandinavian terms were also incorporated into Chinook Jargon.

Though today there are few fluent jargon speakers, some of the vocabulary of the language survives in the American West and Canada, such as *cayuse,* horse; *skookum,* strong; and *kinnikkinnik,* the leaves of a smokable plant; and see *mucka-muck* later in this book.

CHIPMUNK

The eastern chipmunk has five black stripes running down its back and sides—the tiny forest dweller's most conspicuous physical characteristic. Behaviorally, the chipmunk is famous for cramming its cheek pouches with its favorite foods—nuts, berries, seeds, and insects—then hoarding the cache for consumption during the lean months.

The stripes and cheeks of this little rodent earned the chipmunk its classically derived scientific designation: *Tamias striatus*, or "the striped one that stores things."

But the Ojibwe natives, who traditionally dwelt in the Great Lakes region of Canada and the United States, saw something else in the little striped hoarder. The Ojibwe observed that the animal almost always descended a tree with its head pointed downward. The Ojibwe named the creature *atchitimo*, their word for "headfirst." English speakers rendered the word more Anglo-friendly by pronouncing it "chipmunk."

This is one of a handful of native animal words adopted and adapted by European immigrants. Another indigenous language, Algonquin, has given us *skunk*, taken from a term meaning "animal that sprays"; *raccoon*, the word for "it washes with its hands"; and *moose*, which means "it strips off," referring to the creature's manner of browsing bushes and trees.

CHUM

There are at least three *chums* in English: the one that is a pal, companion, or friend; the chum salmon of the Pacific Northwest; and the one referring to the miscellany of food scraps thrown into the water to attract game fish. Are these three *chums* related? No one is certain, but let's take a closer look.

The first *chum,* the one that means "pal" or "friend," predates the others by at least two centuries. According to the *Oxford English Dictionary* it was first recorded in 1684 and originally used by university roommates, who referred to one another as *chums.* One etymological conjecture makes this word a truncation of *chamber-fellow* or *chamber-mate.* But the *OED* is careful to point out that no historical proof of this relationship has been found, so this sense of the word is of uncertain origin.

The name of the *chum* salmon, first cited in 1908, probably derives from a word in Chinook, an indigenous language of the Pacific Northwest. The original term meant "speckled" or "spotted," in reference to the salmon's coloration.

But word watchers are out of luck when it comes to the *chum* that means "fish bait." Most dictionaries state "origin unknown" beside the term. The *OED* offers that the word may be American, and that its first print date is 1857, but beyond that this *chum* is a mystery.

CHUMP

From the catalog of abusive English slang comes the word *chump,* meaning "sucker, dupe, easy mark." Though a bit dated, this moniker is interesting for two reasons.

The first is its origin. When it appeared in print in the early 1700s, *chump* meant "short thick stump of wood." Mary Ann Evans, a.k.a. George Elliot, wrote in her 1863 novel *Romola,* "She fetched a hatchet...and showing him a chump...asked him if he would chop that up for her." The *Oxford English Dictionary* explains that this *chump* was perhaps influenced in form by association with *chop* and *stump.* By the 1860s, the word was being waggishly applied to the human head, likening the cranium or the face to a chunk of wood. The expression *to be off your chump* meant to be out of your head.

From there, it was but a short slide to insult. A human chump was said to be as intelligent as a chump of wood; he was, in essence, a "blockhead," and has remained so to this day.

The second interesting thing about the word is its parallel to another slang insult, *klutz,* or "clumsy fool." This nickname began life as the German term *Klotz,* meaning "block of wood," just like our word *chump.* It passed into Yiddish as *klutz,* a rude moniker for someone judged to be as graceless as a stump.

CLAPTRAP

A slang synonym for nonsense, insincerity, or blather is *claptrap*. This word is but one in the long roster of English reduplications, or expressions formed by combining rhyme and repetition.

Claptrap has been with us since at least 1727, when the word was first printed, according to the *Oxford English Dictionary*. In that era, *claptrap* was a theatrical term—a specific expression referring to sentimental language or music designed to elicit applause from an audience. It was, literally, a playwright's device to "trap claps," thus giving the performance credibility. Swelling patriotic rhapsodies and maudlin sentiments were the claptrap of the 1700 and 1800s that teased audiences to tears and applause.

By the 20th century, the word moved from the theatre to general English metaphor. Conversational claptrap consists of half-truths, insincerity, and foolish banter. Espousals of quack medical cures or improbable religious doctrines might also be considered claptrap.

Many reduplicative terms like this one express contempt. Words like *claptrap, hoity toity, namby pamby,* and *mumbo jumbo* are never complimentary. They are rhyming verbal darts of scorn and derision.

CLEAN AS A WHISTLE

If it's *clean as a whistle,* it's neat, tidy, and pure. But what exactly is the "whistle" doing in this simile? Here is one more familiar English expression whose origin has been forgotten. There are several suggestions that have stepped in to fill the etymological void.

The whistle featured in this cliché may be one of old-fashioned hand-hewn wood—often willow. Perhaps *clean as a whistle* refers to the smooth, clean surface of a willow stick after the bark has been removed to make a whistle. Another account has the original phrase *clean as a whittle,* again evoking the smooth texture of freshly skinned wood.

Other sources claim that whistles, both metal and wood, must literally be clean and dry on the inside to produce their characteristic sound.

Most likely, though, the *clean* in this expression does not refer to the device's sanitary condition but is rather a synonym for "clear" or "sharp." With this in mind, *clean as a whistle* would mean "pure as the sound of a whistle."

CLEAN YOUR CLOCK

When the Democrats threatened a skirmish over the nomination of Samuel Alito to the Supreme Court in January 2006, Republican senator Lindsey Graham of North Carolina rejoined, "I'll just tell you right now, we welcome that debate on our side. We'll clean your clock."

On that January day, Senator Graham enlisted an American slang phrase that's been in circulation now for about a century. To *clean your clock* is to thrash, trounce, or pummel you. Although it's unlikely that any fisticuff-style clock-cleaning would have broken out on the floor, the senator's meaning was clear: he was giving notice that his party aimed to trounce the opponent verbally.

But a physical clock-cleaning usually involves at least a fist in the face. How can this expression be explained?

First, the "clock" part. Since at least World War I, this word has been slang for "face," relying on the notion that both clocks and people have faces, the clock supposedly resembling the human visage.

Though the slang word *clean* can mean many things (*clean* is "innocent," "sober," and "unarmed," for example), its verb form has long meant "to beat or thrash." So *clean your clock* means "punch your face." The phrase's neat alliteration has no doubt been responsible for its long popularity.

CLIPPED WORDS

What do these terms have in common? *dis, za, hood, burbs, zine, morph*. They're all fairly recent examples of words formed by a linguistic process called *clipping*. A word is *clipped* when one or more syllables are dropped from a polysyllabic term. For example, trim the *respect* from *disrespect*, and the result is *dis*, a slangy verb arising in the early 1980s meaning "belittle" or "criticize."

Zine, from *magazine*, generally denotes an amateur or underground publication. When it was popularized in the early 1980s, *zine* almost always appeared with an initial apostrophe. Today, decades after the coinage of the word, this mark is disappearing, an indication that *zine* is beginning to stand on its own lexical legs.

The clipping of *suburbs* gave us *'burbs*, a plural noun that started showing up in the 1970s. This word, like *zine*, is gradually shedding its apostrophe and functioning as a freestanding noun.

Clipping *neighborhood* gives us *hood*, a word fashioned by the hip-hop culture. The clipped form of *vibration* is *vibe*, a word-child of the '60s that refers to a perceived emanation or spiritual intuition.

Morph is the shortcut version of *metamorphosis, app* is the clipped way of saying *application*, and *meds* is a new word for *medications*. Youth slang has given us the very recent clipped arrivals *'rents* for parents and *'za* for pizza.

Do these newfangled words sound a little strange to the ear? Well, consider this: *phone, bus, wig,* and *exam* were once novel and slangy forms of *telephone, omnibus, periwig,* and *examination*.

Cloud Nine

For decades now, American English speakers, when blissfully happy, have claimed to be *on cloud nine.* Though this is a common expression, accounts of its origin are delightfully mottled.

One version has the U.S. Weather Bureau arranging cloud formations in numerical sequence, with level nine clouds, the cumulonimbus, riding the skies at 40,000 feet. Someone sitting on top of such a towering billow—a cloud nine—would be high and blissful indeed.

Another account evokes the mystical quality of the number nine. Nine is a trinity of trinities—three threes equal nine—and as such is considered the perfect number.

In Dante's *Paradise,* the ninth level of heaven is closest to the Divine Presence, which itself dwells at the tenth and highest heaven. This notion may have enhanced the popularity of the expression *on cloud nine.*

The number nine occurs in at least two other common American clichés: *dressed to the nines* and the *whole nine yards.* Coincidentally, these expressions have uncertain origins as well.

Clumsy

One of the very real threats to people of the far northern and southern latitudes is extreme cold. While centuries of human experience in wintry climes have taught us how to dress and shelter ourselves against frigid weather, sometimes overexposure to cold occurs. When it does, the human body responds first by shivering, then by rapidly shutting down its complex functions.

The freezing person becomes uncoordinated, unable to perform otherwise simple tasks such as zipping a jacket or managing a pair of gloves. As the core temperature drops, speech slurs and even walking becomes difficult.

We call this condition *hypothermia,* a Greek term that means "below heat," referring to the body's plummeting core temperature following overexposure to cold.

But in Scandinavia centuries ago, one so affected by frigid temperatures was called *klumsig,* meaning "benumbed with cold."

The word entered the English language in the 17th century as *clumsy,* which originally meant the same as its Scandanavian antecedent. Gradually it lost its association with cold, and *clumsy* has since acquired the meaning "awkward, graceless, coarse"—a feeling that anyone who has suffered the effects of hypothermia can certainly understand.

If spiders construct spider webs, who weaves cobwebs? Cobs do, of course, or at least they did in England in the 13th century. *Cob* is a term, obsolete since the 17th century, that means spider. Actually, *cob* is the clipped version of its former self, which was *attercop*. But here's the story.

Speakers of Old English, believing that all arachnids delivered lethal bites, called spiders *attercops,* a word meaning literally "poison-head," a sensible notion when you consider that a spider appears to be nothing but head and legs. *Attercop* was clipped to *cop,* then slurred to *cob.* By the 1500s, the time of Shakespeare, a *cobweb* was the thing woven by the creature.

Though *cop* and *cob* are obsolete, their synonym, *spider,* lives on in the language. This word, Germanic in origin, literally means "spinner." In German the creature is called *Spinne,* in Dutch, *Spinner,* and in Swedish, *Spindel.* All these terms are kin to the English *spinster,* an older unmarried woman, but one who also etymologically "spins thread."

Back to the old word for spider, *cob.* Is this word related to the *cob* of corn? Most etymologists see a connection between the two senses of the word, with *attercob* meaning "poison-head" and the cob of corn as the "head" or the "top" of the plant.

When someone is laid to rest for the "final sleep," is it in a casket or a coffin? Is there any difference between the two? What are the stories behind the words?

Let's first take a look at the life history of *coffin*. Greek in origin, it originally meant "basket of reeds, rushes, or bark." By the time it found its way to English in the mid-1300s, it meant both "box" and "chest" as well as "basket." Throughout the intervening centuries *coffin* has also referred to a pie dish and the hollow space under a horse's hoof. In the 1500s, *coffin* came to rest on the wooden burial box for the dead, and today that's its primary definition.

Casket is a French word which, from the 1400s through the 1700s, referred to a small ornamented box for jewels, money, or letters. But a curious change came over this term in the mid-1800s when American undertakers started replacing the common word *coffin* with *casket*. Hugh Rawson, author of the word book *Euphemisms and Other Doubletalk*, offers that *casket,* originally a small, exquisite chest for jewels, "makes the happy suggestion that its contents (the remains) are at least as valuable as the container itself."

So *casket* developed into an American euphemism for what in Britian was called a *coffin*. This semantic shift reflects the common tendancy to euphemize topics considered frightening or unpleasant.

COLD FEET

Runaway brides and nervous homebuyers who back out on the deal are said to have gotten *cold feet*. No one is sure what inspired this idiom, but here are some theories.

With its current meaning, the expression has been in common use since the 19th century. There may be a military history to the phrase, since combat soldiers whose feet were frozen out of fear or inadequate footwear were exempted from battle because they *got cold feet*. The saying became associated with loss of nerve at best, and cowardice at worst.

The proliferation of this expression may have been influenced by a scene in an 1862 novel by German writer Fritz Reuter. Losing his money and his nerve in a high-stakes game of cards, one of the novel's characters claimed cold feet as an excuse to withdraw from the game. His cronies, however, suspected feet had nothing to do with his retreat; he was simply fearful of losing more money.

Then again, the cliché might simply refer to a physical response to fear: blood rushing from the extremities—literally giving one cold feet.

COLD TURKEY

In 1969 former Beatle John Lennon recorded a single called "Cold Turkey." The lyrics go: "My body is aching/Goose-pimple bone/Can't see no body/Leave me alone/Thirty-six hours/Rolling in pain/Praying to someone/Free me again/Cold turkey has got me on the run."

For decades before Lennon penned these tortured words, the expression *cold turkey* had been underworld slang for an addict's traumatic withdrawal from narcotics. It was thought that Lennon might have written the song after shaking a heroin habit.

The expression *cold turkey* began showing up in print in the 1920s, though it most likely had been in use years earlier. Junkies thrown in jail suffered the so-called *cold turkey treatment* as they "rolled in pain" in their cells.

Over the years, mainstream America adopted the term to describe sudden withdrawal from the more socially acceptable habits of smoking and caffeine. People even use the expression to suggest the pain of abruptly ending a love relationship.

What links the discomfort of withdrawal to a cold turkey, anyway? The clue may lie in Lennon's phrase "goose pimple bone," which, although alluding to a fowl of a different sort, nevertheless reflects the addict's violent chills, making his flesh resemble that of an uncooked turkey.

Dozens of our most familiar and oft-repeated expressions come from the canon of great literature. English poet Samuel Taylor Coleridge in his 1798 *Rime of the Ancient Mariner* coined a trio of memorable phrases.

The poem recounts the voyage of a sailing ship tossed by fierce winter gales. In spite of the danger, the ship's crew is cheered by the appearance of an albatross, a bird of good omen, which daily follows the ship, even eating bits of food offered by the sailors. But the spell of comfort is broken when, out of boredom or malice, a young mariner shoots the albatross with a crossbow. As punishment, the sailor's shipmates tie the body of the bird around his neck.

Then, misfortune plagues the voyage. The ship lies becalmed, and all the sailors die from hunger and thirst, except for the guilty mariner. When he repents of killing the innocent albatross, he is rescued by a pilot boat.

The Rime of the Ancient Mariner contains three phrases that English speakers use to this day. *"Water, water everywhere, nor any drop to drink"* was Coleridge's comment on the thirsty, dying sailors. Our expression *sadder but wiser* also comes from the lines of this 1798 poem. But perhaps the most famous borrowing from Coleridge's work is *albatross around my neck,* referring to a great burden or sadness.

Condom

The biography of the word *condom* has been a matter of debate for decades. The tale most often associated with the term suggests that it was named eponymously for an 18th century British physician who is said to have invented the device. In written accounts, the surgeon's name is variously Dr. Condum, Quondam, even Conton. Though many sources favor this theory, the *Oxford English Dictionary* states simply, "No 18th century physician named Condom or Conton has been traced, though a doctor so named is often said to be the inventor of the sheath."

Some say the device was named for the southern French village of Condom, a hypothesis advanced in 1904. This theory banks on the traditional notion of the British attributing things erotic and lascivious to the French.

Another possibility is that the word derives from the Latin *condus,* or "that which preserves," from the prophylactic's original use as a preventative for syphilis.

There are more problems in tracing *condom.* For one, the word has been spelled so many different ways over the centuries. Additionally, owing to the delicacy of the subject, the word for it was rarely included in dictionaries. *Condom* did not appear in the *OED* until 1972, though the word is three hundred years old.

COP

The origin of the simple, three-letter word *cop*, the slang term for "law enforcement officer," has a couple of imaginative stories attached to it.

One has the word coming from early London constables, whose uniforms allegedly sported conspicuous copper buttons. This version of the story claims that English police were the first to be called *coppers* and *cops*, names inspired by that sartorial accessory.

Another anecdote associated with the word *cop* makes it an acronym of *constable on patrol* or *constabulary of police*. This abbreviation is said to have been attached to the signature of each policeman: John Doe, C.O.P., or Constable on Patrol.

Despite the appeal of these two stories, they're probably fabrications. The word *cop* for police most likely originated from the 18th century thieves' slang *cop*, meaning to "capture, take hold of." This verb, in turn, probably came ultimately from the Latin *capere*, "to seize." By the 1840s, records indicate that police were *copping* criminals and murderers, and that the officials themselves were becoming known as *coppers*, the apprehenders, the seizers of reprobates. The word *cop* was fairly common in America by the early 1900s.

American English speakers pressed the word *cop* into many creative uses throughout the 20th century. The *Random House Historical Dictionary of American Slang* has several entries under the word. Some of these are obsolete or unfamiliar: *cop a nod*, meaning "to sleep"; *cop a squat*, "to sit down"; and *cop off*, meaning "die." More familiar is *cop a plea*, which this dictionary categorizes as "police and underground slang." The translation of *cop a plea* is "catch a lesser punishment by pleading to a lesser crime." Someone copping a plea etymologically "seizes" or "grasps" at a reduced sentence.

What about the expression *cop out,* counterculture slang for reneging on a commitment or compromising shamefully? When this phrase first appeared in the 1940s, it meant "plead guilty when arrested" or "cop a plea for a lesser sentence." The expression gained national currency in the late 1960s.

CORN, MAIZE

The word *maize* comes from the language of the Taino, a native island people of the West Indies. Harvested throughout the Americas for millennia, maize was a crop foreign to early European explorers, who took both the grain and the word back to their homelands, and to Asia and Africa as well.

When Europeans began to colonize the New World, they found the North American natives cultivating and processing maize, too. The colonists initially considered the indigenous crop unfit for human consumption and fed it to their livestock, but eventually they learned to appreciate its versatility and nutritional value, and gradually maize began to appear on colonial dining tables.

The immigrants were inclined to call the grain *Indian corn,* corn being an Old English word referring to a particle, a small seed, or any type of cereal grain. But gradually the qualifier word *Indian* was nipped off this term, leaving the simple English word *corn.* This was an ironic linguistic development, since most of Europe still knows this grain best by its native name, *maize.*

CORNUCOPIA

An enduring symbol of autumn, the abundance of the land, and the American celebration of Thanksgiving is the *cornucopia,* or "horn of plenty," overflowing with fruits of the harvest. The icon that appears on everything from greeting cards to grade schooler's art projects is symbolic of an event that legend tells us occurred thousands of years ago on the waters of the Mediterranean.

In one version of this ancient tale, the infant Zeus was left an orphan in a cave on the island of Crete by his mother, who feared that her tyrannical and jealous husband would kill her young son.

Zeus was cared for by local nymphs, who suckled him on the milk of a miraculous goat named Amalthea. When Zeus grew to adulthood, he took a horn from Amalthea's head, filled it with fresh fruits and herbs, and gave it to the nymphs as a token of gratitude to the goddesses who had raised him. No matter how much food the nymphs withdrew, the magical horn always replenished itself.

Representations of this eternally abundant horn are found in Greek and Roman symbology and are associated with a variety of pagan deities. The name we use for this icon, *cornucopia,* is Latin and literally means "horn of plenty." The *copia* part of the word is related to *copious,* meaning "abundant."

Couch Potato

The term *couch potato* has been with us long enough now that dictionary editors recognize it as a permanent member of our lexicon. A *couch potato*, according to the *American Heritage College Dictionary*, is "a person who spends much time sitting or lying down, usually watching television."

As far as anyone can tell, the term was first used in July 1976 when Tom Iacino, one of a group of self-described "indiscriminate TV viewers," coined the word *couch potato*, applying it to one of his indolent Southern California chums.

Taken with the name and the concept, the group of television addicts got off the couch to appear in the 1979 "Doo-Dah Parade," a parody of the Tournament of Roses event held in Pasadena. Assembing themselves on a float carrying TVs and "ceremonial couches," the couch potatoes lounged passively, unashamedly watching television for the duration of the parade.

Encouraged by the Doo-Dah crowd's enthusiastic support, the couch potatoes trademarked their name—marketing bumper stickers, caps, and stuffed couch potato dolls, even publising a newsletter called *The Tuber's Voice: The Couch Potato's Newsletter.*

And why the potato emblem for the couch lifestyle? Lumpy, heavy, and inert, the tuber lounges on its soft divan, training its many eyes on the television screen, for endless hours.

COULROPHOBIA

Almost everyone has a phobia—an irrational, persistent fear of something. Familiar terrors are *acrophobia,* fear of high places, and *arachnophobia,* fear of spiders. Those who are terrorized by thunder are *brontophobes*—not a common condition, but significant enough to warrant a name.

More rare yet is an abnormal fear of clowns. Children suffer this terror for the obvious reasons: clowns are large, loud, and freakishly costumed. Adults fear them for more abstract reasons. As tricksters, clowns can be chaotic and unpredictable. Larger-than-life hair and heavy makeup conceal the clown's identity. Clown humor is often expressed in teasing or even cruelty and violence. Many adults fear or dislike these characters and have even been divulging their dread on websites devoted to *coulrophobia,* the abnormal fear of clowns.

Yes, there is a name for this condition—*coulrophobia,* a recently coined term of ancient derivation. *Coulrophobia* may have originated in *kolobathristes,* a Greek word meaning "one who walks on stilts." It seems stilt-walkers were one of the ancient analogues of modern-day clowns.

The verb *creep* means to move slowly, or to crawl close to the ground. But dress the word up as a noun, and it becomes a term of abuse. A *creep* is a despicable person, a low-life, or a strange eccentric. A creep is someone who—well—gives you *the creeps*.

The word began to show up in print in the late 1800s, and it has weathered the decades well. Hugh Rawson, author of the insult lexicon called *Wicked Words,* asserts that *creep* is an abbreviation of the older word *creeper,* a stealthy robber or sneaky thief. Creepers worked in brothels as half of a thieving duo. While one lady of the evening distracted her client, another, called the *creeper,* silently lifted the visitor's money. In this scenario, the *creeper* linguistically became the stealthy, thieving *creep*. The houses of prostitution known for this devious activity were *creep joints*.

Another theory behind the development of this word recalls the ancient loathing humans feel for snakes. A *creep* metaphorically moves like a reptile in the grass with slitherings and creepings—a locomotion style most unnatural to upright bipeds.

Charles Dickens was probably the first to record the expression *the creeps,* a sensation of things crawling across the skin. In his 1849 novel *David Copperfield,* Dickens wrote, "She was constantly complaining of the cold, and of…a visitation in her back which she called 'the creeps.'"

CROCODILE TEARS

Genuine tears of sadness inspire sympathy, but *crying crocodile tears* is merely a show of hypocritical or insincere sorrow.

The expression *crocodile tears* arises from an ancient legend that the fierce reptiles actually weep while luring or devouring their prey. One of the earliest references to this idea comes from the writings of a 12th century Franciscan monk, Bartolomaeus Anglicus, who, in his encyclopedia of the natural sciences, wrote, "If the crocodile findeth a man by the brim of the water…he slayeth him there if he may, and then weepeth upon him and swalloweth him at last."

Another version of the crying crocodile has the beast sobbing to lure a sympathetic passer-by in order to snatch and devour him. In a further twist of the myth, the reptile weeps from greed: after consuming a man's body, the crocodile cries over the bony, tasteless skull.

The origins of these ancient notions have been lost. Crocodiles do produce secretions from their lachrymal glands, located near the eyes, but these are not tears of feigned sorrow. The fluid cleans and moistens the eyes when the creature has been out of the water too long.

While biologists have debunked the myth of the wily, insincere, weeping crocodile, the image is too colorful to dismiss. It has provided us an expression that means "a phony show of sorrow": *crying crocodile tears.*

The expression *as the crow flies,* meaning "the straight-est line between two points," is one example of the way the intelligent, adaptable, ubiquitous crow inhabits our linguistic sensibilities. No one knows who coined this folksy expres-sion, but it was first recorded in 1800. Why the crow was chosen as the star of this simile is unclear. There are plenty of birds whose flight from point to point is straight and true, but would we be as satisfied with expressions like *as the heron flies,* or *as the gull flies?*

Some word (and presumably bird) watchers suggest that the crow wings with singular determination as it flies from one food source to another in a *crow-line,* as it appears in some older documents. Diana Wells, author of the delightful *100 Birds and How They Got Their Names,* writes that, "before the advent of clocks, if the sky was overcast and the sunset was obscured, Hebrews would begin their Sabbath when crows came to roost at sunset, traveling 'as straight as the crow flies.' " Intelligent, resourceful, adaptable, and widely distributed, crows intersect the English language in a variety of expressions. To *eat crow* is to acknowledge a mistake. A story associated with this idiom allegedly occurred during the War of 1812, when a British officer forced an American soldier to eat the meat of a crow in punishment for violating an armistice.

In Australia, however, a *crow-eater* is a lazy man who will live on anything rather than work.

Though crows have many attributes, beauty is not one of them. This sentiment is echoed in the expression *crow's feet,* an unflattering allusion to the lines that crease the corners of the eyes.

A *crowbar,* with its stout hook, functions like the bird's bill, which is designed to pry and turn heavy objects.

In cowboy parlance, a horse that bucks in a series of stiff-legged jumps is a *crowhopper,* and a *crowbait* is an old, lame, worthless horse, good for nothing but carrion for the crows.

CRY ALL THE WAY TO THE BANK

What does it mean to *cry all the way to the bank?* This sarcastic American catchphrase comes with a couple of interpretations. Someone who cries all the way to the bank has made a lot of money and is indifferent to criticism of her wealth, or she makes a substantial income on a substandard performance or product.

The phrase was popularized by Liberace, the flamboyant entertainer famous for his baroque piano style, outrageous feathered costumes, pounds of jeweled rings, and trademark gilt candelabra. In 1956, Liberace played a concert in a sold-out Madison Square Garden. The audience raved, but the critics spewed vitriol. William Connor of the British tabloid the *Daily Mirror* called Liberace a "deadly, winking, snuggling, chromium-plated...quivering, giggling, fruit-flavored, mincing...heap of mother-love." Liberace responded with a telegram that read, "What you said hurt me very much. I cried all the way to the bank."

As the world's highest-paid musician at the time, Liberace felt entitled to his crocodile tears. Some years later he quipped, "You know that bank I used to cry all the way to? I bought it."

Though Liberace made the expression famous in the mid-1950s, evidence suggests the phrase *cry all the way to the bank* was already in place by the 1940s.

CUCKOLD

The common cuckoo of Europe and western Asia was the inspiration, of course, for the little animated bird that hourly appears from behind its shuttered nest in the classic cuckoo clock. The name of the bird is onomatopoeic, *cuckoo* being the verbal representation of its call. But there is also a less quaint association with the word.

Some species of cuckoo are remarkable for their nesting habits, or lack thereof. Instead of building nests in which to raise their broods, some female cuckoos deposit their eggs in other bird's nests, leaving the host birds to raise the chicks.

This parasitic nesting behavior seems to be the explanation for the coinage of the term *cuckold*. This word is of considerable antiquity and appears in the literature of Chaucer, Shakespeare, and many others.

Cuckold is a very insulting term designating the husband of an unfaithful wife, especially one who lacks the power to enforce her fidelity. Such a character was often humiliated by a wife who gave birth to children not belonging to him. The origin of the word *cuckold* is found in the cuckoo's habit of laying her egg in another bird's nest, then wandering afield to repeat the process.

Shakespeare commits this notion to verse in his play *Love's Labour's Lost*. He writes, "The cuckoo...on every tree, Mocks married men: for thus sings he, Cuckoo; Cuckoo, cuckoo: O, word of fear, Unpleasing to a married ear!"

CURIOSITY KILLED THE CAT

In 1993, Russell Baker wrote in the *New York Times:* "Americans have always been of two minds about curiosity. On one hand, children were warned against it. Curiosity killed the cat, didn't it? On the other hand, curiosity was also at the heart of all science, therefore to be treasured."

The curiosity Baker was referring to, the one that "killed the cat," is the form that's akin to nosiness. The proverbial expression *curiosity killed the cat* is one traditionally used to keep children from inquiring too closely, though it's probably futile to expect our young to heed such an odd admonition.

Word watchers are somewhat baffled by the elusive history of this expression. It's unclear where it originated, but it began showing up in American English in about 1910. It probably suggests the quietly inquisitive nature of felines that seems to lure them into buildings that get locked, or cars that drive away, or washing machines that get turned on.

The alliterative charm of *curiosity killed the cat* has no doubt added to its longevity. We tend to treasure phonetically pleasing clichés like this one and others such as *cool as a cucumber, get up and go,* and *right as rain.*

Cut and Dried

Anything that's *cut and dried* is routine, predictable, straightforward. A film plot that's cut and dried is formulaic. Assembly instructions that are cut and dried should be fairly easy to follow.

Some believe this metaphor was inspired by lumber that is cut into standard sizes and then kiln- or air-dried and neatly stacked in an orderly but unimaginative way. Other sources claim the *cut and dried* item is jerky, meat that's been sliced and parched for later consumption. Tobacco is similarly processed. So, too, are flowers and herbs.

Perhaps this type of processing contributed to the establishment of this common American phrase. Whatever has been already cut and dried is no longer fresh; its desiccation has rendered it stiff and immobile. The disposition of such items provides the metaphor.

One of the earliest citations of the expression appears in the lines of a 1730 poem by Jonathan Swift in which he refers to boring speech by saying, "Sets of phrases, cut and dry/Ever more thy tongue supply."

CUT THE MUSTARD

Someone who can't *cut the mustard* doesn't have what it takes to get the job done. If you've ever wondered what cutting mustard has to do with competence, you're not alone. Word watchers have been wondering for decades.

One theory suggests that *mustard* is really a linguistic corruption of *muster*, a military inspection. A soldier failing to meet the assessment standards does not *cut the muster*. Though this makes for a spicy etymological history, most lexicographers dismiss it on lack of written evidence.

Alternatively, the phrase may have an agricultural origin rooted in the harvest of the mustard plant for its seeds. Hand-harvesting the stalks of the plant is arduous work; someone who persevered and completed the harvest was able to *cut the mustard*.

But the theory most phrase dictionaries favor is relatively prosaic. In the late 19th and early 20th centuries, the word *mustard* was American slang for "the best" or "the finest." O. Henry used the word in his 1894 *Cabbages and Kings:* "I'm not headlined in the bills, but I'm the mustard in the salad dressing just the same." In his 1904 story "Heart of the West," the popular author wrote, "I looked around and found a proposition that exactly cut the mustard." This is the first recorded citation of the phrase, and here it means "having what's required for the circumstance."

CYCLOPS, POLYPHEMUS

On his voyage home to Ithaca after waging war at Troy, the Greek hero Odysseus came ashore in the land of the Cyclopes, a dreadful tribe of one-eyed giants. Odysseus and his crew, innocent of the cannibalistic ways of these monsters, entered the cave of one called Polyphemus, whose Greek name means "many voiced" or "much spoken of."

Polyphemus was "much spoken of" because of his cruelty, which led him to murder a pair of sailors and devour them on the spot. He would have gobbled up the rest of the crew had not the clever Odysseus found a way to dispatch him.

Odysseus offered the Cyclops a drink from his wineskin. After many more pulls from the skin of delicious wine, the monster fell asleep on the cave floor. Odysseus then pierced the single, hideous eye of the Cyclops with a lance, blinding him. The mariners quickly escaped the cave of Polyphemus and returned safely to their waiting ship.

This story is linguistically commemorated in the Greek term *cyclops,* which means "round eye," recalling the single orb in the center of the monster's forehead. The name of the Cyclops in the cave is also the common name of a large American silkworm moth. The *Polyphemous moth* was so named, in the 19th century, because of the conspicuous eye-shaped spot on each of its hindwings.

DABBLE

In North America, most wild ducks fall into one of two categories: the divers and the dabblers.

As their name suggests, the divers dart below the water's surface to find food and escape danger. In their search for underwater sustenance like clams, mussels, crustaceans, and vegetation, diving ducks can stay submerged for a considerable time, navigating with their short legs and lobed hind toes.

Dabblers, such as the mallards, pintails, and wood ducks, prefer shallow ponds and sloughs where they can scoop up aquatic vegetation and insects with their broad bills. These ducks typically "up-end" themselves and graze on food from the bottom of the pond. They also dabble or nibble for fare on the muddy shore.

Dabble, the word describing the way these ducks eat, comes from the Dutch verb *dabbleln,* meaning to "spatter or splash in mud or water." Humans, like ducks, can also dabble in water, not for food but for fun, splashing about in the surf, shore, or current.

We also dabble figuratively at hobbies or pastimes, with no professional aspirations. We've all heard someone say something like, "I'm not a serious composer. I just dabble in songwriting." People dabble in astrology, in woodworking, in painting. It's as though we're splashing, nibbling, or trifling at the hobby like dabbling ducks in pursuit of a little sustenance.

DACHSHUND

Short of leg, long of body, and feisty in personality, the dachshund has won the hearts of many dog lovers. The American Kennel Club lists the dachshund among the top ten most popular breeds in the country. Though the most common variety of dachshund is the small, sleek, mahogany-colored version, there are actually several different types: some longhaired or wirehaired, and others with mottles and spots.

The origin of the breed is traced to Europe, where it was developed for hunting in the forests of Germany. A century of selective breeding with hounds and terriers produced a stout, low-slung dog weighing 30–40 pounds. Often used to hunt in packs, dachshunds pursued rabbit, fox, and wild boar. Courageous to the point of rashness, dachshunds have been known to kill prey twice their size.

The true genius of the breed's design lay in badger hunting. The long body and short legs of the dachshund made the animal an efficient hunter in badger tunnels. Breeders even selected individual dogs with broad, paddle-shaped feet for their advantage in digging. Though a badger generally outweighs its dachshund nemesis, the dog's courage served it well in the subterranean hunt. So, it's no surprise that the breed's specialty is revealed in its German name: *dachs* is "badger," and *hund* is "dog."

DANDELION

Though it may be cursed by gardeners, the dandelion, a common weed in lawns and meadows throughout the world's temperate regions, is actually lauded by herbalists.

Dandelion boosters claim the plant has a host of beneficial properties. A tea boiled from its root is said to cure indigestion and allay both infection and skin disease. Dandelion juice has been used as a topical agent for the removal of warts, blisters, and freckles. The greens, which contain four times the iron of spinach, are grown and sold for salads. The plant's diuretic properties earned it the rather graphic contemporary French name *pissenlit,* "piss the bed."

But for those who crave the uniform green of a dandelion-free lawn, the sight of these bright yellow flowers scattered about the grass is anathema. Many American gardeners are given to attacking the persistent plant with sharp digging implements and herbicides.

The English name for this species comes from an older French term, *dent de lion,* or "tooth of the lion," a reference to the deeply notched leaves of the plant, which were said to resemble the jagged dental display of the lion. And the same meaning is found in the German name of the plant, *Löwenzahn.*

Days of Wine and Roses

In December 1962, the film *Days of Wine and Roses* was released to stellar reviews and expectations of Oscar nominations. The production featured the young Jack Lemmon and Lee Remick as Joe and Kirsten Clay, a couple fighting the destructive results of their alcoholism.

The title *Days of Wine and Roses* was inspired by a line of verse from English poet Ernest Dowson. In the late 1800s, Dowson composed "Vitae Summa Brevis," translated as "The Brief Sum of Life." The final verse of the poem reads, "They are not long, the days of wine and roses/Out of a misty dream/Our path emerges for a while, then closes/Within a dream."

Another film title with literary antecedent is *What Dreams May Come,* a 1998 production starring Robin Williams and Annabella Sciorra. When the husband, played by Williams, dies in an automobile accident, his distraught wife commits suicide. Both journey to the afterlife but arrive on different planes. *What Dreams May Come* is a phrase from the well-known "to be or not to be" soliloquy from Shakespeare's *Hamlet,* in which the prince wonders whether he should end his earthly existence and commit himself to the sleep of death: "To sleep: perchance to dream: ay, there's the rub;/For in that sleep of death what dreams may come."

DEADPAN

Buster Keaton, Jack Benny, Bob Newhart, and Steven Colbert are noted for their deadpan comic performances. *Deadpan* is a delivery style characterized by immobile facial expression, an air of bored indifference, and perhaps a flat, monotone vocal inflection, designed to provide an ironic backdrop to the comic situation.

The word *deadpan* is an Americanism coined in the 1920s. One of the first citations of this expression comes from the March 11, 1928, edition of the *New York Times,* which says simply, "Dead pan, playing a role with expressionless face, as for instance the works of Buster Keaton." Actor Keaton, nicknamed the Great Stone Face, was a master of the motionless visage during his silent film career in the 1920s.

The pan in this expression has a long life history. In the 1300s, the word meant "skull" or "head." Manuscripts from that era contain the words *brain-pan* and *head-pan,* both references to the skull. And thus the word remained, until the 19th century, when it was appropriated by theatricals and vaudevillians as a slang term, not for the cranium but the face. So, in actor's jargon, a *dead pan* is a lifeless face, an impassive expression, used to great effect by some of our funniest comedians.

Delicious Dictionaries

In 1625, English philosopher and essayist Francis Bacon wrote, "Some books are to be tasted, others to be swallowed, and some few to be chewed and digested."

This is certainly true of dictionaries. Some are mere appetizers, others fulfill like a month of mom's meals. Read on to sample some delicious dictionaries, the kind Francis Bacon might have considered worthy of full assimilation.

A Dictionary of Euphemisms and Other Doubletalk by Hugh Rawson is an exploration of words we use to mask unpleasant realities, sometimes disingenuously. For example, says Rawson, the term *festival seating* really means *general admission,* and, during World War II, *liberty cabbage* was the acceptable term for the German dish *sauerkraut.*

When Is a Pig a Hog? by Bernice Randall dissects confoundingly related English words. Randall outlines the difference between *violin* and *fiddle, body* and *cadaver, Ginnie Mae* and *Freddie Mac, bottle* and *jar,* and other confusing word pairs.

Zounds! by Mark Dunn is a *Browser's Dictionary of Interjections.* You can read the quirky life histories of *Geeze Louise, d'oh, badabing-badaboom, mamma mia, holy mackerel,* and *yada-yada* in this delightful little compendium.

DELICIOUS DICTIONARIES II

Do you read dictionaries for pleasure? What follows is a review of a trio of dictionaries that read like potato chips taste—one bite, and you must have more.

First up is *Mrs. Byrne's Dictionary,* a collection of six thousand of the weirdest words ever brought into captivity. The editor, Mrs. Byrne, a.k.a. Josefa Heifitz Byrne, investigates such linguistic curiosities as *pozzy-wallah,* British slang for a jam lover. *Merkin,* false pubic hair. *Scotophobia,* fear of darkness.

Howard Rheingold has published a lexicon called *They Have a Word for It,* a collection of untranslatable words and phrases from foreign languages, such as *sentak bangun* (SEN-tock BONG-uhn), the Indonesian term for the phenomenon of awakening with a start, and the German noun *Katzenjammer,* a monumentally severe hangover. With the Chinese word *majie* (MAH-jyeh), literally "to curse the street," one can verbally direct socially unacceptable anger at the road.

In the *Random House Historical Dictionary of American Slang,* editor J. E. Lighter takes a scholarly approach to the study of our nation's casual language. Lighter scrutinizes the slangy words, including *chump, cop-out, air head, buck naked,* and thousands more.

Devil's Dictionary

In 1911, American satirist Ambrose Bierce published a subversive lexicon called *The Devil's Dictionary*. Known best for his fierce social satire, Bierce challenged the most cherished institutions of American society. *The Devil's Dictionary* is an A to Z lexical account of the world according to Bierce, fashioned with words that goad like pitchforks.

Religion, wrote Bierce, is "the daughter of Hope and Fear, explaining to Ignorance the nature of the Unknowable." *Happiness* is "an agreeable sensation arising from contemplating the misery of another"; *responsibility,* "a detachable burden easily shifted to the shoulders of God, Fate, Fortune, Luck, or one's neighbor."

Man is "an animal so lost in rapturous contemplation of what he thinks he is as to overlook what he…ought to be." A *neighbor* is "one whom we are commanded to love as ourselves, and who does all he knows to make us disobedient." And an *egoist,* wrote Bierce, is "a person of low taste, someone more interested in himself than in me." On *dentists:* "prestidigitator[s], who, putting metal in your mouth, pull coins out of your pocket."

Bierce defined a *bride* as "a woman with a fine prospect of happiness behind her." On *beauty,* Bierce wrote, "The power by which a woman charms a lover and terrifies a husband."

Bierce was called "The Wickedest Man in San Francisco" and "Bitter Bierce" for concocting this brew of toxic aphorisms. *The Devil's Dictionary* is still in print, a century after its first publication, and bristles with words that smart to this day.

Have you ever called *dibs* on something like the front seat of the car or the last piece of pie? *Calling dibs* is claiming temporary ownership or priority on a desirable communal resource.

The *Oxford English Dictionary* defines dibs as "a game played by children with pebbles or the knuckle-bones of sheep." The pebbles and bones used in the game are called *dibstones*. The word *dibs* in reference to the pebble game first appeared in print in Britain in the 1730s.

Much later, the word surfaced as an American expression of a claim to ownership. According to British etymologist Michael Quinion, this expression was first recorded in print in *American Speech,* as late as 1932. "It comes into existence seemingly fully formed, with no obvious links to any previous meaning of the word." So, Quinion is saying is that he sees no ready evidence connecting the old bone game dibs to the current Americanism.

The *Dictionary of American Slang,* on the other hand, confidently asserts our *dibs* is an alternate pronunciation of the term *divvy,* meaning to divide or distribute. Though the *DAS* doesn't elaborate, we might speculate that what you want divvied to you is what you call *dibs* on.

DICTIONARY QUOTATIONS

Samuel Johnson, 18th century British author and lexicographer, said that "dictionaries are like watches; the worst is better than none, and the best cannot be expected to go quite true."

In a personal letter dated March 20, 1953, Ernest Hemingway wrote, "Actually if a writer needs a dictionary he should not write. He should have read the dictionary at least three times from beginning to end and then have loaned it to someone who needs it."

Poet Elizabeth Barrett Browning wrote in a letter to a friend, dated April 1839, "At painful times, when composition is impossible and reading is not enough...dictionaries are excellent for distraction."

"A dictionary is the universe in alphabetical order," wrote Anatole France, a French writer awarded the 1921 Nobel Prize in Literature.

In his 1964 autobiography, Malcolm X tells the story of how he hand-copied a dictionary as part of his education. "I [copied] what eventually became the entire dictionary....With every succeeding page, I...learned of people and events and places from history. Actually, the dictionary is like a miniature encyclopedia."

Not all writers have been so sanguine about dictionaries. American journalist Ambrose Bierce, in his *Devil's Dictionary,* defines a dictionary as "a malevolent literary device for cramping the growth of a language and making it hard and inelastic."

Dionysian, Bacchanalia

Dionysus was one of the many sons of the great god Zeus. In the Greek mythological tradition, Dionysus invented wine and developed the cultivation of grapes throughout the ancient world. His festivals, held five times a year in Athens, were frenzied affairs, the celebrants indulging freely in drink and sex. It's said that the theatre, a mirror of Greek social life, developed out of these wild festivals.

The cult of Dionysus was imported to the west in the second century B.C., where it was enthusiastically embraced by the people of central and southern Italy. The god's Roman name was Bacchus, and the citizens continued the Greek tradition of indulging in his feral, orgiastic festivals until the Roman senate outlawed them in 186 B.C.

This dual-named ancient wine god lives on in our 21st century vocabulary. The adjective *Dionysian* means wild, uninhibited, frenzied. A *bacchanalia,* named for the Roman Bacchus, is a drunken orgy, an explosion of uncontrolled, dissolute behavior.

The lives and personalities of the dieties of the classical western world have inspired dozens of colorful words. *Aphrodisiac* comes from the love goddess Aphrodite; *titanic,* from the race of giants called the Titans; *panic,* after the god Pan, whose malicious pranks caused men and animals to run in blind fear.

DISASTER

The Greek word for star, *astron,* and its variant forms *astro* and *aster* appear in several modern English terms. The *aster* flower is named for its starlike shape. *Asterisk,* the term for the distinctive, familiar symbol, means "small star." Etymologically, one who "sails the stars" is an *astronaut,* and an *astronomer* "names the stars." Other Greek-based "star" words are *astrology, astrophysics, asteroid,* and the less-familiar *asteroidean,* a type of starfish.

Another member of this clan is the word *disaster.* Originally related to astrological themes, the term literally means "evil star." This original connotation of *disaster* reflects the belief that human destiny is orchestrated by stellar influence. According to this cosmological view, the disposition of the stars can bring health and good fortune or disease and catastrophe upon humankind.

Shakespeare alluded to these astrological doctrines in his play *King Lear,* in which the character named Edmund proclaims, "When we are sick in fortune...we make guilty of our disasters the sun, the moon, and stars, as if we were...fools by heavenly compulsion...drunkards, liars and adulterers by an inforced obedience of planetary influence."

When Edmund says we make the sun, the moon, and the stars responsible for our disasters, he plays on the original Latin meaning of the word *disaster,* thus reflecting the common belief that stellar bodies are indeed responsible for maladies and mishaps, these being *dis-asters,* or "evil-starred" events.

DOBERMAN PINSCHER

The Doberman pinscher is renowned for its courage, intellegence, and devotion. Sleek, muscular, and proud of bearing, Dobermans stand 24–27 inches at the shoulder and weigh 60–75 pounds. Doberman fanciers claim that the breed's reputation for ferocity has been unfairly fueled by negative media portrayals, especially those of a snarling black animal straining at the end of a leash.

The Doberman was developed in Germany in the late 1860s as a protective animal. Ludwig Dobermann, the eponymous source of the breed's name, collected taxes for the German city of Apolda. Looking for an animal to protect him from angry taxpayers and potential thieves, Dobermann experimented with crossbreeding several types of dog for the right combination of obedience, intellegence, and protective instinct. The Rottweiller, English greyhound, German sheepdog, and Manchester terrier are said to have been early genetic contributors to what was to become the familiar black and tan Doberman pinscher.

It's clear where the first half of this dog's name originated, but how about the word *pinscher?* This is the common German word for "terrier." The *American Heritage Dictionary* suggests the word comes from the English *pinch* and refers to the clipping or "pinching" off of the animal's ears and tail as a traditional grooming style. Or the *pinch* may refer to the terrier's way of making a living by seizing and "pinching" its prey.

DOILY

American English has dozens of terms called *eponyms,* proper names that have become words. Some common eponyms are the word *lynch,* from Captain William Lynch, a Virginia plantation owner who infamously loaned us his name; Tupperware, named after Earl Silas Tupper, inventor of the plastic kitchenware; Doberman, the namesake of Ludwig Dobermann, who bred the famous pinscher in the 19th century; and *masonite,* the building material whose name was fashioned from William H. Mason, an American inventor.

Included in our long list of eponyms is the term *doily,* the dainty lace or paper mat. Although his first name is unknown, most researchers agree that Mr. Doily was a draper who owned a shop in London sometime around 1700. The prosperous Mr. Doily, according to a January 4, 1712, issue of *Spectator* magazine, "raised a Fortune by finding out materials for such Stuffs as might at once be cheap and genteel."

This London shopowner is credited with inventing a lightweight woolen cloth, very popular for ladies' summer frocks. The creation that rendered Mr. Doily's name an eponym, however, was an ornamental table napkin, fringed at either end, to be placed on the table when dessert was served. These crocheted cloths were originally called *Doily napkins.* As the delicate, decorative mats used to protect the finish on tables became more widely used, they became known simply as *doilies.*

Referring to someone who is a stranger to us, we might say, "I don't know him from Adam." This idiom, like dozens of English expressions, is inspired by a biblical reference. The logic driving the phrase is that Adam, created by God as the first man, lived so long ago that, of course, today no one would recognize him.

I don't know him from Adam appears to be a 19th century invention. Charles Dickens used the expression in his 1840 story *The Old Curiosity Shop* when he had a character remark, "He called to see my Governer this morning…and beyond that, I don't know him from Adam."

Quaint elaborations on this cliché have proliferated over the years: *I don't know him from Adam's house cat, from Adam's pet monkey, from Adam's brother, from Adam's left foot,* and so on. Most of these have been consigned to the linguistic boneyard, but one curious variation that surfaces from time to time is *I don't know him from Adam's off ox.*

Teamster history says that an *off ox* is the animal of a pair of draft oxen that was hitched farthest from the driver, the one whose movement is the least monitored. Extending this logic, then, if Adam's off ox was barely seen by Adam himself, how could any of us possibly know the animal?

Dope

The slang term *dope* has a diverse linguistic history. Its meanings have ranged from a simpleton, to narcotics, to a soft drink, and, as late as the 1990s, it took on a new connotation as a synonym for "excellent" or "attractive." Oddly, in tracing the history of *dope,* we find one unexpected source: the Dutch word *doop,* which means "sauce."

American English borrowed this word from Dutch in the early 1800s, when it originally referred to gravy or dipping sauce. By the early 1900s it emerged as a synonym for any thick sauce or liquid preparation, from molasses to lubricants to medicinal ointments.

In many parts of the country, a sweet carbonated soft drink was called a *dope* (for its syrupy base ingredients), and soda fountains regularly advertised flavored *dopes* or toppings to pour over ice cream.

Meanwhile, the *dope* that became synonymous with narcotics may have arisen from the thick, viscous form of prepared opium. This sense of the word arrived on the American wordscape in 1899. By extension, the slow-witted *dope* who appears to be under the influence of narcotics began to show up in the linguistic culture of the early 20th century.

In the late 1980s and 1990s, American rappers turned this term on its head, from a noun meaning a stupid, clueless person to an adjective synonymous with "excellent," "fine," "attractive," and "cool."

DOUBLE WHAMMY

American English speakers often use the expression *double whammy* to mean one hit of misfortune on top of another. Contracting food poisoning while serving jail time for a DUI would certainly be a double whammy of bad luck.

The saying was born and raised on American soil—in a dogpatch, to be specific. It was coined in the 1940s by Al Capp, author and artist of the *Li'l Abner* comic series featuring Li'l Abner himself, Daisy Mae, Jubilation T. Cornpone, and others, residents of the fictitious Southern town of Dogpatch.

One of Capp's characters was the Brooklyn-born, zoot-suited Evil Eye Fleegle. When provoked, Fleegle had the power to effect ocular hexes, claiming he could melt a battleship simply by staring malevolently with his two evil eyes: the famous *double whammy*. Here's how Fleegle bragged about himself in a Capp comic strip from 1951:

> Evil-Eye Fleegle is th' name, an' th' "whammy" is my
> game. Mudder Nature endowed me wit' eyes which can
> putrefy citizens t' th' spot!…There is th' "single whammy"!
> That, friend, is th' full, pure power o' one o' my evil
> eyes!…And, lastly—th' "double whammy"—namely, th'
> full power o' both eyes—which I hopes I never hafta use.

Li'l Abner retired some thirty years ago, but Evil Eye Fleegle's *double whammy* remains a hard-working Americanism.

DOUBTING THOMAS

A *doubting Thomas* is one who remains unconvinced of something until solid, tangible evidence is produced. The inspiration for this ultimate skeptic is a character from the Bible's New Testament. This Thomas was one of the twelve apostles of Christ. The story of Thomas and his famous doubts is in the book of John, chapter 20, which chronicles the first days after Christ's crucifixion.

After he died, was buried, then returned to the living, Christ appeared to some of his disciples, greeted them, and showed them the crucifixion marks on his hands and the spear wound in his side. The followers who had witnessed this appearance then hurried to tell Thomas, who had not been present. Thomas was not convinced of Christ's resurrection. He said, "Unless I see the nail marks in his hands and put my finger where the nails were, and put my hand into his side, I will not believe it."

Later, Christ appeared to all twelve of the disciples. He approached Thomas, the skeptic, and said, "See my hands. Reach out your hand and put it into my side. Stop doubting and believe."

Though this disciple was ultimately convinced of the resurrection because of tangible evidence, he is always remembered as the original *doubting Thomas.*

DOWN THE RABBIT HOLE

Alice grew bored and tired just sitting on the riverbank with her older sister. She was nearly asleep when a white rabbit with pink eyes, a waistcoat, and a pocket watch ran across the meadow and disappeared into a hole. Curious, Alice followed the rabbit into the hole, "never once considering how in the world she was to get out again."

In this opening sequence of Lewis Carroll's *Alice's Adventures in Wonderland,* Alice's disappearance down the rabbit hole drew her into a world of bizarre and improbable events: shrinking and growing in size, conversing with a caterpillar, and playing croquet with a flamingo as a mallet.

Carroll's beloved 1865 classic inspired the expression *down the rabbit hole,* meaning, in everyday language, an adventure into the unknown.

English speakers have kept this phrase circulating over the decades. Journalist William Plummer, in a July 1991 issue of *People* magazine, wrote of "the rabbit hole of cocaine addiction." Moviegoers were treated to this literary allusion with the 1999 release of *The Matrix,* wherein the protagonist Neo is encouraged to go *down the rabbit hole* in his search for an alternate reality. And the computer gaming world has borrowed the phrase to refer to the initial site or clue that brings a player into a new game. With so many metaphorical rabbit holes in life, the future of this evocative phrase seems assured.

DRACONIAN

The adjective *draconian* means "harsh or severe, rigorous." As an example, the term was used in the *New York Times* on August 15, 1988, in an editorial comment on air pollution control: "Air in the New York region...sometimes contains 50 percent more ozone than permitted. The law provides for sanctions, but they are so Draconian that in practice Congress won't let them be applied."

Though the word *draconian* was first recorded in English in the 1700s, the man who inspired its coinage lived in Athens in the 7th century B.C.

Athenian justice in those days was an arbitrary tangle of vendetta and personal revenge. Murder, for example, was considered a private matter, and the family of the victim was allowed to dispense its own style of justice on the perpetrator.

In 621 B.C., Draco, a chief magistrate of Athens, was called upon to write a legal code for public justice in the city-state. But Athenians' cries for a written constitution were quickly muted when Draco mandated the death penalty for almost every offense, even the most trivial infringement. When questioned about his rigorous legal codes, Draco is said to have replied, "Small crimes deserve death, and for great crimes I know of no penalty severer."

Draco's laws were later modified, but his name remains in our synonym for harsh, rigorous, or repressive: *draconian*.

DRESSED TO THE NINES

Someone *dressed to the nines* is nattily attired, spiffily turned out, putting on the dog. What's the story behind *dressed to the nines,* and what does the number signify in this expression?

It turns out that this synonym for "smartly dressed" is clothed in obscurity. No one claims to know its inspiration.

The original expression may have been *dressed to the eyen,* eyen being the Old English plural of *eye.* This gives us the phrase *dressed to the eyes,* or completely and properly accoutered.

Or the *nine* included in this cliché may literally refer to the number nine, the highest numeral before the digits begin to recycle. Nine is mystically significant; a trinity of trinities, or "three threes." If the spiritual perfection of the number is implied in *dressed to the nines,* a fashion bellwether might feel regal indeed.

Nine as a numerical superlative appears in at least two other common English expressions: *the whole nine yards* and *on cloud nine,* but word watchers can only guess at the significance and meaning of this number.

Dud

American English has at least four applications for the word *dud*. An explosive device—such as a shell or fire-cracker—that fails to detonate is a *dud*. So, too, is a person considered worthless or unattractive when good looks are desired. *Dud* can also mean counterfeit (a dud check) or just bad (a dud of a movie). *Dud* pluralized becomes a slang term for clothing: "I unpacked my *duds* and tucked them in a drawer."

According to the *Oxford English Dictionary*, this word showed up in the 1440s but with its origin unknown. The original spelling was *dudde,* which referred to a "coarse cloak." As the centuries passed, the plural form *duds* was applied to dirty, tattered clothing such as a street urchin might wear. By 1825 came the *dud* that is a "worthless per-son," and by World War I a *dud* was a dead torpedo or shell.

Presumably, all these creative applications came from the original sense of the word—a coarse or tattered cloak. The *dud* as a useless person or a worthless weapon, then, is lin-guistically dismissed as one would an old dirty coat.

In the early 1920s, however, Chicago candymaker F. Hoffman put this pejorative term to positive commercial use when he introduced his small, milk-chocolate covered caramels. The candymaker's original idea was to manufacture perfectly spherical confections, but their consistently lumpy shape inspired Hoffman to name the treats *Milk Duds.*

Dude

The original American *dude* was a 19th century dandy. Often accused of vanity and foppery, the dude was "marked particularly by the extreme height of his round white cylinder of a collar...the spoon-shaped crown of his hard hat...the shortness of his fawn overcoat, and...by such tightness of his trousers that no one could explain how he got his feet through them."

That was writer Booth Tarkington's verbal snapshot of the city-dwelling dude of the late 1800s. Sons of prominent American families, these stylish young men often visited the Wild West, where, by the early 1900s, *dude ranches* were established to accommodate them.

The green and tender-footed dude was given a prominent role in the stories of Zane Grey, Mark Twain, and Owen Wister. Stagecoach tourists were sometimes called *dudes,* and even wealthy, adventuresome young women who traveled west were labeled *dudines* as early as 1883.

Though the derivation of *dude* is inconclusive, some suggest it comes from the Middle English *dud,* a rag or an article of clothing. Or it might be a derivative of the dialectal German word *Dudenkop,* "stupid head," or "fool."

During the 1930s, *dude* expanded from the specific moniker meaning "dandy" to a more generic term synonymous with *guy* or *fellow.* Popular with the smartly dressed, zoot suit crowd and the *pachucos* of the Mexican American community, *dude* became an in-group word of address and acceptance.

Dude II

In the 1960s, California surfers enthusiastically embraced the word *dude,* expanding it to cover just about every guy. The term spilled over into the counterculture of the '60s and '70s but has been significantly reworked in the 1980s and later with the advent of the cinema hits *Fast Times at Ridgemont High, Bill and Ted's Excellent Adventure,* and *Clerks.*

Influenced by these films, American youth now lean hard on the word *dude.* No longer just a simple noun, it has evolved into an exclamation, a greeting, and a token of both agreement and commiseration. And, in Dudeland, it behooves one to know who is and is not a dude.

In the fall 2004 edition of the journal *American Speech,* linguist Scott Kiesling decoded and deciphered the word. Kiesling believes that *dude* derives its social significance from what he calls "cool solidarity." For example, young men who know how to use the word appropriately can demonstrate their feelings of solidarity with other males without hinting at intimacy.

Within those parameters, young men—and increasingly, young women—can deploy *dude* in several creative ways. For example, it's incorporated in a greeting: "What's up, dude?" It's a token of commiseration: "Dude, I'm so sorry." And it's a generic exclamation of surprise, agreement, or disgust: "Dude!" Of course, inside dudedom there are rules about who is not a dude: a parent, a teacher, a boss, a significant other. As Kiesling notes, the accepted pronunciation of the word is *dee-ood. Dood* works, but it exposes the speaker's uncoolness.

Someone deeply committed to anything—political party, philosophy, religious conviction, sport, or team—is frequently described as *dyed in the wool:* "He's a dyed-in-the-wool Lutheran." "She's a NASCAR fan, dyed in the wool!" Synonyms of this idiomatic expression are *hard-core, inflexible, confirmed, long-standing,* and *inveterate.*

The phrase *dyed in the wool* derives its literal meaning from England's early textile industry. Raw wool dyed before it was spun into thread was always truer and more colorfast than wool dyed after processing. In 16th century England, this notion provided a metaphor for someone's youthful opinions and inclinations solidifying into a firm—some would say rigid—dedication to a philosophy or cause. You could say that someone figuratively *dyed in the wool* has been permanently "color-treated" with ideals and convictions at the most auspicious moment.

To find the stories behind expressions like this one, go to the library's reference section or a bookstore. Along with the standard Webster's and Random House dictionaries are books that outline the histories of clichés like *dyed in the wool, cool as a cucumber, rule of thumb, mind your P's and Q's,* and thousands of others.

EAVESDROP

Listening in on a private conversation is *eavesdropping*. Who would have guessed that the term is architectural in origin?

The primary element in this word, *eaves*, refers to the edge of a roof that projects over the side of a house. The eavesdrip or eavesdrop of a building is the sheltered area below the eaves where rainwater cascades off the roof. A curious neighbor standing under the projection with an ear to the door or window has, since the 15th century, been labeled an *eavesdropper*.

In a document recorded in 1527, someone named John Rastell wrote, "Eavesdroppers are such as stand under walls or windows by night or day to hear news, and to carry them to others, to make strife and debate amongst their neighbours: those are evil members in the commonwealth, and therefore...are to be punished."

This scenario suggests lodgings not nearly as well insulated as modern houses. Just as wind and rain could creep in through the chinks and cracks of earlier dwellings, conversation could as easily leak out and into the waiting ear of the eavesdropper.

Curious that English has a word for one who secretly listens in on discussions but lacks an analogous term for one who reads others' private mail or documents. How about *eyedropper?*

EPIPHANY

January 6 marks the Christian celebration of the Epiphany. Tradition says that on this day, twelve days after Christmas, the Three Kings from the East, the Magi, came to Bethlehem to honor the Christ child. Symbolically, Epiphany signifies the manifestation of Christ to the Gentiles, who are represented in the story by the Magi from foreign lands.

First recorded in English documents as long ago as 1310, *epiphany* comes from a Greek word meaning "to show forth, to appear or make manifest." But long before the birth of Christ, the Greeks were using this term in reference to the sudden appearances or manifestations of their own gods, Athena, Zeus, Pan, Hermes, Artemis, et al.

Today, we ordinary mortals still experience epiphanies, but perhaps of a more secular nature. No longer exactly divine appearances, as the history of the word suggests, modern epiphanies are personal revelations, sudden insights, moments of clarity that occur randomly, inspired by chance encounters, or words, or gestures.

Epitaph

An *epitaph* is a parting comment composed by, or in honor of, the deceased. Carved in the granite of a headstone or painted on a piece of wood, epitaphs may be tender and sentimental, as is Mark Twain's farewell for his daughter Susy: "Warm summer sun, shine kindly here/Green sod above, lie light, lie light/Good night, dear heart, good night, good night."

Others may be witty and terse. Observed on a Cleveland, Ohio, grave marker: "Once I wasn't/then I was/now I ain't again." In a Georgia cemetery: "I told you I was sick." An obvious nonbeliever in a Maryland graveyard left this message: "Here lies an Atheist/All dressed up/and no place to go."

Julian Skaggs, who died in West Virginia in 1974, had his cremated remains interred in the family burial plot. His parting message reads: "I made an ash of myself." And the good professor John Sumner had this inscription carved on his marker: "An English Teacher, who could not only spell the word epitaph correctly but also knew what it means."

Perhaps John Sumner, rest his soul, knew that *epitaph* is a word of Greek origin, a conjoining of the prefix *epi-,* meaning "upon or over," and *taphos,* "tomb." So, etymologically, an epitaph is a sentiment poised "over the tomb."

ESPERANTO

Esperanto is what linguists call a "universal artificial language." When he conceived Esperanto in the 1870s, Ludovic Lazarus Zamenhof, a Polish ophthalmologist, hoped his invented language would provide the linguistic bridge between people of all ethnic backgrounds.

Dr. Zamenhof, fluent in Yiddish, Polish, Russian, and German, dreamed of an international language of simple, regular grammatical construction with a vocabulary drawn from a variety of European languages.

Zamenhof published the first Esperanto grammar text in July 1887. In 1894 he circulated *Universala Votraro,* the language's first dictionary. Today, there are approximately two million Esperanto speakers throughout the world, most of them living in Central and Eastern Europe, China, and Southwest Asia. Esperanto enthusiasts say the language is a common, easy-to-learn communication system, no matter what the speaker's native language might be.

In 1884, when Zamenhof published his first grammar textbook, he called it *Lingvo Internacia,* Esperanto for "International Language." Under the title appeared the Polish ophthalmologist's pen name, Doktoro Esperanto, which means, in the language, "Dr. Hopeful." The pseudonym reflects the scholar's dream that a universal language would promote peace and understanding. *Esperanto,* meaning literally "one who hopes," eventually became the official name of the language itself.

Dr. Martin Luther King, Jr., once said, "The reason I can't follow the old eye-for-an-eye philosophy is that it ends up leaving everybody blind." King was referring, of course, to the oft-quoted biblical law of fair judgment given to the nation of Israel through the prophet Moses.

The Old Testament book of Exodus traces the movement of the Israelites out of Egypt, the land of their slavery, and into a new country that God had reserved for them. As these people wandered through the desert, God called Moses to the ramparts of Mt. Sinai, where the prophet was given the divine laws for governing the Israelites in their new home. In addition to the Ten Commandments, God also dispensed hundreds of other legal codes directing commerce, domestic life, slavery, and agricultural practices.

One of the laws stated that, if one caused another serious injury, he was to take "life for life, eye for eye, tooth for tooth, hand for hand, foot for foot." This Old Testament "eye for an eye" law has been cited for centuries as justification for revenge and retaliation in kind. The ancient expression is now considered a cliché and has been used as a literary allusion by contemporary writers such as Truman Capote, Mario Puzo, and John Grisham.

Aesop, the Potentate of Proverbs, is probably the inspiration for *familiarity breeds contempt,* a cliché that translates to "overexposure to someone can turn respect into scorn." In his tale of the fox and the lion, a fox bolts in terror the first time he sees a mighty lion. The second time, though, the fox stands his ground, and in their third encounter he initiates a casual conversation with the impressive creature. From there, Aesop implies, the fox is but a hair's breadth from disrespecting the king of beasts.

Aesop told this fable in the 6th century B.C. Five hundred years later, the Roman writer Publilius Syrus recorded the Latin version of Aesop's moral. The expression was subsequently taken up by other writers and thinkers: the Greek Plutarch, Pope Innocent III, Chaucer, Cervantes, and most famously Mark Twain, who flavored it with his own wit by saying, "Familiarity breeds contempt—and children."

In 1603, Miguel de Cervantes said, "Proverbs are short sentences drawn from long experience." William Penn wrote that proverbs are "notable measures and directions for human life." If you're curious about the stories behind the birth of these particular expressions, you can find them in a dictionary of proverbs at your local library or bookstore.

FAR OUT

Synonymous with "great," "excellent," "astonishing," "outstanding," the classic hippie cry *far out* was an integral part of the youth jargon of the 1960s and '70s. *Far out* was both exuberant enough to match the tenor of the counter-culture era and slangy and vague enough to prevent adults from adopting it.

Though the exclamation might give the impression of being as youthful as the baby boomer generation was, *far out* is of older vintage. In the 1950s, jazz players used the expression to describe experimental music. *Far out* in this context simply meant the music was "far out" of the mainstream.

Devoted fans and performers of this brand of jazz had attitude. The *Dictionary of American Slang,* published in 1960, meticulously describes the concept behind the *far out* existence this way: "Extremely 'gone' or far removed from reality...intense; so much in rapport with...one's work, performance, ideas, or mode or way of life that one is as if in a trance...intellectually, psychologically, or spiritually so cool as to be beyond comparison."

In the 1950s, the musician's sense of *far out* had an almost metaphysical dimension, implying a spiritual or intellectual inaccessibility. As the expression gained ground with the hippie culture, *far out* became a high-spirited exclamation of approval.

FERRIS WHEEL

In 1893 it was trumpeted as "Chicago's answer to the Eiffel Tower." The Ferris wheel, like the great steel wonder erected four years earlier in Paris in 1889, was a triumph of engineering. In stunning contradistinction to the Parisian structure, however, the Ferris wheel moved, transporting passengers in a slow rotation that carried them 250 feet in the air before returning them to the ground to begin the cycle again.

The Ferris wheel was installed on the midway of Chicago's World Colombian Exhibition of 1893. Its form and construction were a study in superlatives. Built like a giant bicycle wheel, the device carried up to two thousand passengers in its thirty-six enclosed cars. Its axis was, at the time, the largest single piece of steel ever forged.

The Ferris wheel began operation on June 21, and by the time it closed five months later, 1.4 million thrill seekers had taken the great circular ride.

The brains behind the colossus was a young American steel engineer, already famous for his bridge and tunnel designs. The promoters of the 1893 Colombian Exhibition hired the engineer to showcase the new technology of structural steel. His name? George Washington Gale Ferris. By loaning his surname to the famous wheel, Ferris added yet another entry to the long roster of eponyms, or names that have become words.

Fib

A fable, of course, is a short tale intended to teach a moral lesson. Many of the stories we would call fables are attributed to Greek storyteller Aesop, who spun vignettes filled with talking animals with a full range of human personalities. The well-known fable of the tortoise and the hare, for example, teaches that consistency, not speed, ensures success.

The word *fable* is derived from the Latin *fabula,* meaning "narrative" or "story." But *fable* also denotes a fabrication or a story about as believable as one of Aesop's tales of talking asses and lions. This sense of the word inspired the 16th century construction *fible-fable* for "lies, prevarication." *Fible-fable* is but one in the roster of English nonsense reduplications, or combinations of sound, repetition, and rhyme. It's synonymous with *mumbo-jumbo, hocus pocus,* and *phoney baloney.*

Though the expression *fible-fable* is rather antiquated, its vestige remains in our very current and useful word *fib,* which first appeared in print in the early 1600s. Prolific English critic and playwright John Dryden, in the 1690 comedy *Amphitryon,* wrote, "I do not say he lyes....no, I am too well bred for that: but his Lordship fibbs most abominably." The word *fib,* from the fanciful reduplication *fible-fable,* implies a trivial falsehood, a lie dressed in a fig leaf.

FINK

Born in the waning years of the 19th century, the word *fink* has lived a colorful life in American English slang. The earliest citation of the word comes from the 1892 Homestead strike staged by the workers at Pennsylvania's Carnegie Steel Company. The word *fink* was applied as an insult to the three hundred armed Pinkerton detectives hired to break that strike. Some word watchers suggest *fink* is a rhyme of the *pink* in Pinkerton, surname of Allan Pinkerton, founder of his National Detective Agency in Chicago in 1850.

In the early decades of the 20th century, *fink* was adopted by prison convicts to denote a disloyal inmate who revealed insurgency plans to prison authorities. The word slowly worked its way into America's slang vocabulary as a synonym for "squealer" or "snitch." This leads some lexicographers to surmise that the moniker was taken directly from the German language, where *Fink* means "finch," a metaphor for one who "sings" or tattles on another.

In the 1950s and '60s, American students enthusiastically embraced *fink* as a general term of abuse for someone considered offensive, contemptible, or unreliable. But *fink* was not insulting enough for some; real losers were branded *ratfinks*.

FIRE

If you're terminated from a job in America, you're *fired*. But in Britain you're *given the sack,* or simply *sacked.* What are the life histories behind these two terms for sudden involuntary unemployment?

In the 1870s, to *fire* someone was to simply eject or throw him from a place by force. At the same time, to *fire out* was a phrase often attached to the expulsion of a student. An early 20th century pupil wrote, "He spanked me with a club and fired me out of the school." By the 1880s, laborers were said to be *fired out* of their jobs.

Gradually, the *out* was dropped from the phrase, leaving the familiar word for dismissal from a job: *fired.* Not related at all to burning, this fire seems to derive from the sense of rapid ejection, specifically, the discharge or "firing" of a bullet or a cannonball.

As for *sack,* the British analogue, here's what lexicographer Stuart B. Flexner writes in his book *Listening to America:* "The concept of being 'sacked' had been widespread throughout Europe since the Middle Ages, some say because craftsmen were given back their tools in a sack when they were dismissed, while others say it comes from the method of execution of being tied in a sack and drowned, a punishment...going back to ancient Roman days when [murderers] were tied in a sack and drowned in the Tiber River."

FLABBERGAST

Have you ever been so shocked and astonished that you were *flabbergasted?* Have you ever wondered how one's "gast" comes to be "flabbered"? Though most of us know what this word means, no one seems to know for certain why it's constructed the way it is.

The *Oxford English Dictionary* tells us the term was first mentioned in 1772 as a new piece of fashionable slang possibly generated by some playful wordsmith in Suffolk, England.

Word watchers are fairly sure the *gast* part of *flabbergast* derives from the Middle English verb *agasten,* "to terrify," and is related to "aghast," "ghastly," and even "ghost."

It's the *flabber* part that's troublesome, really, but here are some guesses about its genesis. It could suggest "flap" or "disturbance," as in to make a flap about something. If so, *flabbergast* would mean "to be frightened over a flap or uproar."

Or, the flabber could suggest trembling. So, our word might mean being so thunderstruck that one "flabs" and quakes with "gast," or fear.

It's not so important to know the precise derivation of *flabbergast,* or any such tasty polysyllable. What matters is that you use it, often, and with gusto!

FOGEY, GEEZER

The male elders among us must frequently endure derogatory nicknames. *Fogey* is a slightly condescending slang term for one who holds fast to antiquated notions. Fogies are often elderly, but not necessarily so. Even a young man can be a *fogey* if his ideas are outdated enough.

The origin of this term has been a matter of some discussion. It may be a variant of an older sense of the word *foggy*, a Scottish term meaning "moss-covered," or, by extension, "old and inert," just like a fogey.

On the other hand, the term may have had a specialized military meaning. In 18th and 19th century England, *fogey* and *old fogey* were nicknames for an invalid or elderly soldier. *Fogey pay*, a term current during the 19th and 20th centuries, was longevity pay or a pay increase awarded to a soldier after a given number of years of service.

Another unflattering term aimed at older men is *geezer*. The *Oxford English Dictionary* has this as a dialectal pronunciation of the word *guiser*, one who goes about in disguise. Such a character is whimsically attired and peculiar in personality, a common observation made about elderly eccentric men.

Other opprobrious nicknames for older or hidebound males are *duffer, codger,* and *fuddy duddy*. The interesting stories behind these terms are on the pages of any good dictionary.

A mélange of spiced and chopped meat stuffed in a casing, sausage has been a popular source of nutrition since antiquity. The Greeks were probably making and eating sausage in the 6th century B.C., and the Romans are credited with introducing the culinary preparation to Northern Europe six hundred years later.

Europeans experimented with the concept, eventually innovating their own local varieties. A butcher's guild was in place in Frankfurt Germany by 1484, showcasing a regional sausage that became known as the *Frankfurter*, meaning literally "of Frankfurt." Imported to the States by 19th century German immigrants, this sausage became the American *frank*.

The liver sausage called *Braunschweiger* was originally the local preparation of butchers from Braunschweig, Germany. The *brat* in *bratwurst*, the name of a pork sausage, comes from an ancient Germanic term meaning "roast meat." *Wurst*, the German word for "sausage," evolved from the Latin *vertere*, "to turn, roll," a reference to the cylindrical shape of the prepared meat.

Bologna in northeast Italy is the home of a fully cooked and smoked sausage, and the word *salami* comes from *sal*, the Latin word for salt.

The word *freak* has a long and checkered etymological career. According to the *Oxford English Dictionary*, the ultimate ancestor of freak is an Old English verb meaning "to dance." When the word began appearing in print in the 1500s, it meant "a sudden causeless change or turn of the mind; a capricious humour, [or] notion." Authors of the 16th century wrote poetically of "fickle freaks of fortune" and "freaks of tyrannical fury."

The term remained fairly stable until the 1800s. Since the natural world itself was sometimes considered whimsical and capricious, the word *freak* was called into service to describe nature's abnormally developed organisms: *freaks of nature,* or simply *freaks.* A dwarf this, a two-headed that, a hairy something else—all these *freaks* were typical 19th century sideshow exhibit fare. Later, in the 20th century, the word became a term of abuse; someone considered odd in any way might be labeled a *freak.*

So when the hairy, peace-loving hippies began appearing on the streets of San Francisco in the 1960s, they were dubbed *freaks* by the less whimsically inclined. Counterculture youth delighted in the moniker, embracing the notion that they were considered abnormal and deviant.

After the original countercultural movement, there were freaks everywhere: speed freaks, eco-freaks, Jesus freaks, guitar freaks. The word used in this sense is a synonym of "enthusiast." Another stripe of *freak* is the sexual deviant, usually a woman who explores many sensual frontiers.

The expression *freak flag,* meaning "long hair," got its

moment in the sun in David Crosby's 1970 song "Almost Cut My Hair":

> Almost cut my hair
> It happened just the other day
> Was gettin' kinda long
> I could've said it was in my way
> But I didn't and I wonder why
> I feel like letting my freak flag fly
> 'Cause I feel like I owe it to someone

The unfortunate freak who experienced a bad hallucinogenic experience was said to *freak out* when she lost control. This phrase has since passed into mainstream English. It's no longer necessary to ingest chemicals to freak out. Today, the expression means to be "overcome by fear, anger, or excitement."

FREE LUNCH

It may be offered here and there, but *there's no such thing as a free lunch*—or so the common-sense American catchphrase goes, warning that you can't get something of value for nothing. The source of this expression cannot be verified, but most dictionaries place its appearance somewhere in the early 20th century. It may have been inspired by saloon customers partaking of a heavily advertised "free lunch" only to pay inflated drink prices.

The catchphrase was popularized in Robert A. Heinlein's 1967 science fiction novel *The Moon is a Harsh Mistress.* But Heinlein turned the phrase into an acronym: TANSTAAFL, which stands for *there ain't no such thing as a free lunch.* The expression enjoyed another brush with fame in 1975 when economist Milton Friedman published a book titled *There's No Such Thing as a Free Lunch.*

Advertisers and writers lean heavily on this phrase. In a Dallas restaurant review blog of May 2005, Glenn Eddie Gill wrote, "There's no such thing as a free lunch…but if you work downtown…there's a damn cheap lunch for just $3.95." In an op-ed column about U.S. trade with Vietnam in the June 20, 2003, issue of the *Chicago Times,* economics professor Van Pham wrote, "As free market proponents like to point out 'there's no such thing as a free lunch.' Now, from the freest of market economies, comes another piece of wisdom, 'there's no such thing as free trade.'"

For millennia, thinkers have pondered the nature of friendship. Roman statesman Cicero considered friendship important enough to be judiciously cultivated and carefully maintained. An early Latin poet and the so-called Father of Latin literature, Quintus Ennius, who lived from 239 to 169 B.C., said, "Uncertain times distinguish the certain friend."

This ancient sentiment has been expressed in a variety of ways throughout the centuries. In 200 B.C., playwright Plautus proclaimed, "Nothing is there more friendly to a man than a friend in need." Englishman William Caxton, translating the fables of Aesop in 1485, wrote, "The very and trewe friend is fond in the extreme nede." A French proverb likewise says, "Prosperity gives friends, adversity proves them."

None of these observations on friendship is commonly quoted in its original form. Instead, all seem to have been conflated into the modern proverb *a friend in need is a friend indeed,* a pithy rhyme that has been in circulation since the late 1600s.

Interested in proverbs and the stories behind their coinage? I recommend an excellent tome called *Dictionary of Proverbs and Their Origins,* by Linda and Roger Flavell. The Flavells combine their passion for the proverb with insight and careful scholarship.

The Full Monty

It wasn't until the 1997 release of a British movie that Americans were exposed to the expression *the full monty,* meaning "everything, the total amount." The film tells the story of six unemployed steelworkers who turn to stripping for some extra cash. Before an enthusiastic female audience, the men molt their garb, finally revealing *the full monty.*

Unfortunately, the history of this expression does not reveal itself as easily. The phrase has sparse recorded evidence before the late 1980s, but it quickly gained currency throughout Britain in the early 1990s. Those who track the sources of words and phrases can only take an educated guess at the origin of *the full monty.*

One theory involves a card game called *monte;* the winner of the high-stakes game would rake in the whole kitty, or *the full monte.*

Another story links the expression to World War II British Field Marshal Bernard Montgomery, who insisted on a complete daily breakfast, even in the field. His morning meals became known as *the full Monty.*

Others say one Sir Montague Burton, a British tailor, is responsible for today's phrase. A proper gentleman's suit, complete with waistcoat and a spare pair of trousers fashioned by Sir Montague Burton, may have been the original *full Monty.*

FUZZ

Remember the word *fuzz,* the insulting nickname for police that was last heard coming from the mouths of war protesters sometime in the early 1970s? Though this term emitted a bright, brief spark in the 20th century, no one has been able to identify its source. But it's not for lack of effort. Almost every American etymologist has floated a theory to explain the existence of *fuzz.*

Fuzz appears to have originated in the 1920s as part of tramp and underworld slang. Then, as now, *fuzz* was a disrespectful moniker for police. The earliest explanation for the nickname is that *fuzz* was based on the word *fuss,* suggesting that cops were "fussy" about enforcing the details of the law.

Another theory that's been circulating for decades has *fuzz* as a slurred pronunciation of "Feds." Others say the word is a direct reference to the "fuzz," or extravagant facial hair, sported by "old fashioned," turn-of-the-century cops.

In a more exotic account, the nickname comes from the West African word *fas,* meaning "horse." From there, the term, modified to *fuzz,* passed to mounted policemen, then to cops in general.

Recently, Evan Morris, the master of an excellent website—*The Word Detective*—suggested that the word could be based on the adjective *fuzzy.* He says, "To be 'fuzzy' [is] to be unmanly, incompetent, and soft. How better to insult the police, after all, than to mock them as ineffectual?"

GADFLY

Greek philosopher Socrates earned the moniker "gadfly of Athens" for his relentless public questioning of the city's leaders on their understanding of philosophical and political issues. Pleased with the metaphor, Socrates imagined Athens a large, well-bred horse and himself a gadfly keeping the animal alert by his maddening, stinging discourse.

Such agitators derive their label from the common family name of Tabanidae, or biting flies, a scourge on nearly every continent. Called horseflies, deerflies, or blue-tail flies in North America, their European analogue is *gadfly*. These swarming, stinging insects can drive livestock and wild herds mad, providing metaphor for the human gadflies that infuriate powerful corporations and political entities.

The *gad* in this term comes from an Old Norse word meaning "sharp spike of metal." The word *goad,* referring to a pointed rod for driving cattle, is a close relative. Etymologically, when the gadfly bites, it's as if a metal spike is piercing the skin.

One of the meanings of the verb *galvanize* is "to stimulate to sudden action, to startle, to excite"—as in "The devastating loss galvanized the entire team to claim subsequent victories." The term *galvanize* has an impressive life history, one that involves frog's legs and an Italian anatomist.

Luigi Galvani was born in Bologna, Italy, in 1737. As professor of anatomy at the famous university in his hometown, Galvani's research projects were diverse—from the structure of the ear in birds and humans to the electrical properties of the torpedo ray. But a series of experiments with frog's legs was what placed Luigi Galvani conspicuously on the scientific and etymological landscape.

After dissecting a frog in his laboratory one day, Galvani discovered that the creature's lifeless limbs twitched and contracted when touched with electrically charged metal contacts. Galvani attributed this reaction to a force he called "animal electricity," a mysterious power that made dead tissue quiver, even for a moment, with life. Hundreds of subsequent experiments convinced him of the validity of his conclusions.

But Galvani's academic peers exploded his theory with counterclaims that it was merely the externally generated electricity that was responsible for muscle movement in dead animals. Galvani nevertheless remains enshrined in the verb *galvanize:* "to stimulate or rouse as if by electric current."

GENERATION GAP

When the baby boomers began to come of age in the 1960s, they embraced values antithetical to those of their parents. Abandoning American organized religion, for example, boomers turned to mysticism, astrology, Buddhism. And Vietnam War protests shocked the older generation that had just been involved in a cooperative effort to claim a world war victory.

Boomers dismantled the sexual regulations their parents had defined and observed. Youth fashion and musical tastes strained the tolerance of the "GI Generation," who were mystified by their children's willingness to experiment openly with recreational drugs.

This significant moral, political, and social distance between boomer youth and their elders was, in about 1967, given a name: the *generation gap*. This phenomenon became a national obsession for the remainder of the 1960s.

So fashionable was the moniker *generation gap* that two San Francisco entrepreneurs claimed part of it as a name for their small clothing store. In 1969, Don and Doris Fisher opened a shop in downtown San Francisco that sold nothing but jeans, the essential component of the counterculture wardrobe. They called it *The Gap*, hoping to attract the people on the youthful side of the generational divide.

The plan worked, with sales escalating steadily throughout the 20th century. In the new millennium, its namesake chain store Gap serves millions of boomers—most of whom are now older than their parents were at the apex of the 1960s generation gap.

Have you ever been so annoyed that you could say with relative confidence that someone *got your goat?* We've been using this idiom to express annoyance or irritation for at least a century, and probably longer. What's the story behind this inscrutable phrase?

Unfortunately, the origin of *get one's goat* is fugitive. Although one of the first literary citations of the expression appeared in a 1912 Jack London novel called *Smoke Bellew,* the source of the cliché remains elusive.

American editor and critic H. L. Mencken offered a somewhat fanciful theory in 1945, speculating that the expression derived from the horse racing industry. Goats, said Mencken, were often stabled beside high-strung thoroughbreds to calm them between races. A goat stolen (or "gotten") from a paddock by the owners of a rival racehorse would be missed by its equine stablemate. The scheme was to upset the horse enough to cause him to falter in the next race.

It's not a good idea to find fault with something that someone freely gives you. That's the plain English translation of the common expression "don't look a gift horse in the mouth."

The logic supporting this notion is that one can evaluate a horse's age and health by examining its teeth. A young animal's mouth is full of smooth, clean, compact teeth, but as the horse ages, the teeth become increasingly dark and more grooved, and they appear to lengthen year by year.

So, if someone is kind enough to *give* you a horse, don't insult his generosity or ruin a friendship by immediately inspecting the animal's teeth—that's what this proverb literally tells us. You gratefully accept the horse, whether it's young or old, sound or sick.

Versions of this expression appear in Latin, Spanish, Portuguese, and Russian. The Germans say "Einem geschenkten Gaul nicht ins Maul sehen." In its earliest English citation, from 1510, the expression reads "A gyuen hors may not be loked in the tethe."

Ginger, Gingerly

There are two *gingers* in the English language: one is the fragrant spice for flavoring and cooking, and the other is the largest part of the adverb *gingerly,* meaning "delicately, carefully." *Ginger* and *gingerly,* alike as they are, would appear to rest on the same branch of the tree of etymology. But do they?

Let's begin by shining the light on ginger, the pungent spice derived from a plant root. Native to Southeast Asia, ginger has been a popular trade item for thousands of years. The word has an incredibly complicated life history, but its ultimate language of origin is thought to be Sanskrit, the classical language of the Hindus of India. *Ginger* arises from a word meaning "horn-body," a reference to its branching form.

Though *gingerly* is nearly a mirror image of *ginger,* their similarities are merely coincidental. *Gingerly* is more closely related to the words *genteel, gentleman,* and *generous,* whose ultimate ancestor is a Latin term meaning "well-born, noble." So, someone moving about *gingerly* is etymologically comporting herself daintily and gracefully, as befitting one of noble birth.

GLADIATOR

Gladiator exhibitions were popular attractions throughout the ancient Roman empire. The first known gladiator contest was held in Rome in 264 B.C. The tradition flourished for about 600 years until it was finally abolished in about A.D. 400.

Trained to fight battles with men and wild beasts, gladiators were mostly criminals, slaves, or prisoners of war, destined for a likely death in the arena. There were various classes of gladiators—some fighting with nets, lassos, and tridents; others battling on horseback or from chariots.

Their most common implement of combat was the Roman legionary's short sword, called the *gladius*. The ancient warriors earned their name from this weapon: *gladiator* means "one who fights with the *gladius*, or short sword."

The Latin word *gladiator* shares etymological history with the name of a popular garden flower, the gladiolus. Sometimes called the sword lily, the gladiolus grows tall and slender, with brilliant spikes of flowers and long blade-shaped leaves. The plant is native to Africa, Europe, and the Mediterranean. In A.D. 70, Roman historian Pliny the Elder named this plant gladiolus, or "little sword," after the shape of its distinctive leaves, which resembled the *gladius* of the sword-wielding gladiators.

GOING TO THE DOGS, TO POT, TO HELL

On the losing end, no American English speaker need merely "deteriorate," or "fail." She can, more colorfully, *go to the dogs, go to pot,* or *go to hell in a handbasket.*

Going to the dogs expresses a sentiment as old as the human-canine relationship itself. In places where dogs are not revered, they're often reviled; a person *gone to the dogs* has metaphorically joined the ranks of the inferior, sleeping outside and scavenging for scraps. The expression *go to the dogs* has been popular since the 17th century.

The synonymous cliché *go to pot* was inspired by substandard portions of meat being chopped up and added to a boiling stew, where they eventually grew tough and unpalatable. Someone *gone to pot* has disintegrated and lost flavor, suffering the same fate as low-grade stew meat.

And how about its sinister sister, *going to hell in a handbasket?* Christine Ammer, researcher for several cliché dictionaries, says this phrase owes its appeal to alliteration. Ammer notes that, since "something carried in a handbasket is necessarily light and easily conveyed...the term means going to hell easily and rapidly."

GOLDWYNISMS

Film baron Samuel Goldwyn, born in Warsaw, Poland, in 1882, emigrated to the States at age 13 with twenty dollars in his pocket. He died in 1974, a multimillionaire and respected producer of some seventy American cinema classics, including *Wuthering Heights* and *Porgy and Bess*.

Samuel Goldwyn was not only a trailblazer in the film industry, he was also something of a linguistic oddball, and the author of countless malapropisms. With a twinkle in his eye and English as his second language, Goldwyn mangled America's mother tongue just enough to keep the public chuckling. His 1937 assessment of Hollywood directors was, "They're always biting the hand that lays the golden egg."

When Goldwyn resigned from the Motion Picture Producers and Distributors of America in 1933, he quipped, "Gentlemen, include me out!" Discussing the quality of his films in 1969, he said, "Our comedies are not to be laughed at." Of psychotherapy, the rage of Hollywood, Goldwyn opined that "anyone who goes to a psychiatrist ought to have his head examined."

Because Goldwyn fractured the language with such frequency, he was often called Mr. Malaprop, after the comic character Mrs. Malaprop, the verbicidal aunt in the 18th century English play *The Rivals*. Goldwyn, a shameless self-promoter, didn't seem to mind his reputation. He is said to have gleefully quipped, "Let's have some new clichés!"

Good Samaritan

Someone who selflessly helps a stranger in distress is a *good Samaritan*. This noble title alludes to one of Christ's parables in the New Testament.

Jesus tells a story illustrating how a good neighbor ought to behave: One day, a Jewish traveler was on a journey from Jerusalem to Jericho. Along the road, he was ambushed by bandits, stripped and robbed, then beaten so badly that he was near death. A priest who was taking the same path came across the bleeding man but quickly crossed to the other side of the road. Next, a Levite, a sort of priest's assistant, came along, but he was in such a hurry that he also refused to help the injured traveler.

Soon a Samaritan—a member of an outcast society among the Jews—came upon the injured man. The Samaritan took pity on him, dressed his wounds, and then paid for his lodging at an inn. Jesus used this parable to illustrate that the Samaritan—the traditional pariah—was the true and good neighbor.

Interestingly, the exact phrase *good Samaritan* does not appear in the Bible. It evolved over the centuries through various references and allusions to this parable.

A confederation of American RV owners called the "Good Sam Club" named its organization in 1966 for the ancient Samaritan who helped the needy stranger on the road.

GORGONIZE

According to Greek mythology, the Gorgons were three monstrous sisters with necks covered in dragon's scales, claws of bronze, and teeth of curled boar's tusks. Live snakes writhed and hissed from the Gorgon's heads where hair should have grown.

The most fabled of the horrible sisters was Medusa, whom tradition says was once a beautiful woman. Unfortunately, Medusa made herself a rival of Athena, the goddess of beauty itself. Jealous Athena turned upon Medusa and cursed her with terrible disfigurements and a spite like poison.

So fierce was Medusa's hatred that a glance from her eyes turned animals and humans to stone. Petrified corpses littered the entrance to her cavern; even the immortals feared the wrath of the hideous Gorgon.

But finally, a warrior god named Perseus vanquished Medusa. Guided by the reflection on his shield, so her glance could not kill him, Perseus drew near the sleeping Gorgon and beheaded her. He gave the head to Athena, who attached it to the middle of her shield as a protective talisman.

The legend of the Gorgon Medusa inspired a splendid but woefully underused English verb: *gorgonize*. *The American Heritage Dictionary* defines *gorgonize* as "have a paralyzing or stupifying effect upon." In the poem "Maud," Alfred, Lord Tennyson, writes, "He gorgonized me from head to foot with a stony British stare."

GRAMMY

The first Grammy Award ceremony was held on May 4, 1959. The album of the year was Henry Mancini's *Music from Peter Gunn,* and Perry Como won best male performance of the year with "Catch a Falling Star."

The Grammy, an award presented annually by the National Academy of Recording Arts and Sciences—the Recording Academy—in a range of performance categories, is the holy grail of musicians of every genre. Grammy winners, selected by the voting members of the Recording Academy, receive a gilded statuette of a gramophone, the namesake for the award.

But what exactly is a gramophone, and how did it get its name?

Gramophone was the name of a recording device patented in 1887 by German inventor Emile Berliner. This machine, the first of its kind to generate mass-produced disks from a master recording, was outfitted with turntable, a metal arm with a stylus, and a trumpet-shaped speaker—the familiar model for the Grammy statuettes.

Berliner created the name for the device by reversing the syllables of *phonogram,* a word already in use referring to a device for recording phonographic messages. *Phonogram* means something like "sound writing," but Berliner inverted the whole concept with *gramophone,* which literally means "writing sound." The slangy abbreviation *grammy* was appropriated by the Recording Academy in 1959.

THE GRASS IS ALWAYS GREENER

The proverbial phrase *the grass is always greener on the other side of the fence* expresses a common human suspicion that someone else's situation may be more desirable than one's own. Also implied in the proverb is the notion that whatever is inaccessible is pleasing and fascinating.

Roman poet Ovid may have been the first to record an ancient statement analogous to this one. His version was "The harvest is always more fruitful in another man's fields." According to an English proverb recorded in 1640, "The apples on the other side of the wall are the sweetest," and a Scottish expression from 1678 claims that "The fairest apple hangs on the highest bough."

Perhaps *the grass is always greener on the other side of the fence* was inspired by the habit of grazing livestock escaping to a neighboring pasture for better, or at least different, forage. Today, of course, this proverb is often cited as an excuse for infidelity, with the "greener grass" a metaphor for the illicit lover.

Proverbs, like any formulaic expression, invite parody. Some of the recent waggish variants of this proverb are "The grass is always greener when you take care of it"; "The grass may seem greener on the other side, but it still needs mowing"; and "The grass is really never greener on the other side, but rather 'differently shaded.'"

GUINEA PIG

The little guinea pig is native to South America, specifically Ecuador, Peru, Bolivia, and Brazil. In the wild, these rodents live in grassy areas, moving about in small family groups. As crepuscular creatures, they tend to be active at dawn and dusk when they are least visible to predators. Guinea pigs were domesticated for their meat thousands of years ago and are still used as a source of protein by people living in the mountainous regions of South America.

In North America and Europe, however, these timid creatures are enjoyed as pets, and they have been selectively bred into several varieties.

The label *guinea pig* is a misnomer, for the animals are neither of West African origin—as the first part of their name might suggest—nor related to pigs in any way. So, whence the name? The *Facts on File Encyclopedia of Word and Phrase Origins* by Robert Hendrickson advances one possibility—that the creature was first brought to Europe on slave ships that originally sailed from Guinea to South America. On the return trip from the Americas, so-called *guinea pigs* were brought aboard and may early on have been compared to pigs because of their round rumps, stout necks, and edible flesh.

Because these rodents are often used in laboratory experiments, the extended moniker *guinea pig* informally refers to a person on whom something new is tested.

When was the last time you *let your hair down,* or relaxed and abandoned formality? This is a phrase that's long outlived the custom that inspired it. *Letting the hair down* alluded to the carefully tended, old-fashioned tresses atop a woman's head that were allowed to fall loosely only in the informal atmosphere of the home.

When you *get in someone's hair,* you're being an annoyance. Though the origin of the phrase is uncertain, to *get in one's hair* may suggest the intrusive irritation of head lice. The expression was certainly in use by the mid-19th century, and probably much earlier.

People who *split hairs* quibble over insignificant details. The analogy between painstakingly dividing a single hair and formulating an overrefined argument was known in Shakespeare's time. In his 1597 drama *King Henry IV,* Shakespeare writes, "I'll cavil on the ninth part of a hair," meaning, "I'll argue over a tiny portion."

The phrase *bad hair day* is of more recent vintage. First appearing in print in 1991, this expression literally describes unruly hair, and, by extension, refers to a day when everything seems similarly unmanageable. The phrase showed up in 1993 in *Glamour, Time,* and *Science* magazines and soon made its mark in popular culture. In 1994, complaints about the *bad hair day* were featured on the Oprah Winfrey show.

Hair Expressions II

It's been said for decades that swallowing strong liquor or coffee will *put hair on your chest,* that is, make you "manlier." One early use of this phrase occurred in the 1931 film *Painted Desert,* in which a character holds out a bottle and says, "Take a swig of this. It'll put hair on your chest."

The slang adjective *hairy* has at least two undertones. Early in the 20th century, *hairy* was a synonym for "old" or "passé." A hairy joke was old enough to have grown tangles of hair. But in the 1950s the word was used to mean "frightening" or "difficult," like a turbulent airplane flight or a steep ski run. This sense of *hairy* could be a version of the expression *hair-raising*—describing a circumstance so frightening it makes the hair stand on end.

What about the curious phrase *hair of the dog?* In modern incarnation, this expression is hairless...*and* dogless, for that matter. *Hair of the dog* is a cure for a hangover, consisting of a nip or two of the alcohol that got you drunk the night before, on the logic that "like cures like." This is an idiomatic echo of the ancient practice of curing the effects of a dog-bite with a poultice made of the hair of the very dog that mauled your flesh. So the full expression is really *hair of the dog that bit you,* though of course today the dog bite is a metaphor for the savage effects of overindulgence.

This phrase has been with English speakers for centuries. It showed up in print for the first time in 1546 in a collection of English proverbs. The compiler, John Heywood, wrote, "I pray thee, let me and my fellow have a haire of the dog that bit us last night."

HAMBURGER

Ah, the hamburger. The anchor of the classic American restaurant menu and the staple of backyard barbeques. With the burger so solidly entrenched in American culture, it's surprising that so little is known about its origin.

Some say that what would later become fried ground beef served on a bun was originally poor-quality spiced and shredded meat cooked or eaten raw by lower-class Germans. In the northern city of Hamburg, the dish became known as *Hamburg steak,* and, imported stateside, ultimately became the familiar American *hamburger.* No one knows when or where the bun was added to the concoction.

Another story has the town of Hamburg, New York, as the birthplace of the burger. It's said to be the invention of brothers Frank and Charles Menches, food vendors at the 1885 Erie County Fair. When they ran out of pork for their sandwiches one day, the Menches brothers improvised with ground, cooked beef. If the tale is true, the sandwich was named after an American Hamburg.

By about 1910, the word *hamburger* and the sandwich it represents were familiar to many Americans. Around 1935, diners began serving hamburgers topped with cheese, inspiring the novel moniker *cheeseburger.* By the close of the 1930s, Americans, comfortable with this ground beef fare, clipped the name of the dish to simply *burger.*

Handsome

The proverb *handsome is as handsome does* is English and dates from the mid-1600s. Actually, the original rendering was *he is handsome that handsome doth,* but both versions mean the same thing: "The mark of good character is deeds, not appearance." Have you ever wondered why the adjective *handsome* means "attractive"?

Let's dissect the word, starting with the last syllable, *-some.* This is the very suffix that occurs in *wholesome, bothersome, adventuresome, awesome,* and *others.* The *-some* ending denotes the quality, condition, or character of the preceding element. So, a quarrelsome person likes to quarrel, that which is wholesome is complete, something awesome inspires awe, and so forth.

Hand-some, then, literally means "handy, easy to manipulate, convenient," since the *hand* in the word is in fact the one on the end of the human arm. The word starts to appear in English documents in the early 1400s and was originally applied to the convenience or handiness of a sword, ax, or pike.

By the 1500s, *handsome* became synonymous with "appropriate, clever, apt." Writers from the 15th and 16th centuries record such expressions as *handsome speech* and *handsome letter.* Other synonyms of the word are "gracious," "generous," and "admirable." In the end, the positive attributes of something handy, apt, generous, and admirable have developed an association with men and women of fine form: they are considered *handsome.*

Scores of common English expressions come from the pages of the Bible. Some examples of biblical clichés are "cast the first stone," "feet of clay," "a drop in the bucket," "an eye for an eye." Another expression from the pages of holy writ is *handwriting on the wall,* a foretelling of ill fortune.

The players in the story that inspired this phrase are Belshazzar, a splendidly wealthy king of ancient Babylon; Daniel, an Israelite prophet; and a mysterious, disembodied hand.

One day King Belshazzar arranged an opulent feast for his entire court. Feeling expansive from drinking wine, Belshazzar commanded that all the plundered goods from the temple of Jerusalem be brought out and laid on the banquet tables. This scheme angered the god of the Israelites, who decided to take revenge upon the arrogant Babylonian king.

Suddenly, as the royal guests were eating and drinking from the stolen vessels, the fingers of a man's hand magically appeared and wrote a cryptic message on the plaster wall of the palace. Terrified, Belshazzar called Daniel the prophet to interpret the mysterious hieroglyph.

According to Daniel, the text said that the king had been tested by God and found wanting. His reign was coming to an end and his kingdom was about to fall and be divided among his enemies.

This was the original *handwriting on the wall* that later came to allude to any portent of doom or misfortune.

Hanky Panky

To engage in *hanky-panky* is to be involved in infidelity or sexual misbehavior. This term is a relative newcomer to the English language, having appeared in print in 1841. So, what's the story behind this saucy little rhyming expression *hanky panky?*

Some etymological sources suggest it comes from Romany, one of the languages spoken by European gypsies. The Romany phrase, spelled in dictionaries *hakkni panki,* is said to mean "sleight of hand," "trickery," or, to use an old-fashioned term, "legerdemain."

The *Oxford English Dictionary* considers *hanky panky* to be a variation on the much older expression *hocus pocus,* a term originally used by magicians while performing tricks.

Robert Hendrickson, in his *Facts on File Encyclopedia of Word and Phrase Origins,* writes that this reduplication "may have been coined...from the magician's handkerchief, or *hanky,* under which so many things have appeared and disappeared through clever sleight of hand."

The expression also appears in carnival jargon as *hanky-pank,* meaning, a tawdry trinket or a midway game so designed that every player would win a cheap souvenir.

By the 1940s, *hanky panky* had lost its denotation of trickery or deceit and acquired sexual overtones, referring to covert extramarital dalliances.

Happy as a Clam

One of the more absurd idioms in the English language surely must be *happy as a clam,* meaning "perfectly contented." Placing it under the cliché microscope, the expression becomes moment by moment more unreasonable. Are clams more felicitous than any other organism? How is clam happiness gauged, anyway? Though the idiom makes no sense, our faith in its ability to express a concept is astounding.

Some clarity is gained when we learn that *happy as a clam* is a truncated version of its original form *happy as a clam at high tide.* The saying originated on the East Coast, where clam diggers know that the mollusks can be extricated from the sand only when the tide is out. So, if we are to believe anything about this phrase, clams are happiest at high tide, when clam diggers must cease their search.

Happy as a clam isn't alone in the absurd cliché category: in this volume, you can also read about *cat got your tongue, busy as a bee,* and *apple of my eye.*

He Can Run, but He Can't Hide

When an expression that's been generated by advertisement, novels, television serials, or movie dialogue becomes popular, it's called a *catchphrase*. Some examples are "I yam what I yam," from the animated *Popeye* series; and "Let your fingers do the walking," an advertising slogan for Yellow Pages.

During the 2004 presidential campaign, both candidates for office, George W. Bush and Senator John Kerry, reprised an old American catchphrase during the October debates. President Bush started it all when he said of John Kerry, "He can't have it both ways. To pay for the big spending program he's outlined during his campaign, he will have to raise your taxes. He can run but he cannot hide." In a subsequent debate, Kerry recycled the catchphrase when he retorted, "To borrow a saying, when it comes to George Bush's record on gas prices, he can run but he can't hide."

Though this phrase was oft-repeated in a political context in 2004, it originated in the boxing arena. When American heavyweight boxer Joe Louis was preparing for a title match against his fast-moving opponent, Billy Conn, in 1946, a reporter asked him how he would deal with Conn's lightning moves. Louis replied, "He can run, but he can't hide."

In the intervening decades, Louis's famous retort has become a catchphrase meaning "a wrongdoer or a fraud will eventually be exposed."

HEART ON THE SLEEVE

We English speakers are especially fond of expressions that include the cardiac organ, clichés such as *heart of gold, heart to heart, home is where the heart is,* and *absence makes the heart grow fonder.*

These sayings reflect the traditional belief that the heart governs the emotions, the intellect, and even the memory: have you ever learned something *by heart?*

For that matter, have you ever *worn your heart on your sleeve?* Nonsensical when interpreted literally, this expression describes the aspect of a romantic, a committed lover, or a demonstrably emotional person.

Shakespeare didn't invent this phrase, but he was one of the first to record it, in his tragedy *Othello.* The story has the villain Iago proclaiming his false and feigned devotion to his master Othello. Iago says "For when my outward action doth demonstrate/the native act and figure of my heart/In compliment extern, 'tis not long after/But I will wear my heart upon my sleeve/For daws to peck at."

Shakespeare's line was referencing a custom of young men of the day to attach to their sleeves small gifts and tokens from their lovers, thus advertising a mutual and public affection.

The coinage of this expression is most often attributed to American cartoonist Billy De Beck, originator of *Barney Google,* a syndicated comic strip that ran in the early 20th century. De Beck's cartoon characters used the phrase *heebie jeebies* to describe the jitters or the fidgets.

No one is sure how De Beck came up with this expression, but one source speculates that it may be a "reduplicated perversion" of *creepy* or the *creeps.* The late etymologist John Ciardi, in his book *Good Words to You,* wondered if De Beck might have coined *heebie jeebies* from a euphemism like *holy jeepers* or *heeper jeepers.*

De Beck's reduplication was propelled to national recognition when Louis Armstrong recorded his novelty hit "Heebie Jeebies" in Chicago in 1926. The tune was full of scat syllables, with *heebie jeebies* in the starring role. The recording sold 40,000 copies and inspired a dance of the same name that enjoyed a brief but frantic life among American youth in the late 1920s.

No one dances the Heebie Jeebies any more, but we still *get* the *heebie jeebies,* or feelings of anxiety, the creeps, the jitters.

Reduplications—*pell-mell, hocus pocus,* and *helter skelter*—are expressions formed by the repetition of a sound, syllable, or word. *Helter skelter* brings to mind disordered haste. The term is recorded in Shakespeare's 1597 drama *King Henry IV,* where a harried horseman says, "Helter-skelter have I rode to thee, and tidings do I bring."

Helter skelter was once someone's idea of the sound of hurried confusion, such as the rapid clatter of feet. It is also the name of an amusement ride in Britain, which is constructed like a lighthouse tower with an external spiraling slide, which riders career down on mats. The Beatles, in their *White Album* song "Helter Skelter," referred to this ride in their lyrics: "When I get to the bottom I go back to the top of the slide/where I stop and I turn for a ride."

In 1974, the expression *helter skelter* was given a sensational new life as the title of a book featuring the lives and deeds of the Manson family, a California communal group who followed the teachings of cult guru Charles Manson. In the late 1960s, Manson attracted a group of young followers who believed, like he did, that a worldwide holocaust was coming.

Convinced that apocalyptic prophesies were encoded in the Beatles' *White Album,* Manson took the title of the song "Helter Skelter" to be a synonym for the coming armageddon. Obeying the supposed instructions recorded in the song, Manson ordered his followers to commit random murders in the Los Angeles area, and to graffiti the words "helter skelter" at the crime scenes.

HICKORY

Because European immigrants to the Americas had no names for most indigenous New World plants and animals, they relied on native terms. *Opossum, raccoon, persimmon, avocado, cougar, moose, tomato, chocolate*—all these are native American words adopted and modified by English speakers.

Add the word *hickory* to this list. Early colonists in the North American east and south found the durable wood of this deciduous tree excellent for ax and hatchet handles, for the rims and spokes of wheels, for singletrees and buggy shafts. Hickory switches were used on recalcitrant children and mules, and hickory smoke was considered best for curing hams and bacons. The seventh U.S. president, Andrew Jackson, was nicknamed "Old Hickory" for his steadfastness and endurance in battle.

Native peoples of North America used hickory nuts and bark for food and dyes. The Algonquin of the East Coast prized a beverage made from this tree—an oily, milky-looking liquid of pounded hickory nuts and water. The name *hickory* comes from the Algonquin word for this nutritious beverage, which was *powcohiccora,* or at least that's what it sounded like to 17th century Europeans, who recorded it that way in about 1618. The word was subjected to many spellings and pronunciations over the decades, but *hickory* became the standard in the early 19th century.

HIGH MUCKAMUCK

Chinook Jargon is a trade language developed among natives of the Pacific Northwest. Consisting of some 500–1,000 words drawn from several native languages of the area, Chinook Jargon facilitated commerce in food and goods between the inhabitants of this linguistically diverse region.

One lexical survivor of this trade language is the expression *high muckamuck,* or *mucketymuck,* which is the Jargon-derived way of referring to one of elevated professional or social status. Originally, the Chinook Jargon word *muckamuck* meant, depending on the context, choice whale meat, a meal, food, or to eat or feast.

When the Chinook Jargon adjective *hayu,* meaning "big, important" was attached, the resulting *hayu muckamuck* meant plenty of food, big feast—the kind of spread enjoyed and offered by the wealthy.

English speakers, adopting and adapting this phrase, rendered it *high muckamuck,* figuratively someone who eats well, but by extension the wealthy, powerful one; the boss. The *Oxford English Dictionary* cites the printed expression from 1856 in the *Democratic State Journal* of Sacramento. In current American English, the term *high muckamuck* or *muckety-muck* is contemptuous and generally reserved for political or corporate bigshots with an inflated sense of power and influence.

What's your hobby? Building boats in bottles? Collecting Elvis memorabilia? We cultivate hobbies, not for their financial rewards, but for the amusement they provide. But what about the word itself? If we retrace the somewhat tangled history of *hobby*, we find that the story begins with the name of a horse.

Centuries ago on the British Isles, small, sturdy horses were developed and bred as all-purpose cart and plow animals. In the 1400s and 1500s, favorite names for these ubiquitous animals were Dobbin, Hobin, and Hobby, nicknames for the very common Robin or Robert.

The nickname *Hobby* became permanently attached to these all-purpose work horses, and in some areas the word became synonymous with "horse," just as we recognize "Rover" as a dog.

By the 16th century, people dressed as horses, or *hobbies*, began participating in the revelry of the English folk celebrations known as morris dances. *Hobbyhorse* dancers kicked and bucked and neighed just like their four-legged namesakes. The word *hobbyhorse* in this sense was first recorded in print in 1557; in later years came to refer to a child's toy, also known as a *stick-horse*.

This word acquired the extended meaning of "a favorite pastime" by the end of the 17th century, with *hobbyhorse* referring to an adult's toy horse to play with. The final version *hobby*, meaning "pleasurable activity," evolved from this sense of horseplay.

To *hobnob* is to socialize with the elite or the power-ful, in a more or less elegant atmosphere while seeing and being seen. We might say the socially prominent hobnob, while commoners simply hang out.

The expression *hobnob* is another example of reduplica-tion, the kind of rhyming phrase so common in the English language. This word has been dated to at least 1601, because Shakespeare used it in his play *Twelfth Night.*

The linguistic antecedent to *hobnob* is thought to be the Middle English expression *habbe nabbe,* which in turn comes from a pair of words: *habben,* which means "to have," and *nabben,* or "not to have." The Middle English *habbe nabbe* meant approximately "have and have not," or "give and take."

The actions depicted in this phrase derive from a tradi-tion of cordial feasting and drinking in which friends exchanged toasts and meals. In this scenario, the revelers gave, or "hosted" and took, or "were hosted," in a spirit of reciprocity. Give and take, have and have not, hob and nob. This Middle English sense of the reduplicative phrase seems appropriate still, for social hobnobbers must always under-stand the subtle rules of giving and taking, of "having and having not."

HOCUS POCUS

Deceit, trickery, flim-flam—that's *hocus pocus.* Word hunters have offered several explanations for the origin of this reduplication. The story most often cited in respectable dictionaries evokes the Latin words uttered in a Catholic mass at the moment of transubstantiation: *hoc est corpus,* "this is the body." It's said that magicians and conjurers, in an attempt to dazzle audiences, would shout out a corruption of this solemn Latin formula, *hocus pocus,* at the climax of a trick. By the 17th century, the magician's acts of trickery and prestidigitation became known generally as *hocus pocus.*

By the 1600s, *hocus pocus* had become a nickname for not only magicians but jugglers as well, as in this quotation from 1634: "A Persian Hocus-Pocus…performed rare tricks with hands and feet." And in *King Henry IV,* Shakespeare writes, "I incline to call him hocus-pocus, or some juggler, or attendant upon the master of the hobbyhorse."

Hocus pocus—the art of trickery and deceit: what does your dictionary say about the origin of this ancient reduplication?

HOLD THE FORT

War tends to be linguistically productive. Those who have engineered or fought in armed conflict over the centuries have coined countless words and phrases to identify the events and inventions of warfare, many of which are now useful members of our daily lexicon: *jeep, blockbuster, deadline, flash in the pan,* and *I came, I saw, I conquered* were all inspired by the culture of armed conflict.

The expression *hold the fort* derives from an order given by Union General William Tecumseh Sherman in 1864 near the end of the Civil War. Confederate General J. B. Hood, expelled from Atlanta after its devastating fall, was moving his troops northward out of the ruined city when he encountered a Union stronghold at Allatoona, Georgia, commanded by General John M. Corse. Hood demanded the surrender of Corse's Union troops, but Corse refused, insisting he had a received a communiqué from Sherman that said, "Hold the fort at all costs, for I am coming." Corse did just that, standing his ground until reinforcements arrived.

The circumstances surrounding the coinage of this expression inspired the American imagination. Now, more than a century after its conception, *hold the fort* has been extracted from its combat context and is used colloquially to mean "take care of things until I return."

After the death of John Paul II in April 2005, a conclave of cardinals gathered at the Vatican to elect a new pope. Sequestered in the Sistine Chapel, each of the 115 cardinals cast his vote for a papal successor. After each round of voting, the paper ballots were burned in a fireplace. Twice, chemicals added to the ballots created black smoke, which issued from the Vatican chimney and signaled a failure of the cardinals to agree on a papal candidate. Finally, white smoke poured out of the chimney, announcing that a new pope had been elected.

This Vatican tradition prompted many word lovers, in the spring of 2005, to wonder if the exclamation *holy smoke* arose from the ancient election custom.

Though it makes a good story, there's no evidence linking papal ballot-burning to the expression *holy smoke*. Instead, our exclamation appears to be part of a family of religious euphemisms that includes *holy cats, holy cripes, holy cow, holy heck,* and even *holy Toledo.* Today's expression could be an oblique reference to some verses in the Bible's Old Testament, where the "holy" smoke of burnt sacrifices symbolizes prayers ascending to heaven.

HOOCH

American English speakers have always been splendidly equipped with a profusion of slang synonyms for alcohol: *firewater, rot gut, white lightning, suds, juice, brewski, booze,* and many more.

Another generic term for liquor, *hooch,* has been traced to the years following America's 1867 purchase of the Alaska territory. American soldiers, dispatched to lonely Alaskan outposts in the late 1800s, were severed from any reliable source of alcohol. One thirsty group, stationed on Admiralty Island near present-day Juneau, found a way to fashion molasses, yeast, berries, sugar, and graham flour into what one critical observer called a "villainous decoction" of intoxicating spirits.

The compound became a trade item between American soldiers and a group of neighboring natives who, depending on which account you read, were called the Hoocheenoo, possibly after a village by the same name. Adopting the Americans' brewing technique, the Hoocheenoo Indians made, drank, and shared the villainous decoction with their neighbors.

The eponymously named *hoocheenoo* liquor was cheap and potent, soon becoming a favorite of Klondike gold seekers in the 1890s. The abbreviated *hooch* was quickly adopted to designate any low-quality, illegal, or extraordinarily potent liquor. The word found a permanent home in the American English slang vocabulary of the 20th century and was enthusiastically embraced by tipplers and gin makers during Prohibition.

Although the word *hooker* has been cited as a synonym for *prostitute* since at least the mid-19th century, no one can claim with certainty where the term originated. Several respected etymologists have offered a handful of theories on the genesis of *hooker*.

Scholar and poet John Ciardi believed it arose from British slang and cited a volume of interviews with London prostitutes published in 1857. Says one: "We hooks [a clergyman] now and then." Another states, "I've hooked many a man by showing an ankle on a wet day." This may be an analogy to hooking a fish, or simply the action of a prostitute hooking arms with a client to draw him in.

Meanwhile, John Bartlett, the compiler of *Bartlett's Familiar Quotations,* has the term coming from Corlear's Hook, a district in New York City. He said a hooker is "a resident of the Hook, i.e., a strumpet....So called from the number of houses of ill-fame frequented by the sailors at the Hook [Corlear's Hook] in the city of New York."

Etymologist Eric Partridge suggests that *hooker* is based on the word *huckster,* meaning "hawker" or "peddler."

The most colorful but least probable theory makes Civil War general Joseph Hooker the eponym of the word in question. It's often been cited that hordes of sex peddlers followed Hooker's Union soldiers from camp to camp and were often called Hooker's Reserves. Tempting as it is to lean on this theory, most word watchers dismiss it, since the term *hooker* seems to predate the Civil War by decades.

One of the challenging aspects of the our English mother tongue is its abundance of almost-synonymous word pairs, like *world* and *earth, garbage* and *trash, brain* and *mind.* It's not easy to articulate the differences, if any, between these pairs of terms.

Another potentially perplexing linguistic couple is *horn* and *antler.* Who wears the horns and who the antlers? And what are the stories behind the two words?

In North America, antlers grow on elk, deer, moose, and caribou. Antlers are branched structures that are shed and regrown annually, and, with the caribou as the exception, are present only in males.

Horns are curved, pointed, unbranched projections, and they're permanent. Males of the Bovidae family have horns, but females often bear them as well. Bison, bighorn sheep, musk oxen, and domestic cattle are all horn bearers.

But enough of the biology—what about the word histories? The ultimate ancestor of *antler* is a slurred pronunciation of the Latin term *anteocularis,* meaning "positioned in front of the eye," probably referring to the brow tine that often protrudes in the center of the forehead over the eye. *Horn* is also Latin in origin, from the word *cornu.* This is also the source of the word *unicorn,* meaning "one horn."

Hot Dog

Throughout the 19th century, immigrant European butchers were transporting their signature sausages with them to the New World. From Frankfurt, Germany, came the Frankfurter, which ultimately became the American *frank*. The Weinerwurst, a traditional sausage from Vienna (Wien in German), found a new identity as the *wiener* or *weenie*.

But the American term *hot dog*, referring to a mongrel offspring of a variety of German sausages, is unlike its European counterparts, since no one is certain of its origins.

Most sources quote, but cannot verify, a colorful legend of the birth of the term *hot dog* that involves a dachshund, a ballpark, and a cartoonist.

In the early 1900s, sausages were a favorite food at New York area baseball games. The story has it that one local vendor was hawking what he called "hot dachshund sausages," a name suggesting the shape and German origins of the preparation. A local sports cartoonist named T. A. Dorgan came home from a game one day and rendered an illustration of the vendor at his stand. Dorgan drew a scene of a barking dachshund nestled in a bun, but, unable to spell the German word *dachshund,* he captioned the cartoon "Get your hot dogs here!" Though this makes a compelling story, the illustration that allegedly inspired the name of one of America's favorite fast foods has never surfaced.

Other sources claim that the Germans had for decades affectionately nicknamed their Frankfurter sausages *dachshunds* for their obvious shape. In the 19th century, American college students adopted this notion, but with the sly implication that the sausage was literally made of dog meat. So a freshly cooked dachshund sausage became a *hot dog* among college students of the time.

Word watcher John Ayto, in his *20th Century Words,* departs from both of these explanations. He claims that this American-style sausage may owe its name to the hot dog who's a daredevil, a hot shot, one who is skilled or daring. This sense of *hot dog,* Ayto says, was in place in the language since 1900, so the edible hot dog "would be a super sausage sandwich."

"A merry Christmas, uncle! God save you!" cried a cheerful voice. It was the voice of Scrooge's nephew.

"Bah!" said Scrooge, "Humbug!"

"Christmas a humbug, uncle!" said Scrooge's nephew. "You don't mean that, I'm sure?..."

Scrooge, having no better answer ready on the spur of the moment, said "Bah!" again; and followed it up with "Humbug."

Charles Dicken's tight-fisted misanthrope Ebenezer Scrooge had no use for Christmas and its traditions of merrymaking and charity. Though surrounded by goodhearted relatives and neighbors, Scrooge recoiled from their holiday greetings, disdainfully spitting back, "Humbug!"

By the time Dickens had written his famous *Christmas Carol* in 1843, the slang word *humbug* had been around for a century. Then, as now, it meant "fraud, hoax, worthless nonsense."

Its origin is unknown. The *Oxford English Dictionary* suggests it was borrowed from underworld slang. In 1751, a student recorded this rather jaundiced observation about the epithet: *humbug* "is a word very much in vogue with the people of taste and fashion....it is indeed a blackguard of a sound....some great men deceive themselves so egregiously as to think they mean something by it!"

But by 1843, Dickens had immortalized this "blackguard" of a word. Its popularity was further reinforced in the late 1800s, when circus impresario P. T. Barnum was dubbed the "Prince of Humbug."

Hunky-Dory

In the mid-19th century, the distinctly American phrase *hunky-dory* began appearing in print as a synonym of "splendid, fine, satisfactory." The biography of this obliquely rhyming phrase reveals two stories of linguistic cross-pollination.

The first tale implicates Yokohama, Japan, a city inhabited by international traders since the 1860s. A favorite Yokohaman playground for U.S. sailors on leave was Honcho-dori, a business and entertainment avenue running through the city center, *dori* being the Japanese word for "street." Some sources suggest that *hunky-dory*, a sailor's riff on *Honcho-dori,* came to mean anything as pleasant and delightful as one might find on that Yokohama street.

Another etymological possibility involves a borrowing from an entirely different language, Dutch, as spoken by immigrants from Holland in the New World. In a Dutch version of the game of tag, the word *honk* or *hunk* referred to "goal" or "home" or the "safe place." This in turn engendered the slang terms *on hunk* and *hunky,* which referred to being in the right place, or safe and sound.

Who added the *dory* to *hunky* is not known. The *dory* in this expression may be a grafting of the same Japanese *dori* that means "street." The *Oxford English Dictionary* has *hunky-dory* first appearing in 1866. By the time it appeared in print, it meant exactly what it means today: fine, splendid, all right.

In the Greek mythological tradition, the god Hypnos personified sleep. The son of Night and the twin brother of Death, Hypnos lived in a misty cavern through which the river of Forgetfulness flowed. Artistic renderings represent the winged Hypnos gliding silently over land and sea to lull mortals to sleep.

In the 18th and 19th centuries, academics borrowed this god's name and applied it in various ways to the science of sleep. The first to do so was James Braid, a Scot surgeon who invented the term *hypnotism* in 1843. Braid called hypnotism the condition of "nervous sleep," but a more modern definition of the word is "the process of putting one into a sleep-like trance."

In 1901, the science of psychology introduced the term *hypnopompic,* an adjective referring to the state of drowsiness between sleep and waking. Greek from end to end, the word *hypnopompic* literally means "sending away from sleep."

The opposite condition is the *hypnogogic,* which identifies the moments of drowsiness just before sleep takes hold. This word, first appearing in print in the late 1880s, means etymologically "leading into sleep."

In God We Trust

In 1956, the phrase *In God We Trust* was established by Congress as the official motto of the United States—its most familiar appearance being on U.S. currency. The first coin to bear the motto "In God We Trust" was the 1864 two-cent piece. In 1955, an act of Congress made it mandatory for all coins to be inscribed with the motto, and by 1957 it began appearing on paper currency too.

The phrase *In God we trust* was inspired nearly three centuries ago after Francis Scott Key penned the lyrics to what has now become our national anthem, the "Star-Spangled Banner." In the fourth and final verse of the song, Key wrote, "Then conquer we must, when our cause it is just/And this be our motto: "In God is our trust,"/And the star-spangled banner in triumph shall wave/O'er the land of the free and the home of the brave!"

Some have advocated the removal of the motto from U.S. currency, arguing that any endorsement of God by the government is unconstitutional. Nevertheless, the expression is deeply ingrained in our linguistic sensibilities. Mark Twain said, "It always sounds well—In God We Trust. I don't believe it would sound any better if it were true." Another tongue-in-cheek adaptation of the phrase is often posted in retail stores: "In God We Trust. All others pay cash."

Someone who's *in like Flynn* is assured of favor or success. This rhyming cliché has been in circulation since the 1940s. Is there an actual Flynn behind this slangy expression, and, if so, why is he the icon of easy access?

Some phrase watchers allege *in like Flynn* is an allusion to Edward J. "Boss" Flynn, Democratic campaign manager during Franklin D. Roosevelt's presidency. Flynn's campaign machine never lost an election; his candidates always seemed to be in office. So, by extension, to be *in like Flynn* would be to achieve automatic success like "Boss" Flynn's favored politicos.

The phrase is also attached to Errol Flynn, the Australian-born Hollywood actor. Flynn was the debonair, romantic leading man of such productions as *The Adventures of Robin Hood* and *Captain Blood*. He was Hollywood's biggest box office draw during the 1930s, '40s, and early '50s.

Handsome Errol had a reputation as a libertine and notorious seducer of women. In 1942 he was charged with the statutory rape of a teenage girl. An all-female jury acquitted him, but he purportedly had an airplane—engine running—waiting to fly him out of the country had the jury ruled against him.

It seemed as if Flynn had everything: fame, women, talent, and, ultimately, luck. In this picture, those who succeed like the charismatic actor are said to be *in like Flynn*.

INFLUENZA

In 1918 and 1919, an influenza outbreak, cited as the most devastating epidemic in history, claimed between 20 and 40 million lives worldwide. A fifth of the world's population was infected by this virulent strain of virus, which acquired the moniker *Spanish flu*. Since the unprecedented devastation of the 1918 pandemic, several other influenza outbreaks have encircled the globe, including occurrences of the swine flu and bird flu.

Influenza epidemics were also known to ravage human populations throughout antiquity. Hippocrates observed and recorded what is now believed to be a flu pandemic in 412 B.C. At least thirty-one widespread influenza outbreaks have been recorded since 1580.

The word *influenza* came directly to English from Italian, where it simply means "influence." The term was originally associated with astrology; influenza was believed to be an ethereal fluid flowing from the stars to the earth, where it literally influenced the destinies of human beings.

Throughout the 1600s, the sudden emergence of diseases whose terrestrial causes were not apparent was blamed on the *influenza* of the stars. In 1743, Italy was struck with what has since been identified as the flu but at the time was called *influenza di cattaro*, or the "influence of catarrh." By the time the illness and its name had reached England, it was known simply as *influenza*. The clipped form, *flu*, began to appear in print in the 1830s.

Ivory Tower

An *ivory tower* is not a literal structure, of course. It's a metaphorical edifice that suggests a state of intellectual isolation or a tranquil, lofty retreat from the distractions of terrestrial existence.

An ivory tower is mentioned in the Old Testament's Song of Solomon. Praising the beauty of his beloved, the writer declares, "Your neck is like an ivory tower." Here, the simile alludes to the beauty of a woman's form.

But the "intellectual isolation" sense of *ivory tower* probably came from a French poet named Charles-Augustin Saint-Beuve. In 1837, Saint-Beuve wrote a poem mentioning two of his peers, Victor Hugo and another writer, Alfred de Vigny. In translation, Saint-Beuve wrote:

> Hugo, strong partisan…fought in armor,
> And held high his banner in the middle of the tumult;
> He holds it still; and Vigny, more discreet,
> As if in his ivory tower, retired before noon.

The expression suggests passionless and elegant detachment in a cool, white aerie where a poet or philosopher might retreat to think and write.

Since the publication of this 1837 poem, many writers have adopted the phrase, including Ezra Pound, H. G. Wells, and Aldous Huxley. A relatively recent example comes from an October 12, 1963, edition of the *Daily Telegraph:* "Pity the poor parson!…If he eschews all worldly contact, he's accused of being ivory-towerish and out of touch."

The jaeger has a well-deserved reputation as an aerobatic pirate of the high seas. This agile marine bird generally resembles its close relative, the gull, in size and coloration. In flight, however, the jaeger is sleek and streamlined, with the long, pointed wings of a falcon and stinger-like central tail feathers.

The jaeger nests in the Arctic during the northern summer but migrates to the open oceans of the Southern Hemisphere for the winter, making its living as a "kleptoparasite," stealing food from other birds. Darting and swooping, jaegers harass not only their gull cousins but other species too, like terns and kittiwakes, pestering them in midflight until they finally drop their prey. The jaeger then dives for the food as it plunges to the ground.

This avian species, specially equipped for aerial harassment, was given its common name in the 19th century. *Jaeger* is a German word that means "hunter," from the verb *jagen,* "chase, pursue, drive."

Interestingly, the term *yacht* is related to the name of this bird that hunts and steals. A yacht is etymologically a boat for "chasing" others. The antecedent of *yacht* is the Dutch word *jaghtschip,* literally meaning "chase ship."

JUGGERNAUT

In the 14th century, strange tales began to circulate throughout Europe of a religious ritual held in the city of Puri, in northeastern India. It was the annual procession of Jagganath, or the "Lord of the World," one of the many titles of the god Vishnu.

In a colossal display of veneration, Jagganath disciples mounted an image of their god on a wheeled cart 45 feet high. Pilgrims moved in unison, many bodies deep, pushing and pulling at the vehicle as it rolled in procession from the city temple.

Stories multiplied about Jagganath supplicants throwing themselves under the moving wheels of the carriage in an act of ecstatic sacrifice. Scandalized Europeans no doubt exaggerated accounts of these "religious suicides." The fatalities were most likely accidental, with devotees simply falling in the crush of the crowd.

Nevertheless, tales of this religious festival inspired the term *juggernaut,* after the god whose Hindi name means "Lord of the World." In modern English, a *juggernaut* is an inexorable, implacable force that consumes all in its path. Early steam locomotives were the juggernauts of 19th century rails; armored tanks were the juggernauts of the battlefield during the first two world wars.

JUMBO

On a summer day in 1865, hundreds of Londoners lined up for their first look at an elephant. The celebrated pachyderm was Jumbo, a four-year-old African bull elephant who arrived at the London Zoo on June 26, 1865. During his seventeen-year residency at the zoo, Jumbo gave rides to thousands of children, endearing himself to a generation of Britons.

This behemoth might have been named after *Mumbo-Jumbo*, a West African Mandingo deity. In another account, Jumbo acquired his name from the Zulu word *jumba*, meaning "large packet or parcel." A large one indeed: in adulthood Jumbo grew to a ponderous 7 tons, at nearly 11 feet in height.

Thousands of North Americans saw the African colossus in 1882 when he was purchased by the Barnum and Bailey Circus and toured throughout North America. Though Jumbo died in 1885, this popular elephant's name is preserved in the colloquial adjective meaning "gigantic, king-sized." There are many examples: *jumbo peaches, jumbo pack, jumbo burgers, jumbo-sized,* and the absurdly monikered *jumbo shrimp.* Front and center in this lexical family is *jumbo-jet,* the name of the gigantic Boeing 747 that took to the skies in the late 1960s.

Ever heard of *jump the shark?* If you're a devoted television watcher, you probably know what the phrase means. For those who don't, read on for the story behind the coinage of a new phrase.

To appreciate the expression *jump the shark,* first consider how important ratings have been to such popular weekly television shows as *Friends, Seinfeld, M*A*S*H,* and *Little House on the Prairie.* Trendy series like these are destined to die when their viewership plummets. As the production begins to twist slowly in the wind, the writers may devise a gimmicky scenario designed to bolster ratings. Against logic, a character gets married, pregnant, terminally ill. If the gimmick doesn't work, it may cause the series to *jump the shark,* or turn from good to decaying.

According to Jon Hein, creator of the website www.jumptheshark.com, the expression was inspired by an episode of *Happy Days* (1974–84) in which Fonzie literally jumps over a shark during a daredevil waterskiing stunt. That, according to Hein and hundreds of *Happy Days* fans, was the absurdity that doomed the series.

This phrase has potential. Any popular band, movie star, automobile manufacturer, or anything else that falls from grace by abandoning quality could be accused of *jumping the shark.*

Jury-Rigged, Jerry-Built

Something that's *jury-rigged* is assembled in a makeshift fashion. *Jury-rig* and its antecedents *jury-mast, jury-rudder,* and *jury-tiller* are nautical terms for emergency replacements for broken equipment. Some sources have this *jury* short for "injury," so an *injury-rig,* or *jury-rig,* is one that replaces the disabled rig. Other dictionaries define the word as a form of the old French term *ajurie,* "help or relief."

But the companion phrase *jerry-built* appears to come from an entirely different source. The *Oxford English Dictionary* defines *jerry-built* as "built unsubstantially of bad materials; built to sell but not to last." Though the definition sounds sure and simple, the origin is not so.

It's often said that this *jerry,* which dates to 19th century England, comes from the name of a building firm out of Liverpool with a reputation for shoddy construction.

Another story attached to *jerry-built* dates all the way back to the Old Testament account of the city of Jericho, whose walls crumbled at the sound of a few trumpets.

Yet another possibility has *jerry* coming from the French word *jour* for "day." Construction workers hired by the day are less likely to do quality work than long-term laborers. Of course, it could be that *jerry-built* is simply another form of the earlier, nautical *jury-rig,* an emergency replacement for the real thing.

Have you ever heard the expression *Katy bar the door* and wondered where it came from? People use it to mean "get ready for trouble," or "watch out—something bad is about to happen." This phrase is another example of a firmly established American idiom with an uncertain origin.

The development of the expression may lie in a poem by Gabriel Dante Rossetti called *The King's Tragedy,* written in 1881, which chronicles the 1437 assassination of Scotland's King James I.

As co-conspirator in the murder plot, the king's own chamberlain removed the security bar of the royal bedroom door one night to clear the way for would-be murderers. A lady-in-waiting to the queen, one Catherine Douglas, over-heard the killers as they opened the door to the king's chamber. When Catherine valiantly attempted to block the open doorway with her arm, the assassins first broke the brave lady's arm, then killed the king.

It's been suggested that the poet's line "Catherine, keep the door!" which commemorates the brave deed, may have inspired the more popular *Katy, bar the door!*

KIBITZ, KIBITZER

We've all experienced the unsolicited, meddlesome commentary of the *kibitzer*. The primary definition of the word *kibitzer* in most dictionaries reads something like "an interfering looker-on, especially at a card game." But a kibitzer can also be a josher or a wisecracking friend, or simply someone who indulges in light conversation. *Kibitzer* derives from the German and Yiddish verb *kibitz,* meaning "to tease, comment, or gibe."

A deeper look at this verb reveals a most delightful pedigree, one that involves a European bird called the *lapwing,* sometimes known as the *peewit,* and in certain regions of Germany, the *Kiebitz.*

When their nesting sites are disturbed, adult lapwings feign injury to distract the intruder, or they circle very close with loud cries and complaints. To the ears of locals, the creatures' calls sounded something like *peewit* or *kiebitz,* imitative terms that ultimately became names for the bird.

The German version, *Kiebitz* or *Kibitz,* was eventually applied to human busybodies, *kibitzers,* who hover in the background of activity, crying out advice and commentary like the anxious lapwing. The late Leo Rosten, in his Yiddish-English dictionary *The New Joys of Yiddish,* says that such lookers-on "are rarely knowledgeable or respected; if they were, they would be advisers, not kibitzers."

KID

The word *kid* has three definitions in modern English. One is a noun meaning "young goat," another is a slang synonym for "child," and the third *kid* is a verb meaning "tease" or "joke." What thread ties together this trio of kids?

Originating in the Scandinavian languages, the word *kid* first referred to the young of a goat. This *kid* began appearing in English manuscripts as early as 1200. The offspring of the European roe deer are called *kids,* as are the progeny of the North American antelope.

Written references to human children as *kids* showed up in the late 1500s. The word was considered crude slang until the mid-19th century, when it became a common, affectionate moniker for young *Homo sapiens.* The connection between juvenile goats and juvenile humans is obvious to anyone who's seen both creatures at play.

How is the verb *kid,* meaning "to fool or joke," associated with the goat and the child? When you *kid* someone, you etymologically treat him like a youngster, playfully teasing him as if he were a naïve kid.

To *kidnap* is literally to "nap" or "nab" a child. Kidnapping was common in 17th century London, where children were spirited away on ships bound for the American colonies, where they were pressed into service on plantations—hard work for kids.

KITH AND KIN

The brief alliterative cliché *kith* and *kin* refers to one's family and acquaintances. Breaking this expression into parts, we have *kin,* relatives and possibly in-laws, and *kith,* which means what?

According to the *Oxford English Dictionary*, that muscular repository of etymology, *kith* derives from an Old English word meaning "the country or place that is known or familiar, one's native land, home"—and by extension, one's countrymen or peers. The *OED* cites a document in 888 as the word's first recording. Though itself obsolete, *kith* exists as a linguistic fossil in the expression *kith and kin.*

Fossil words like this one are preserved in several modern English expressions. The *hue* of *hue and cry* is the remnant of an Old French verb meaning "to shout."

The fossil words *hem* and *haw,* conjoined, create an expression meaning "to avoid making a decision." But what do they signify separately? According to phrase watcher Christine Ammer, the words are syllabic imitations of sounds made in clearing the throat, as one might do when expressing discomfort or doubt.

Do felines lurk in the history of the colloquial expressions *catty-corner* and *kitty-corner?*

First, to define these terms: *catty-corner* and *kitty-corner* are simply two ways of saying the same thing: "to be in a diagonal relation."

The *catty* of *catty-corner* began life as the French word for the number four, *quatre.* The word was Anglicized to *cater* in the 1500s, when it was used to indicate the four of dice or cards. Michael Quinion, in his excellent on-line etymology site *World Wide Words,* explains the next step in the word's evolution: "The standard placement of the four dots at the corners of a square almost certainly introduced the idea of diagonals. From this came a verb *cater,* to place something diagonally opposite another or to move diagonally....By the early years of the nineteenth century it was...recorded in the USA in the compound form of *cater-cornered.*"

American English speakers of the 19th century no longer associated the word *cater* with the French term for four. The spelling and pronunciation of the word linked it with cats, which gave us such formations as *catty-corner* and *kitty-corner.*

The American word *catawampus,* meaning "askew, aslant, out of square," is a playful offspring of *catty-corner.* The origin of the *wampus* in this word remains a mystery.

KLUTZ

In 1976, Stanford graduate John Cassidy's first attempts at juggling inspired him to create an instruction booklet to assist others in getting started with the sport's tricky maneuvers. *Juggling for the Complete Klutz* was sold with a trio of bean-stuffed cloth cubes for the novice juggler to practice with. The instruction kit sold well and was followed by another, in 1982, for complete klutzes who wanted to learn hackey sack.

Cassidy's initial Klutz products were marketed to those who considered themselves clumsy, slow, bungling, and non-athletic, since that's exactly what the word *klutz* means.

A term that gained currency in English in the mid-20th century, klutz comes directly from Yiddish, a language that has borrowed many words from German. The German term *Klotz* means "a block of wood, a lump, a butt, a stump." In the spirit of biting wit and sarcastic wordplay, Yiddish speakers appropriated the German term and fashioned it into *klutz,* a moniker reserved for someone with all the grace and charm of a chunk of wood.

Beneath the brightly spotted wing case of the little ladybug is a voracious predator. Both larval and adult ladybugs dine exclusively on aphids, thrips, and other agricultural pests. Gardeners and orchard growers often order ladybugs by the gallon, releasing them on crops as natural agents of biological pest control.

Ladybugs are found on almost every continent. Most species are conspicuously marked with bright yellow or red wing cases, which are mottled with black spots, varying in both number and shape.

In the Western world, these beneficial insects have long been regarded with affection. The British call them *ladybirds,* or *ladybird beetles.* Even Shakespeare used the moniker *ladybird* as a term of endearment synonymous with "sweetheart" or "darling."

The *ladybird* or *ladybug* was so named not because every specimen is female, but in tribute to "our Lady," the Virgin Mary. Since the Middle Ages, the insect has been associated with the mother of Christ. The ladybug's Spanish name is *mariquita,* the "Little Mary"; in German it's *Marienkafer,* or "Mary-beetle."

The expression *the last straw* is an idiomatic way of indicating the final, often insignificant event that makes a bad situation simply unbearable. *The last straw* is a truncation of the complete phrase "It's the last straw which breaks the camel's back"—suggesting that even though a camel can manage massive loads, the beast will finally collapse under a straw's-weight too much.

This proverb has analogues in several languages. In the 16th century, Spaniards said, "A cord may be finally broken by the feeblest of pulls." In 17th century France, people said, "A glass may overflow with the last tiny drop." An older English version, which has not survived, was "It's the last feather that breaks the horse's back."

Though our camel cliché is several centuries old, its variations still emerge from the tongues and pens of modern English speakers and writers. In the 1936 novel *Gone With the Wind,* Margaret Mitchell wrote of Scarlett O'Hara's widowhood: "She behaved as she had behaved before her marriage, went to parties, danced...flirted, did everything she had done as a girl, except stop wearing mourning. This she knew would be a straw that would break the backs of Pittypat and Melanie." In an up-to-the-minute context, "The Last Straw" is the rather cutesy name of a web journal of straw bale construction techniques.

LEAD A HORSE TO WATER

In 1546, an English dramatist named John Heywood compiled a 200-page tome entitled *A dialogue conteinying the nomber in effect of all the proverbes in the Englishe tongue*. Later retitled simply *The Proverbs of John Heywood*, the book was a catalogue of the proverbs current in the mid-16th century.

Now, going on five hundred years later, many of Heywood's expressions seem familiar. Consider this one: "A man may well bryng a horse to the water, But he can not make him drink without he will"—the modern English version being, of course, "You can lead a horse to water, but you can't make him drink."

Especially meaningful in an age when horses provided most of the transport for commerce, this cliché suggests the effort of providing water for the animals, since this often meant going to the trouble of finding a stream, trough, or well and then perhaps unhitching the horse from the plough or wagon and removing the bit from its mouth. All this effort would be wasted if the animal refused to drink.

The proverb is now a metaphor for human behavior. When repeating the expression "You can lead a horse to water, but you can't make him drink," we imply that that even though we might create an auspicious environment for success, ultimately we can't force someone to take advantage of it.

"**D**o you want to be adored by the ladies?...instead of draping yourself in unflattering clothes...put on a more natural garb, which does not hide your best features."

This sartorial suggestion is included in the 19th century memoir of France's most famous trapeze artist. This high-flying Frenchman, who—incidentally—invented the trapeze, performed before delighted circus audiences in Paris and London during the 1850s and '60s, dazzling crowds with his spectacular aerial somersaults.

Our French acrobat's memoir hints that he was destined for the circus life, since, as he claims, his infant cries were silenced only when he was hung upside-down from a horizontal bar. Later in life he would be the inspiration for the popular novelty song "That Daring Young Man on the Flying Trapeze," written in 1860.

The Daring Young Man was so serious about his appearance that he designed and wore a novel costume for his aerial performances—a tightly clinging, low-necked, one-piece garment. The 19th century acrobat's skin-tight garb was the prototype for the garment still worn by dancers, gymnasts, and other athletes today. It is called the *leotard,* after its inventor and promoter, Jules Leotard, the original Daring Young Man on the Flying Trapeze, who boasted that his special attire did not "hide his best features."

Greek poet Sappho dedicated her life to music and poetry. Born around 610 B.C. in Asia Minor, Sappho is regarded as one of the finest poets of any age. The Greeks have called her "the tenth muse" and "the mortal muse." Her verses, preserved on papyrus and in the citations of other writers, are simple, powerful, and passionate.

Sappho was married to a wealthy and aristocratic man and spent most of her life on the island of Lesbos in the Aegean Sea. It was common in Sappho's time for women of elite families to assemble in informal societies for the composition and recitation of poetry. Sappho was a celebrity in her coterie of poets, attracting admirers on her home island and in many other parts of Greece.

It appears that Sappho clearly enjoyed the society of women; her verses are ripe with declarations of affection and devotion toward her female friends. Many Sapphic scholars have assumed that the Greek poet was homosexual, though nothing in her verses connects her specifically with same-sex passion.

Nevertheless, Sappho's home, the island of Lesbos, inspired the term *lesbian* to denote female homosexuality. The word was first recorded in 1870, in a diary entry by a writer named A. J. Munby.

LETHE

Styx was the name of the principal river flowing through the Greek underworld. Mortal souls, newly departed from the land of the living, were ferried across the river Styx to gain entrance to Hades.

When the time came for the residents of the underworld to return to earth as reincarnated souls, they approached another river, Lethe, the Stream of Forgetfulness. Drinking of Lethe's waters, the soul entered oblivion, forgetting its past lives, including its visits to Hades. The spirit was then free to return to earth with an unencumbered memory.

Lethe, the river's name, comes from the Greek word for oblivion or concealment. It's also the name of an ancient goddess who personified forgetfulness.

The word *lethe* is the source of our modern English terms *lethargy, lethargic,* and possibly *lethal. Lethargy* is a state of drowsiness, apathy, or inactivity, as if one has lost the memory of purpose or movement. One who is *lethargic* is torpid and sluggish, given to sleep, the time when memory is least active. Some scholars think that the Greek *lethe* also influenced the coinage of the term *lethal,* or sent into oblivion.

The story behind the development of this family of English words is another example of how the sensibilities of the ancient Greeks find their way into our modern lives through words.

Someone who "comes on like gangbusters" is enthusiastic, forceful, and perhaps even aggressive. A *gangbuster* musical or theatrical performance is an energetic success. But what exactly is a gangbuster, and what makes the allusion so winning?

Gangbuster was originally an American term referring to a law enforcement official who broke up organized criminal groups, or "gangs." In the mid-1930s, CBS appropriated the word *gangbusters* as the title for a radio drama that premiered on January 15, 1936, and ran for over twenty years. The series followed the exploits of police and FBI officials as they pursued and "busted up" gangs of scofflaws and criminals. The opening theme of the drama featured a battery of dramatic sound effects: machine-gun fire, squealing tires, sirens, and angry shouts. So popular was the *Gang Busters* radio series that by as early as 1940, only four years after its debut, the expressions *coming on like gangbusters* and *going on like gangbusters* had come into vogue.

Though the CBS radio drama has faded from memory, the cliché is very much alive here in the 21st century. A web search of the expression reveals its use in such verbal variations as *growing like gangbusters, selling like gangbusters, getting along like gangbusters,* and *she's built like gangbusters.*

LIMBO

In the Catholic tradition, *limbo* denotes the afterlife status of those who lived good lives but died before the time of Christ, along with the innocent unbaptized who died in infancy. In the limbo otherworld, souls experience neither the sublime bliss of communion with God nor the tortures of hell. While "supernatural joy" is reserved for those who attain heaven, souls who are sent to limbo can only hope for what Catholic theologians call "natural joy."

Because the word derives from a Latin source meaning "border," "edge," or "boundary," those in limbo etymologically stand on the "borderline" between heaven and hell.

In its nonreligious context, *limbo* refers to another type of borderline—the state of an activity or process being suspended in anticipation of future resolution. A house plan halted by absentee roofers, for example, would be held in "construction limbo." Court delays and a morass of unfinished paperwork might maroon a law case in "legal limbo."

But what about the *limbo* dance sensation that swept America in the 1960s? Its connection to the spiritual disposition of the departed is uncertain, but some sources claim this dance, which originated on the island of Trinidad, was performed one week after a death to help the soul escape the state of limbo. A successful crossing under the limbo stick ensured entrance into heaven.

A lion, a fox, and a wolf, hungry for meat, mounted a hunting party. They dispatched a stag, then gathered around to quarter the spoil. That done, the lion placed himself between the carcass and his hunting partners. "The first quarter is mine," he announced, "for I am king of beasts. The second is mine, too, because I brought down the stag. My mate and cubs need the third quarter, and as for the remainder, well, touch it if you dare." The fox and the wolf slinked away, not daring to challenge the mighty lion.

This fable, one of the hundreds attributed to Aesop, is the inspiration for the expression *lion's share*. In the traditional telling of the story, the lion's share is everything—the whole enchilada or, in this case, the whole stag.

But in most modern contexts, the *lion's share* is the greater portion. The expression was recorded in English in the late 1700s and has held up quite well over the centuries. The June 2, 1872, issue of the British publication *Punch* provides instructions on "The art of finding a rich friend to make a tour with you in autumn, and leaving him to bear the lion's share of expenses."

LOLLYGAG

The venerable *Oxford English Dictionary* indicates that the origin of the verb *lollygag* or *lallygag,* meaning "dawdle or waste time," is unknown. But of course, this doesn't discourage imaginative word watchers from formulating their own educated opinions. Though apparently an etymological orphan, *lollygag* does provide some tantalizing clues about its life history.

The word first appeared in print in American magazines and newspapers in the early 1860s. Tucked inside its syllables is the word *loll,* a Middle English word meaning "to recline in a relaxed or indolent manner," or "droop or dangle" like a dog's tongue. There seems to be a logical relationship between the relaxation in both *lolling* and *lollygagging.*

Here's another possibility. *Lolly* is British English slang for "tongue." Adding *gag* to this word makes *lollygag*—literally "gag with the tongue," or "French kiss," an activity that might have been perceived as an inappropriate use of time.

This notion seems to be supported in a quotation from an 1868 publication of the *Northern Vindicator,* an Iowa newspaper that complained about "the lascivious lolly-gagging lumps of licentiousness who disgrace the common decencies of life by their love-sick fawnings at our public dances."

MACARONI

One of the classic folk tunes we've all heard from childhood is "Yankee Doodle went to town/riding on a pony/stuck a feather in his hat/and called it macaroni." Have you ever wondered who Yankee Doodle was, and why *macaroni* was the name of his plumed headgear? To appreciate the significance of this American ditty, we need to look at the history of macaroni.

This curvy, tube-shaped pasta was developed, of course, in Italy, but the word itself was derived from a Greek term meaning simply "barley food."

Though macaroni had been known in Britain since the late 1500s, it wasn't until a group of young city dandies began to advertise their preference for this continental dish that it became popular in London. In the mid-1700s, members of the so-called Macaroni Club, rich and well-traveled dilettantes, began to affect Continental styles and mannerisms, eating exotic foods, wearing long curls, and sporting what one observer called "spying glasses." The preening Macaroni Club members inspired the use of the word *macaroni* as a synonym for "dandy" or "fop."

Here's where the word intersects with the jingle. "Yankee Doodle" was a sneering nickname the British had for American colonists in the late 1700s. The joke was that a rustic, poorly dressed and uneducated Yankee Doodle would consider himself as fashionable as a London Macaroni if he only had a feather to stick in his tricorn or coonskin cap.

MAGIC

The Magi, or "Three Wise Men," are an important tradition in the story of the nativity of Christ. American minister John Henry Hopkins immortalized the Magi in his 1857 Christmas carol "We Three Kings," the traditional story, in song, of the Magi's star-led journey from the Orient to Bethlehem.

The identity of the Magi and their homeland has been a matter of debate among biblical scholars for centuries. A theory favored by many is that the "wise men" were not kings, as songwriter Hopkins proposed, but educated Persian astrologer-priests. A new light in the heavens inspired the astrologers to seek its earthly significance. According to the New Testament account, their search led them to Bethlehem, where they met the Christ child, whose birth the star heralded.

The plural noun *magi* (the singular is *magus*) has its origins in a Persian word meaning "sorcerer." From Persian, the word passed to Greek, to Latin, to French, and, finally in the 1500s, to English.

The word *magi* is significant to modern English because from it came the noun and adjective *magic,* which developed out of the perceived supernatural aspects of the sorcerer's or astrologer's art.

MAKE HAY WHILE THE SUN SHINES

A proverb urging us to take advantage of opportunity—to act while conditions are favorable—is *make hay while the sun shines*. This proverb is of course rooted in agriculture. After hay is cut, it needs to be stacked or baled while it is dry so that it won't turn moldy or rotten. *Make hay while the sun shines* implies that if the hay is dry and the weather fair, the harvesters are wise to work as long as possible before it rains.

This wisdom is centuries old. One of its first recordings is found in a 1546 collection of English proverbs, as "when the sunne shyneth make hey." Though it may have earlier analogues in German and Latin, at least one scholar believed the aphorism was English in origin. In 1853, an Anglican archbishop of Dublin and noted poet, Richard Trench, wrote, *"Make hay while the sun shines* is truly English, and could have had its birth only under such variable skies as ours."

This early proverb, inspired by the harvesting of grass to make fodder for animals, is still a vital expression in 21st century English. Type the phrase into a search engine, and thousands of citations will appear for this well-worn old English proverb.

Make No Bones about It

Have you ever really thought about the odd cliché *make no bones about it?* Almost every native English speaker can use it in context, and we all know what it means, that is, to "speak frankly or take direct action." But it's difficult to imagine how bones have any place in this idiom.

The origin of *make no bones about it* is long lost but frequently debated. Through the years, etymologists have offered various theories. One involves games played with dice, which for centuries were called *bones,* having been originally carved from animal bone. Those who grabbed the dice and threw them quickly and directly, without murmuring incantations for luck, were said to *make no bones about* the cast.

Other phrase watchers give this expression a culinary context. It may have originally alluded to a diner, who, encountering a bone in his soup, simply removed it from his dinner without complaint. He took direct action against the problem in *making no bones about it.*

Journalists and other writers are not shy about appropriating this phrase. In www.Dailyrecord.com, Morris County, New Jersey's online business magazine, staff writer Tim O'Reilly filed an article titled "No bones about it: Dog treat business is hard to sell." In an article by Marylin Linton of the *Toronto Sun* we read, "Make no bones about it. Stronger bones for women is…a worthy goal."

How would you like to learn some new "bad" words? Almost every word headed up with *mal-* is bad. Consider *malicious, malevolent, malignant, malign, malady, malaria.* Bad, even evil: that's what this Latin-based prefix literally means.

Let's look at *malaria.* This word, taken directly from Italian, means "bad air." It reflects the former belief that the disease was caused by the foul, dank atmosphere arising from swamps—the "bad air," or *mal-aria* of damp places.

Badness also occurs in *malady,* a lingering illness or deep-seated disorder. Etymologically, *malady* means "bad condition."

A *malediction* is a curse, a denunciation. It comes from a Latin verb that means "to speak evilly." The antonym of *malediction* is *benediction,* or "good speech."

Malaise is a vague sensation of uneasiness or discomfort or a general sense of depression. The word literally means "badly at ease."

One retiring member of the rather sizeable *mal-* family is the term *malapert,* meaning "impudently bold or sassy," from an old French word meaning "badly clever." *Malversation* is a woefully underused *mal-* word. Defined as "misconduct in public office," *malversation* is etymologically "bad behavior." Find a good dictionary and look up some additional cousins in the *mal-* family: *mal de mer,* sea-sickness; *malign, malicious, malcontent, maladaptive:* there they sit on the page, in all their malevolent glory.

Malapropisms

"She's as headstrong as an allegory on the banks of Nile....Oh! It gives me the hydrostatics to such a degree!"

Such are the mangled pronouncements of Mrs. Malaprop, a character in the 1775 play *The Rivals* by Irish playwright Richard Sheridan. The affected, busybody aunt of the play's heroine, Mrs. Malaprop tries to fashion her niece into a proper young lady, albeit with hilarious lexical absurdity. The aunt claims that her niece should "have a supercilious knowledge in accounts." Mrs. Malaprop goes on to say, "I would have her instructed in geometry, that she might know something of the contagious countries...and likewise that she might reprehend the true meaning of what she is saying."

We've all played the part of Mrs. Malaprop from time to time, unintentionally scrambling and misappropriating words: saying "prostate" instead of "prostrate" or "state the oblivious" or "on the spur of the cuff."

These kinds of lexical misappropriation are called *malapropisms,* from the name of the vain and pompous Mrs. Malaprop. Playwright Sheridan fashioned her character name from the French expression *mal a propos,* meaning "out of place, unsuitable."

A Man's Home

The proverbial expression *a man's home is his castle* has weathered the years well. It was first attested in a document from 1581 and has appeared in English and American manuscripts throughout the centuries. On the other side of the Atlantic, the proverb is often rendered an *Englishman's home is his castle.*

The saying was considered a general legal expression in its early history, associated as it was with the notion that each man's domicile is a haven, and that none may enter without his permission. In 1603, English jurist Sir Edward Coke published a summation of this common law. He wrote, "The house of everyone is to him as his castle and his fortress, as well for his defence against injury and violence as for his repose."

Established expressions such as *a man's home is his castle* are traditionally singled out in playful and sometimes banal reinterpretations by journalists and others. In 1976, Art Buchwald wrote, "Car pooling is a drag.... Who wants to talk to four guys every morning? I think a man's automobile is his castle, and there's no reason he should share it with anyone else."

This statement appeared in a 1994 *New York Times Magazine* article: "A man's home is his castle, but his apartment lobby belongs equally to the tasteless boob down the hall."

MAY-DECEMBER

An amorous relationship between an older and a much younger person is often linguistically marked as a *May-December* love. Traditionally, the players in a May-December affair have been an older man with a much younger woman, but the moniker can also be applied to the inverse relationship.

Here, December, the final month of the calendar year, is a metaphor for someone of advanced age, while May suggests the freshness and fecundity of spring.

The notion is at least as old as Chaucer, the 14th century English poet who, in his *Canterbury Tales,* wrote of a knight named January, a bachelor of 60 years who seeks and finds a very young bride named May. Chaucer probably chose the name January to invoke the snow white hair of the old man, but later writers changed the month to December when alluding to the disparate pairing, possibly to illustrate an end of year/end of life analogy.

More than seven centuries have passed since Chaucer spun the yarn of the young bride and her antique groom, but the image is timeless. Today, you can access a user group called "May/December Love," which is dedicated to pairing older lovers to younger.

McPrefix

In 1955, a 52-year-old entrepreneur named Ray Kroc partnered with brothers Richard and Maurice McDonald to franchise a chain of hamburger restaurants. Called McDonald's, after the surname of the brothers, the first eatery opened in Des Plaines, Illinois, in 1955.

Kroc purchased the exclusive rights to the name "McDonald's" in 1961 and established a hamburger empire that would eventually serve countless millions throughout the United States and in more than one hundred other countries.

McDonald's is one of the most recognizable trade names in the world. It's also managed to impress itself on the slangscape of our language. American journalists started it all in the early 1980s when they nicknamed *USA Today* the *McPaper*. The construction of this word with the prefix *Mc-* aligns the contents of *USA Today* with the perceived negative values of the fast food industry: homogeneity, lack of nutritional quality, superficiality.

The prefix also inspired the recently minted term *McJob,* employment in the service industry where the pay is low and the benefits scanty. *McDoctor* is the McDonald's of the medical industry; it's what some have nicknamed urgent care facilities.

MELTING POT

America has often been called the *melting pot* of nationalities, where immigrants from around the world amalgamate their various beliefs, religions, and languages into a new, homogeneous culture.

The expression began circulating early in the 20th century as a result of Israel Zangwill's play *The Melting Pot*. The English playwright's successful production, which debuted in 1908 in Washington, D.C., featured a climactic scene in which the lead character proclaimed,

> America is God's Crucible, the great Melting-Pot where
> all the races of Europe are melting and reforming!...Here
> you stand in your fifty groups, with your fifty languages
> and histories, and your fifty blood hatreds and rival-
> ries....A fig for your feuds and vendettas! Germans
> and Frenchmen, Irishmen and Englishmen, Jews and
> Russians—into the crucible with you all! God is
> making the American.

The term has become an important part of the American English lexicon, providing a powerful metaphor for the nation's emerging character.

But there are critics of this metaphor who prefer to see the blending of cultures in America as occurring not in a melting pot but rather a salad bowl, where each ingredient retains its integrity and flavor while contributing to a successful final product. The term *salad bowl* in this sociological context was first recorded in American English in 1975.

MESMERIZE

Some denounced him as a charlatan; others proclaimed him a visionary healer. Franz Anton Mesmer, an Austrian born in 1734, studied traditional medicine in Vienna, but by 1775 he had developed some unusual healing techniques. Mesmer proposed that the planets emitted a powerful, invisible vapor that flowed to earth and directly influenced all matter on the planet. He called this vapor "animal magnetism" and claimed that magnets could activate this force and turn it into a source of healing.

Mesmer was accused of practicing magic and sorcery and was drummed out of Austria. He became wildly popular in France, however, where he attracted the attention of the science-mad Parisians. When Marie Antoinette endorsed his practices, the public could not get enough of Mesmer's animal magnetism.

Throngs of followers came to his sessions, which Mesmer conducted in a dimly lit room. Dressed in purple robes, Mesmer requested that his patients join hands in a circle while music from a glass harmonica floated throughout the room. Moving from patient to patient, he looked each person directly in the eyes, murmuring and stroking them softly. Many claimed to be cured of their maladies through Mesmer's animal magnetism techniques.

Mesmer died in Austria in 1815, long after his practice ended. But he loaned his name to the verb *mesmerize,* which means "to captivate, charm, or fascinate."

The word of the year for 2003, according to the American Dialect Society, was *metrosexual.* Trendy and provocative, the term created a lot of media buzz in the early years of the new century.

Though he may not have coined the term *metrosexual,* British satirist Mark Simpson was the first to get it in print— in a 1994 issue of the London newspaper *The Independent.* Observing a new aesthetic trend among urban males, Simpson wrote, "The typical metrosexual is a young man with money to spend, living in or within easy reach of a metropolis— because that's where all the best shops, clubs, gyms and hairdressers are. He might be officially gay, straight or bisexual, but this is utterly immaterial because he has clearly taken himself as his own love object, and pleasure as his sexual preference."

The avatar of the metrosexual is the young, chiseled, impeccably dressed model in men's fashion magazines. The real-life metrosexual strives for that image, buying the latest in designer clothes and accessories, working out to stay trim and solid, and primping with a range of hair and body products.

Metrosexual is a blend word consisting of *metro,* meaning "metropolis or city," and *sexual,* which some sources interpret as a clipping of the word *heterosexual.* Indeed, one of the definitions of a metrosexual is "a young man who is seen, sociologically, as having attributes common to homosexuals, but is in fact heterosexual."

Someone with a *Midas touch* has a talent for turning any venture into a success. This allusion comes from the legend of King Midas of ancient Phrygia, known today as Turkey.

The story opens with the mighty god Dionysus granting King Midas a wish as a reward for his hospitality. The king accepted the offer, his wish being that everything he touched would turn to gold. Dionysus made it so, and the ecstatic king began experimenting with his new power. The apples in his orchard and the crimson roses in his garden all turned to pure gold at the king's touch. Even where Midas walked, he left golden footprints.

Dreaming of wealth unimaginable, the king called for a celebratory feast. But, of course, his food and wine were impossible to eat because they turned to gold when he touched them. So, too, did his beloved daughter when he reached to embrace her. King Midas realized the folly of his desire and begged Dionysus to let him withdraw his wish. Midas washed away the curse of gold by bathing in the river Pactolus.

Though the moral of this tale is a cautionary one, the modern use of the phrase *Midas touch* is almost always positive. Those with the *Midas touch* seem to be unfailingly successful at whatever they put their hands to.

Minced Oaths

Consider the quaint and archaic interjections *gad-zooks* and *zounds*. These oaths are linguistic relics that may have had a sharp bite in Shakespeare's day, but here in the 21st century they're nearly toothless.

A close look at oaths like *gadzooks* and *zounds* reveals some secrets about both the morality of the 17th and 18th century English and their sense of wordplay. Parliament passed a bill in 1606 called "The Act to Restraine Abuses of Players." A portion of this law read, "If...any person...shall in any Stage play, Interlude, Shewe...or Pageant...prophanely speake or use the holy name of God or of Christ Jesus, or of the Holy Ghoste...[they] shall forfeite for every such Offence by...them committed Tenne pounds."

And so Shakespeare and his contemporaries used clever euphemisms—sometimes called "minced oaths"—to avoid fines. When actors uttered *gadzooks* onstage, it was a euphemized version of the blasphemous oath *God's hooks*—a reference to the nails by which Christ was crucified. *Gad* also appeared in *by gad, gad's bodlikins* ("God's little body"), *gads-precious, gadslids,* and *gadswoons,* more minced references to Christ's suffering.

Zounds has a similar pedigree. It was originally pronounced *God's wounds,* but after the Act to Restraine Abuses of Players, the curse became *zwounds,* and finally *zounds.* Then as now, actors in the theatre just couldn't afford a ten-pound fine every time they swore.

And there were more oaths, some of which may seem to us utterly absurd. Consider Shakespeare's *'sblood.* The apostrophe signifies the excision of the name *God,* so *'sblood* was the euphemism of "God's blood," considered a scandalous curse in the 16th century. Oaths of similar construction, which implied a swearing by some portion of divine anatomy, were *'slid, 'sfoot,* and *'sbody.*

Shakespeare's contemporary Ben Jonson also found ingenious ways to conceal the oaths in his plays. Jonson's "by Heaven" was altered to *by these hilts,* "by the gods" was changed to *by my sword,* and "by Jesu" became *believe me.*

Mind Your P's and Q's

There are certain American clichés whose origins defy investigation. *Mind your p's and q's* is one of them. Everyone agrees the expression is an admonition to behave properly or judiciously. But when we try to grasp the source of *mind your p's and q's,* the cliché squirms away from us, leaving us with nothing but a handful of theories.

One theory makes Britain's pub owners responsible. In this scenario, *p's and q's* stands for pints and quarts of beer recorded on a tally slate. Patrons charging their drinks exhorted the bartender to *mind his p's and q's* and not charge them for a quart when only a pint was consumed.

Some claim the phrase was advice to young printer's apprentices to not confuse the lower-case *p's and q's*. This would be an especially apt warning in the printing trade, since the metal-type letters appear backwards.

Or perhaps it has a French origin, with the letters abbreviating *pieds*, meaning "feet," and *queues,* or "wigs." Young, inexperienced dancers were told to mind their feet—*pied*s or *p's*—so as not to appear clumsy, and their *queues,* their wigs, so they wouldn't fall to the floor while bowing to a partner.

MISTLETOE

Stand under a sprig of mistletoe during the holidays, and sooner or later you're liable to get kissed. The origin of this tradition reaches back to a pre-Christian Norse myth about the death and resurrection of Baldur, the god of love and light.

When the evil trickster Loki struck Baldur with a dart made of mistletoe wood, the gentle love god perished on the spot. Baldur's mother Frigga, grieving deeply, begged the gods for his resurrection. When he was miraculously restored to life, Frigga declared that the mistletoe would forever be a symbol of peace, promising a kiss and an embrace to all who passed beneath it.

Mistletoe was revered by the Druids, who gathered the plant to burn it in religious rituals. It was also prescribed for female infertility and even as an antidote for poison. Pre-Christian Romans decorated their homes with garlands of mistletoe during their winter solstice feasts.

Mistletoe is a quasi-parasitic plant that frequently grows on poplar, oak, apple, and hawthorn trees. In Europe it enjoys a symbiotic relationship with the mistle thrush, a bird that eats the plant's white berries. Mistletoe grows directly out of the thrush's droppings, which contain digested seeds—hence the Germanic word *mistletoe,* meaning "dung on a twig."

Mollusk

Clams, oysters, slugs, snails, cuttlefish, and octopuses: these are a few familiar examples of the thousands of species of the phylum Mollusca, commonly known as mollusks. These invertebrates are plentiful on our planet, with over 100,000 species identified and more being described every year.

Most mollusks are buttressed and protected by their shells, which the animals construct by secreting a special material from an organ called the mantle. But underneath that protective shell is a soft, unsegmented, and vulnerable body. The 17th century Swedish botanist Carolus Linnaeus, inventor of the modern biological naming system, classified these creatures by their most obvious attribute: *mollusk* comes from the Latin *mollis,* meaning "soft."

The word *mollusk* has some unexpected etymological kin. Consider the term *mollify,* meaning "to soothe or to calm in temper." Sharing linguistic DNA with *mollusk,* meaning "soft animal," *mollify* etymologically means "to soften in intensity."

An *emollient* is a medicinal agent to soothe and soften living tissue. This word, too, is a sibling of *mollusk* and *mollify* by virtue of its Latin progenitor, *mollis,* or "soft."

It's happened to nearly everyone who listens to vocal music. We sometimes don't understand the lyrics, so we make up our own. There are two classic examples of this phenomenon in rock music. Many listeners refashioned Jimi Hendrix's musical line "'Scuse me while I kiss the sky," to "'Scuse me while I kiss this guy." When Creedence Clearwater Revival sang "There's a bad moon on the rise," some heard "there's a bathroom on the right."

Our language actually has a name for this type of "revision": *mondegreen,* a word introduced by Sylvia Wright in a 1954 article in *Harper's.* As a child, Wright explained, she often heard a lovely ballad called "The Bonny Earl of Murray." One of the stanzas, as heard by the young Sylvia, went: "Ye Highlands and Ye Lowlands/Oh, where hae ye been?/They hae slay the Earl of Murray/And Lady Mondegreen."

Noble and unfortunate Lady Mondegreen, slain with her lover, perhaps? Well, Wright later learned that there was no such lady, and that the actual lyrics were, "They hae slay the Earl of Murray/And laid him on the green." So Sylvia Wright enshrined her phantom Lady Mondegreen in a noun referring to the very phenomenon that conjured her up in the first place.

Another example comes from the lovely song Louis Armstrong made famous, "What a Wonderful World." He sings, "I see skies of blue/clouds of white/the bright blessed day/the dark sacred night." But what was someone thinking when he heard, "the bright blessed day/and the dog said goodnight?"

All of us have misheard song lyrics or words to popular recitations at some time in our lives. A misinterpretation of a familiar refrain is called a *mondegreen*. A common example is the refashioning of the classic Christmas tune into "while shepherds washed their socks by night."

Because pop tunes play constantly in the backdrop of our lives, scores of mondegreens come from this type of music. A classic instance of mondegreenage occurred when someone heard Bob Marley sing, "I shop and share it," when he was really confessing, "I shot the sheriff."

Van Morrison crooned. "Can I just have one more moondance with you, my love?" The mondegreen: "Can I have just one Mormon dance with you, my love?"

Thousands of us misheard words to songs by the 1980s pop trio, the Police. In the tune "Canary in a Coal Mine," the trio was thought by mondegreeners to have sung "you live your life like a canary in a coma." Some heard the Police sing, "When the world is running down, you make the best homemade stew around," instead of "you make the best of what's still around."

When the Rolling Stones sang, "I'll never be your beast of burden," scores of people heard "I'll never leave your pizza burning." Joe Cocker—known for being difficult to understand—sang "Give me a ticket for an air-o-plane" in his song "The Letter," but others heard "Give me a chicken for an air-o-plane."

A fan of the song "Angel of the Morning" mondegreened vocalist Merrilee Rush's plea for a touch on the cheek this way: "Just call me angel of the morning, angel, just brush my teeth before you leave me."

Some mondegreens seem like logical misinterpretations. My sister, a practical-minded child, had a slightly different reading of "God Bless America": "...stand beside her/and guide her/through the night/with a light from a bulb."

But what about another child's version of the first line of the Pledge of Allegiance: "I led the pigeons to the flag?" It seems that the oft-quoted pledge has always been vulnerable to mondegreening by uncomprehending children. Here's another: "and to the republic for Richard Stans, one naked individual, with liver tea and just this for all."

The same type of misinterpretation inspired "Chipmunks roasting on an open fire"; "While shepherds washed their socks at night"; and "When a man loves a walnut"—mondegreens all.

Clichés can be mondegreened too. I once had an employer who warned me that it's a "doggy-dog world out there."

One of my favorite mondegreens is the mangling of the closing tune of Lawrence Welk's weekly TV series. The correct lyrics are "And now, 'til we meet again/Adios, au revoir, auf Wiedersehen." But someone who didn't hear the exotic goodbyes turned it into "And now, 'til we meet again/Oddie oats, or a vowel/All mean the same."

But my very favorite mondegreen comes from a friend of a friend who heard John Denver singing "Rocky Mountain high, bongo bongo."

The strange history of *mumbo jumbo* begins with English explorer Francis Moore, who published his memoir, *Travels into the Inland Parts of Africa,* in 1738.

Moore wrote of a spirit-god among the Mandingoes of western Africa whom the men summoned to frighten their wives into submission. Calling the spirit *Mumbo Jumbo,* probably an Anglicization of a Mandingo term, Moore writes: "At Night, I was visited by a Mumbo-Jumbo, an Idol, which is among the Mundingoes a kind of cunning Mystery....This is a Thing invented by the Men to keep their Wives in awe."

Travelers who later followed Moore's route into Africa also spoke of this strange idol Mumbo-Jumbo, the fearsome god of the Niger River.

The notion captured the European mind, and by the 1840s the name suggested any object or idea inspiring senseless veneration. By the turn of the 20th century, the expression was a synonym for jargon or meaningless talk.

And, of course, we've taken this ancient phrase into the digital age with complaints about the "technical mumbo jumbo" that can so often bedevil us.

NAMBY-PAMBY

Some of our most banal English expressions come from fairly unlikely sources. Take *namby-pamby,* for instance. This epithet, meaning "indecisive, weak, or insipid," was actually coined in the heat of a literary feud between two respected English poets.

The leading man in this lexical drama was Ambrose Philips, born in 1679. The other player was Alexander Pope, the satirist best known for his poems *An Essay on Criticism* and the *Rape of the Lock.* Pope's acerbic wit earned him the moniker "Wasp of Twickenham," from the name of his birthplace in England.

In 1709, both Philips and Pope contributed poems to a popular literary publication. The Twickenham Wasp was incensed when his works were ignored while Philips's verse received favorable reviews. The rivalry ignited a quarrel between the two that persisted for years.

It was Ambrose Philips's misfortune in this case to have written a series of sentimental rhymes for the infant child of close friends. Alexander Pope and his literary ally, Henry Carey, printed biting satires of these simple poems, referring to the writer as Namby-Pamby, a mocking baby-talk reduplication of the name Ambrose. From then on, the poet was lexically associated with insipid sentimentality, deserved or not.

Nepenthe

Edgar Allen Poe's poem *The Raven* weaves the tale of a young man, lonely and grieving his deceased lover, who admits a tame raven into his chambers one cold December evening. Grateful for the company, the man speaks to the bird, and it replies with three repeated syllables: "Nevermore."

This is the word most often associated with *The Raven*, but a closer look at the verses reveals a term far more engaging than the bird's, another three-syllable word: *nepenthe*. Stirred by painful memories of his sweetheart Lenore, the man cries to the bird, "by these angels he hath/Sent thee respite—respite and nepenthe from thy memories of Lenore!/Quaff, O quaff this kind nepenthe and forget this lost Lenore!"

This word *nepenthe* is Greek in origin, composed of the prefix *ne-*, meaning "not," and *penthos*, meaning "grief, sorrow." It is the name of an ancient elixir that erases the pain of grief. Homer used the word in a way that scholars believe is a reference to opium. An herb called *nepenthe*, when steeped in wine, was once thought to possess the power to dispel sadness.

Modern writers use this beautiful little term more figuratively; they speak of alcohol as a type of nepenthe, or of the nepenthe of obsessive busyness and hard work that can blunt the agony of sorrow.

What's in a nickname? People sometimes get their nicknames from physical characteristics: Shrimpy, Curly, Stretch. Or from personality traits: Gabby, Sweetness, Pokey. Even U.S. states have official nicknames: New Mexico is the Land of Enchantment, and Hawaii is the Aloha State.

But what's in the word *nickname?* This term began life way back in the 1300s as *ekename,* with *eke* meaning "additional." So an *ekename,* etymologically, was a "name added on."

Then, in the 1600s, *ekename,* preceded by the indefinite article *an (an ekename),* was misinterpreted as *a nekename,* which ultimately became *a nickname,* and so the word has remained to this day.

Incidentally, the word *eke,* a verb, still survives in the expression "eke out a living," which means to supplement or add to ones income with various means, just as an *eke-name* was once a title "added on" to one's given name.

The amazing stories behind such words as *nickname* are just an etymological dictionary away.

When Europeans began acquiring surnames in the 13th through the 15th centuries, many became known by their given occupations, some of which are familiar to us today, such as *Miller* and *Baker,* and others less so, like *Mather,* which means "hay harvester." Others acquired the name of their village or a conspicuous landscape feature nearby. For example, the name *Olmo*—an Italian word meaning "elm"— might have been given to one who dwelt near an elm grove.

Some of the most delightful surnames, however, came from nicknames, monikers often given in reference to a person's appearance or personality. For example, the English name *Doolittle* was originally given to a lazy man. A German fellow of diminutive stature was often nicknamed *Klein,* which means "small."

Frost was bestowed on a white-haired man, or one of icy and unyielding disposition. *Funke,* a German word meaning "spark," became a name for a lively individual. *Roy* is a Scottish nickname for someone with red hair.

The German word for "rooster," *Hahn,* often became a nickname for a proud or lusty man. *Lever* is a Norman nickname for either a fleet-footed man or a timid person, deriving from the Old French noun *levre,* meaning "rabbit or hare."

NICOTINE

In 1559, a French scholar named Jean Nicot was sent to Lisbon to negotiate a marriage between the royal houses of France and Portugal. It so happened that Nicot's ambassadorial tenure coincided with the arrival of a strange and exciting new plant from the West Indies: tobacco.

Nicot obtained some tobacco seeds and carefully cultivated the plants. He then sent some of it—ground into powder—to the French queen, who quickly became a tobacco enthusiast. When Nicot returned to Paris in 1560, he brought with him a ship's cargo of tobacco. Soon thereafter, fashionable Parisians were inhaling Nicot's new powdered snuff.

Fast forward to 1753. In commemoration of the French ambassador Jean Nicot, Swedish naturalist Carolus Linnaeus gave the tobacco plant the genus name *Nicotiana.* Then, in 1828, two German medical students isolated the tobacco alkaloid, which they called *nicotine,* in keeping with the Linnaean tradition.

The term *nicotine* is an eponym, a word derived from a proper name. Other examples of eponyms include Nobel Prize, named after Alfred Nobel, and Levi's, from Levi Strauss, a Bavarian immigrant to California who sold canvas work pants to sailors in the late 19th century.

NIGHTMARE

A *nightmare* is a bad dream. The term is so familiar we rarely consider its compound construction: *night* plus *mare*. Does the mare in this word have any connection to a mature female horse?

It turns out that the only things the two mares have in common are spelling and pronunciation. The "horse" sense of *mare* comes from the Old English tongue, spoken from about A.D. 450 to 1100. This word has, for over a thousand years, denoted a female horse.

The *mare* in *nightmare* is not a horse at all but an evil spirit or goblin. Originally spelled *maere* or *moere,* this word is also of Old English vintage and referred very specifically to a female spirit said to visit sleepers and sit upon their chests, causing a feeling of suffocation, oppression, and anxiety. Latin speakers called this type of goblin *incubus,* a word meaning "one that lies down upon." The English "maeres of the night" were also thought to bring disturbing visions, a belief that ultimately engendered the word *nightmare,* a synonym for "bad dream," in the 13th century.

In England, the word *mare* is still used to refer to an unpleasant, frightening, or frustrating experience. American English speakers often call difficult people or situations *nightmares.* The same term may be applied to the many little disasters that occur during the course of everyone's waking lives.

NIKE

In 1971, retired track coach Bill Bowerman and athlete Phil Knight named their newly formed shoe company *Nike*. Nike's first shoe design, the "Waffle Trainer," sold for $3.30 per pair and became popular after four 1972 Olympic marathon finalists cruised to the finish line shod in newly minted Nike Waffle Trainers.

Nike's commercial success both galvanized and paralleled the nation's growing interest in physical fitness during the 1970s and '80s. Signing professional athletes such as Michael Jordan and Tiger Woods to endorsement contracts enhanced the corporation's visibility. Nike's reputation was somewhat tarnished when it was criticized for labor exploitation in Indonesia and Mexico. Nevertheless, by 1999, Nike was the number-one shoe company in the world, with its swoosh logo—the lazy checkmark—recognized everywhere.

Back in 1971, Bowerman and Knight named their fledgling company for the Greek goddess Nike, an ancient personification of battlefield and athletic victory. Nike is portrayed most famously as the so-called Winged Victory, the imposing marble statue of the headless goddess with her wings unfurled.

Even the Nike corporation's famous swoosh logo was designed with the victory goddess in mind. The symbol represents the curve of Nike's wings.

OCCUPATIONAL SURNAMES

In the 13th through the 15th century, Europeans from Scotland to Spain to Hungary began acquiring surnames, official identities given to individuals by local bureaucrats for the tax rolls.

Surnames were often assigned for common occupations—like Butcher, Tailor, Shepherd, and Glover. Today, many folks of European descent bear surnames of long-obsolete occupations.

For example, a medieval candlemaker might have been given the surname *Chandler,* which denominated his profession. *Collier* is the occupational surname for a coal seller. In Germany, a butcher may have been named *Fleischmann,* literally, "one who cuts flesh," and a tanner or leather craftsman was often named *Gerber. Ferro* was the surname in both Italian and Portuguese given to an iron worker; the name ultimately comes from the Latin word for iron, *ferrum.*

Stoddard, literally meaning "stud-herd," is an English name originally assigned to a horse breeder. A keeper of falcons in central Europe might very well have been named *Sokol,* the Czech word for a falcon.

And those with the German surname Zimmerman may have the blood of carpenters flowing through their veins. *Zimmerman* means "woodworker."

The original English Kelloggs were hog butchers, with the name being taken from the Middle English verb *kellen,* "to kill." *Kellogg* literally means "kill-hog."

The surname Lorimer was given to makers of spurs, bits, and small attachments to the harness. The derivation of *Lorimer* goes all the way back to the Latin word *lorum,* a harness or strap.

The Coopers of Europe were barrel makers—the crafters of casks, wooden tubs, buckets, and vats. *Cooper* is also Latin in origin, coming from *cupa,* or "cask."

The rhyming *Hoopers* fashioned the wooden or metal bands or hoops used to bind the vats, barrels, and buckets made by their fellow artisans, the Coopers.

What was the trade of an English *Barker?* The Barkers were leather tanners. These artisans regularly harvested tree bark for its tannin, which was used in processing animal hides.

Mahler is a German occupational surname that identified a painter of stained glass. *Mahler* comes from the German verb *mahlen,* "to paint."

The *Tuckers* processed raw cloth by beating and trampling it in water. This surname derives from an Old English verb meaning "to torment." The *Trotters* were the wine pressers, since they were the ones who trod or "trotted" the grapes. Someone with the surname *Minter* probably has a European ancestor who stamped metal coins; a Minter, of course, worked in a mint.

If you're interested in the meaning of your surname, check your library or bookstore for a dictionary of names. One excellent title is *A Dictionary of Surnames,* by Patrick Hanks and Flavia Hodges, published by Oxford University Press.

OFF THE GRID

Households or communities that are *off the grid* operate independently of utility companies. These self-sufficient pioneers heat with woodstoves, cook with propane, collect rainwater and snowmelt, and create their own electrical power with wind turbines or solar panels. Unlike the rest of us, committed off-gridders never pay a utility bill.

What exactly is the grid these energy mavericks are avoiding? Sources differ in their definitions. Paul McFedries's *Word Spy,* www.wordspy.com, a website devoted to monitoring new words in the English language, suggests the phrase *off the grid* began showing up in popular media sources during the early 1990s. McFedries defines the new *grid* this way, "The grid in [this] phrase is the informal name given to the electricity network's interlocking system of transmission lines and power stations. So...*off the grid* originally meant only a disconnection from the electricity supply, and has been used in that sense in the power industry for some time."

But lexicographer Anne Soukhanov, editor of *Atlantic Monthly* magazine's column "Word Watch," asserts that this phrase was inspired by a military sense of the word *grid.* Soukhanov writes, "The Joint Chiefs of Staff's dictionary of military terms defines grid as 'two sets of parallel lines intersecting at right angles and forming squares; the grid is superimposed on maps...to permit identification of ground locations.' When you're off the grid, you're off the map."

Many of our most common expressions have long outlasted the circumstances or technologies of their inspiration. Such is the case with the cliché *in the limelight,* which derives from the bright stage lighting produced by burning a block of calcium carbonate, or lime.

On tenterhooks is another expression living beyond its original derivation. In a metaphorical sense, the phrase means to be suspended in a state of anxious uncertainty. It is unlikely that anyone in the 21st century has used tenters or their hooks, yet, remarkably, the phrase persists.

The idiom was derived from the now-obsolete technology of manufacturing woolen cloth. Newly woven woolen strips, still full of oil, dirt, and plant residue, were washed and cleaned in a process called *fulling.* The wool had to then be stretched and dried to prevent shrinkage.

The fabric was pulled across a wooden frame called a *tenter* and secured by metal hooks, called, appropriately enough, *tenterhooks.* During the Middle Ages, open fields surrounding European towns were often covered with tenter frames and drying woolen fabric.

By the 16th century, tenterhooks were appropriated as a metaphor for the trouble that plagues the mind or the conscience. The expression *to be on tenterhooks* has survived its literal origin and now means to be figuratively stretched on the hooks of anxiety or suspense.

ON THE BLINK, ON THE FRITZ

When something is broken or malfunctioning and in need of repair, we say it's *on the fritz*—or *on the blink,* another slangy expression that works just as well.

The origin of the phrase *on the fritz* has preoccupied wordmongers for a long time. Some connect it with the *Fritz* that was the derogatory nickname for the common German soldier during World War I. Others see the inspiration for this expression coming from a character named Fritz in the comic strip *The Katzenjammer Kids,* popular in the early 20th century. Fritz and his brother Hans, hijinxing twins, were such troublemakers that it's said they put the whole town *on the Fritz.*

Alas, there seems to be no definitive origin for the synonymous phrase *on the blink,* either. *The Random House Historical Dictionary of American Slang* indicates the expression showed up in print in 1899, and that it might have been derived from early electric lights "blinking" when the electricity, or the bulb itself, was about to fail.

A web search for modern uses of this phrase reveals that a whole host of broken things can be considered *on the blink:* TVs, computers, cash machines, cell phones, websites, water heaters, even someone's hearing or memory can be said to be *on the blink.*

On the Lam

When an escaped convict is a fugitive from the law, he's said to be *on the lam*. Where does this expression have its origin?

The word *lam* can be traced to Old Norse, a language related to the Icelandic tongue and spoken in Norway around the 9th century. *Lam* comes from the word *lamja,* meaning "to make lame." *Lamja* became the English *lamme* in 16th and 17th century documents.

The English version of the word means "to beat soundly, to thrash or whack, to make lame." And though it generally referred to one person "lamming" another, one could also lam or strike out with a whip or a ball. Lam is an element in the word *lambaste,* which also means "to thrash." An English document dated 1895 speaks of *lamming for eels,* or "thrashing the water to force eels into a net."

In 20th century America, the phrase *on the lam* became a synonym for "beat it"—but this time, it is the feet of a wrongdoer "beating" or "lamming" the road as they carry their guilty owner away.

So, diners or lodgers running out on the bill, escaped convicts, and fugitive criminals *on the lam* are etymologically "beating it" from the scene of the crime. In the early decades of the 20th century, fleeing scofflaws were sometimes called *lammisters.*

On the Wagon

Someone who refrains from drinking alcohol is, in the world of slang, *on the wagon*. So just what wagon might these erstwhile tipplers be riding on?

The vehicle in this late 19th century expression of abstinence was a horse-drawn water wagon, used to sprinkle water on dirt roads to keep dust from flying. It's said that during the apex of the Temperance movement of the 1890s, men pledging abstinence from spirits claimed they would rather climb aboard the wagon for a drink of dirty water than touch a drop of alcohol.

The expression was quite common in America by 1904. The American Dialect Society distributed a publication in that year that said, "'To be on the water wagon' [means] to abstain from hard drinks." Today, of course, we know this phrase best without the "water" in it.

Predictably, an antonym quickly arose to describe someone who had abandoned her pledge of sobriety. Thirsty for something stronger than water, the backslider was said to have *fallen off the water wagon,* or just *fallen off the wagon.*

The Greek-based element *-onym* is included in an interesting array of modern English words. *-Onym* comes from the Greek word for "name" and is found in such terms as *synonym, eponym, patronym, antonym, pseudonym, acronym,* and *homonym.*

Take a closer look at the last one: *homonym.* Homonyms are words that are pronounced alike but have different meanings, such as *flour* and *flower, caught* and *cot.* The word *homonym* literally means "same name."

An acronym is a pronounceable word formed from the initial letters of a phrase: FEMA from Federal Emergency Management Agency, for example. *Acronym* means "name from the top," or a name formed from the "topmost" or first letters of words.

A *pseudonym* is a "false name" taken by an author; pseudonyms are sometimes called "pen names." *Antonym* means "opposite name" and refers to a word whose meaning is contrary to another's, as *high* is to *low* or *night* is to *day.*

How about *patronym?* This word refers to names like *Johnson,* "son of John," *Thompson,* "son of Tom," or *MacDonald,* an Irish and Scottish name for "son of Donald." In Spanish, the suffix *-ez* creates a patronym: *Fernandez* means "son of Fernando." *Patronym* derives from the Latin word for father, *pater,* and today's Greek element *onym,* meaning "name." A patronym is etymologically a "father's name."

In 1612, English explorer John Smith published the first complete description of the New World settlement of Jamestown, Virginia. The 39-page volume was titled *Map of Virginia, with a Description of the Countrey, the Commodities, People, Government and Religion.* In his account, Smith recorded this: "An Opassom hath an head like a Swine, and a taile like a Rat, and is of the bigness of a Cat. Under her belly she hath a bagge, wherein shee lodgeth, carrieth, and suckleth her young."

Baffled by the strangeness of this creature, whose Indian name he spelled *opassom*, John Smith was obliged to describe the New World opossum in terms of familiar European creatures: swine, rat, and cat. And who can blame him? The beast had no European cognate.

A marsupial, the opossum female carries her young in a pouch. The hairless prehensile tail steadies the creature as it climbs. The mouth of the opossum is packed with teeth—fifty, to be exact—the most of any North American mammal. When threatened, the creature "plays possum," feigning a gruesome death, complete with protruding tongue and drooling mouth.

Lacking an importable name for this singular creature, John Smith and his contemporaries adopted and recorded the Algonquin term *opossum,* meaning simply "white animal."

In 1796, Irish painter Robert Barker invented the word *panorama* to denote a scene painted on the interior of a large cylinder, giving the viewer, standing in the center of the cylinder, a 360-degree view of the painting. Barker's word, *panorama,* is a blending of the prefix *pan-,* meaning "all," and *-orama,* from a Greek verb meaning "to see."

The Greek-based *-orama* made a significant appearance again in the early 1950s with the development of *Cinerama,* a wide screen process of film projection that surrounded movie audiences with exciting, lifelike sound and movement. This thrilling technology launched a new, slangy, 20th century career for the ancient Greek element *-orama,* which was resurrected as a noun-forming suffix.

Stuart Berg Flexner, in his history book *Listening to America,* says *-orama* was "in wide fad use by the 1950s, especially to name or describe a...cheap or flashy business establishment." So by the late '50s, Americans could go to a *drink-orama* for cocktails or knock down some pins at a *bowl-orama.* Even into the 21st century, you can look for used goods in the neighborhood at a *garagarama.* An Internet search yielded some delightful information about *Spongarama,* a Florida museum dedicated to—you guessed it—sponges.

ORTHO-

The Greek-based prefix *ortho-* heads up an august assemblage of modern English words. *Ortho-* means "straight" or "perpendicular"; metaphorically, it can also imply correctness and rightness. This element is the vanguard of many obscure medical, zoological, and botanical terms that you won't see on the pages of any standard dictionary, words like *orthocarpous, orthocoelic,* and *orthoaxial.*

But this lexical element is also useful to most English speakers in the words *orthodontist, orthodox,* and *orthopedics.* Consider *orthodontist.* Here, *ortho-,* meaning "correct" or "straight," is attached to another Greek based element, *odontos,* "tooth." Literally and etymologically, an orthodontist is a "tooth straightener."

An orthopedist, on the other hand, deals with abnormalities in bones and joints, especially in children. The *pedist* comes from the Greek word for "child," so, etymologically, this specialist is concerned with the "straight" development of children's bones.

What about *orthodox,* another member of this linguistic family portrait? This adjective means "having generally accepted opinions, especially in faith or religious doctrine." An orthodox Methodist, for example, adheres to the established customs and traditions of that branch of Christianity. *Orthodoxy,* appearing in English in the 1500s, literally means "straight or correct opinion."

Here are two others worth mentioning: *orthochromatic,* having to do with photographically reproducing the "right" color, and *orthography,* which is the study of "correct" spelling.

Oxymora

A word or phrase that contains two seemingly opposite or contradictory elements—*bittersweet, definite maybe, cruel kindness, freezer burn*—is a rhetorical device known as *oxymoron*. The venerable 20th century English lexicographer H. W. Fowler defined the device this way: "The combining in one expression of two terms that are ordinarily contradictory, and whose exceptional coincidence is therefore arresting." More oxymoronic examples are *cheerful pessimist, alone together,* and *proud humility.*

The strange-looking and odd-sounding term *oxymoron* has an engaging etymology. It combines the Greek element *oxys,* meaning "sharp, keen," with *moros,* "foolish, dull," to produce "sharp dullness, keen foolishness." *Oxymoron* is itself oxymoronic. So is the related word sophomore, which literally means "wise foolish." Etymologically, a *sophomore,* while no longer an academic novice, is still emotionally immature.

American linguist and verbivore Richard Lederer wrote that the contradiction inherent in oxymoronic expression "engages our hearts and minds because…paradox has always been at the center of the human condition." We wrestle daily with good and evil, birth and death, day and night, agony and bliss. Contradictory expressions like *idiot savant, deafening silence,* and *loner's club* are linguistic reflections of our paradoxical lives.

Oxymora II

Last time on this series we examined oxymoronic expressions such as *deafening silence, genuine imitation,* and *proud humility.* Though such terms contain seemingly contradictory notions, they nevertheless can reveal profound truths.

Generations of writers have relied on the oxymoronic device to stimulate both reader and audience. With compelling paradox, Shakespeare's Hamlet said, "I must be cruel only to be kind." The Bard's Juliet oxymoronically sighed to her lover, "Goodnight, goodnight, parting is such sweet sorrow."

In his epic poem *Paradise Lost,* John Milton described hell as a place with "no light, but rather darkness visible." In his 1891 mystery *A Case of Identity,* Arthur Conan Doyle joined two opposites when he wrote, "Depend upon it, there's nothing so unnatural as the commonplace." And Mark Twain is reported to have said, "It takes a heap of sense to write good nonsense."

By the way, if you want to refer to more than one oxymoron, you can say either *oxymorons* or *oxymora;* both are used.

Pan-

In the mid–17th century, English poet John Milton coined the word *pandemonium* in his epic poem *Paradise Lost*. Irish artist Robert Barker, in 1796, invented the term *panorama* to denote his painted wrap-around landscapes. Both men employed the Greek *pan-* in their linguistic innovations—a prefix meaning "all." Milton's *pandemonium* means "dwelling of all demons," and Barker's *panorama* can be translated as "a place to see all."

Pan- is a hard-working prefix in the English language. It's the vanguard of such words as *pandemic,* which literally means "all the people." A pandemic disease, for example, can affect a whole continent, or the entire world: all the people.

Pan- heads up the word *panacea,* meaning "universal remedy." The word literally means "all-healing."

The recently coined adjectival phrase *Pan-American* means "relating to all of North, Central, and South America." Similar prefix-related terms are *Pan-African, Pan-Arabic,* and *Pan-Hellenic.*

Pantomime is also included in this prefix tribe. A word of Greek heritage, *pantomime* means "all-imitator."

A cruise through the *pan-* section of your dictionary will reveal more lexical delights headed up by this prefix.

In 1667, English poet John Milton published his most celebrated work, *Paradise Lost,* an epic account of the biblical stories of Lucifer's rebellion against heaven and the creation of the earth and its first couple, Adam and Eve.

Milton's poem opens with the satanic hosts plotting to thwart God's plan of creation. The devil and his cohorts are gathered in a place Milton calls *Pandemonium,* or, in the words of the poet, "the high Capital Of Satan and his Peers...Citie and proud seate Of Lucifer."

Milton, a classical language scholar, fashioned his word from the Greek prefix *pan-,* meaning "all," and *daimon,* "demon." Milton's satanic city, *Pandemonium,* is literally and etymologically the "dwelling place of all the demons."

The poet's literary successors adopted this word as a synonym for hell. By the late 18th century, *pandemonium* came to represent any place of notorious wickedness. The word was colored a slightly different shade in the mid-1800s when writers used it as a general reference to chaos, confusion, and tumult—the kind that might have been generated in Milton's hellish Pandemonium, "the high Capital of Satan and his Peers," and "the dwelling place of all the demons."

The prefix *pan-,* meaning "all," heads up such words as *pantomime,* etymologically the "imitator of all," and *panacea,* which means "all-healing."

We can add the name of the mythological character Pandora to this lexical family portrait, because the pan in her name is identical to the one that occurs in *pantomime* and *panacea.*

One version of her story asserts that Pandora was the world's first mortal woman, created by Zeus to punish mortal men for their offensive deeds. Beautiful Pandora was sent to earth with a wooden box of baleful gifts from the gods: sickness, hunger, death, and others. When she reached the world of mortals, she flung open the box and unleashed the divine calamities upon humanity.

Another story has Pandora going to earth as a courier of blessings. When she left Mt. Olympus, the gods gave her a boxful of helpful gifts for humankind. Pandora prematurely opened the box, however, and all the blessings escaped.

In any case, the name *Pandora* means "all-gifts," because, depending upon which tale you prefer, the young mortal woman brought to earth either all the curses or all the blessings from the immortals of Mt. Olympus.

PANORAMA

In 1788, citizens of Edinburgh Scotland swarmed to see a representation of their city painted around the inside of a colossal cylinder measuring 60 feet in diameter. Amazed visitors stood on a platform in the center of the cylinder, and, by turning slowly in a circle, were able to view a painted 360-degree cityscape of Edinburgh.

The inventor of this curious novelty was an Irishman, Robert Barker, who seemed to have a genius for painting accurate and lifelike scenes on such an unlikely canvas. After the successful run of his Edinburgh exhibition, Barker mounted cylindrical paintings of the London cityscape and of the Napoleonic Wars.

The device needed a title, and the artist himself provided it. He called his wraparound scenes *panoramas,* a word Barker fashioned from the Greek prefix *pan-,* meaning "all," added to *-orama,* a derivative of a Greek verb which means "to see."

Though the memory of Barker's cylinder paintings has faded, his word *panorama* survives, now generally to denote an overview of a cityscape or landscape. *Panorama* is etymologically a place to "see all."

"Parents Pay Through the Nose for Kid's Admissions." "Phone Callers Pay Through the Nose." "Paying Through the Nose for Blogs."

These are titles of recent articles appearing in newspapers and journals from India, New Zealand, and the United States. Each story, of course, bewails the high price of a service.

The bizarre-sounding idiom *pay through the nose,* used with gusto throughout the English-speaking world, has some explaining to do. How could this combination of words possibly have any synonymy with "pay too much" or "pay until it hurts?"

The tale commonly associated with this cliché alludes to a tax the Danes levied on the Irish in the 9th century under the code of Scandinavian rules called the Danelaw. Anyone failing to satisfy the tax assessor's request was punished by getting his nose slit; he literally "paid through the nose."

But this is only one suggestion for the origin of this strange idiom. Another is that a severe bout of nasal hemorrhaging is about as irksome as excessive payment.

Wilfred Funk, in his *Phrase and Word Origins,* writes this about the expression: "The very fact that the process of delivering up tribute money via the passages of the nose would be uncomfortable and indeed impossible makes the expression the more vigorous."

PECKING ORDER

Anyone who has ever been part of a corporation, organization, or club has discovered their place in the *pecking order*—the social or institutional hierarchy.

One's position in the pecking order might be predicated on job title, age, size, or even personality. Schoolchildren can be ruthless in jockeying for status on the playground, and a corporate pecking order is established through countless nuanced workplace interactions.

The expression *pecking order* is of recent vintage, first appearing in popular media sources in the mid-20th century. But years before it was applied to human interaction, it was a biologist's term, inspired by the observations of a Norwegian zoologist named Thorlief Schjelderup-Ebbe.

In the 1920s, Schjelderup-Ebbe, in a scientific observation of a flock of hens, concluded that the birds established a ranking system through pecking relationships. One hen might peck at another of lower status while submitting to the pecking of a higher-ranking bird. Through this means, the hens established which one had first feeding rights and which one ate last. Shjelderup-Ebbe called this behavior *Hackliste,* a German word that was eventually translated to the English *pecking order.*

The expression was later appropriated as a metaphor for the prestige patterns of human interactions. It became popular in the 1950s and has weathered the decades well.

PEZ

In their signature character dispensers, PEZ candies have been a favorite in America's confectionary cupboard for decades. Since 1952, candy lovers have been popping fruit-flavored PEZ pellets out of the fliptop heads of Snoopy, Daffy Duck, Fred Flintstone, and about 270 other characters.

What might be considered the quintessential American "interactive candy" was, originally, never intended for kids. Nor was it domestically produced. PEZ was invented in 1927 by one Edward Haas, an Austrian food company executive. Sold in tins, the original PEZ was intended as a breath mint for smokers.

In 1948, Haas began selling PEZ in dispensers. There were no cartoon heads involved—this was Austria in 1948, after all—but by the time Haas began marketing PEZ to American children in 1952, he found a market ripe for eating candies out of the tiny plastic heads of Mickey Mouse, Santa Claus, Goofy, et al.

What about the unusual name PEZ? Originally a breath freshener, the confection was made with extract of peppermint. The name is actually an acronym constructed from the German word for peppermint, which is *Pfefferminz*. If you line up the first, middle, and last letters in *PfeffErminZ*, you get *PEZ*.

PHAETHON

Helios, the Greek sun god, drove his flaming chariot across the sky every day to give light and heat to the earth below. One day, his young son Phaethon, eager to prove his strength, demanded a turn at the reins of the sun-chariot. Though Helios protested, the young god harnessed his father's fiery steeds and embarked on his journey across the sky.

The inexperienced Phaethon failed to keep the chariot on course. The horses, out of control, plunged so low that the sun scorched the earth and desiccated the rivers. Then the animals flew so far skyward that the frightened stars cried out for Zeus's protection. To prevent the conflagration of the earth and the heavens, Zeus struck poor Phaethon down with a thunderbolt.

The callow Phaethon, like so many characters from classical myth, eventually found his way into the English language, though now, in the 21st century, he may be fading from view.

In the 1500s and for several centuries thereafter, rash, impetuous, and destructive young men were referred to as *phaethons,* especially those who drove carriages recklessly through the streets.

In the 1880s, a type of light, four-wheeled, horse-drawn carriage was dubbed the *phaeton* for the aspiring charioteer. Phaetons were often driven by women, and the *Oxford English Dictionary* includes this citation: "The emancipated woman of the 1890s was sure to drive her own 'lady's phaeton.'"

What's love got to do with it? *Philosophy, philanthropy,* and *Philadelphia* are related through the Greek term *philos,* meaning "loving." Etymologically, a *philosopher* is a "lover of wisdom," and *philosophy* itself the "love of wisdom." The Greek noun *sophos,* meaning "wisdom," combined with *philos* rounds out the picture.

One who loves mankind is a *philanthropist.* The *anthropist* comes from the Greek *anthropos,* meaning men collectively, or "mankind." Philanthropists express themselves by generously contributing to charities and other humanitarian causes—thus engaging in *philanthropy,* the "love of mankind."

In 1862, the Quaker William Penn named a new colonial settlement in Pennsylvania. Founded on principles of religious tolerance and freedom, the city was given the name *Philadelphia,* meaning "city of brotherly love"; *adelphos* means "brother."

The *philodendron,* a common broad-leafed houseplant seems to have nothing in common with the noble *philosophy* and *philanthropy.* Vining plants, philodendrons are native to the South American tropics and adorned homes since Victorian times. In the tropics, they attach themselves to tree trunks, twisting and climbing their way upwards toward the light. This characteristic prompted botanists in the 1800s to give the plant its Greek-based name *philodendron,* meaning "tree-loving." The *dendron* portion of the name also occurs in *dendritic,* or "tree-like," and *dendrology,* the technical term for the scientific study of trees.

PHOBIAS

In his inaugural address of March 4, 1933, President Franklin D. Roosevelt said, "The only thing we have to fear is fear itself."

Comforting words to some, but try telling that to the multitudes who suffer psychological aversions known as *phobias*. The word *phobia* comes from a Greek term meaning "fear." For many people, fears lurk everywhere, if our nomenclature to categorize them is any evidence.

One common fear is *acrophobia,* an aversion to heights. *Acro,* meaning "high," is also found in *acrobat,* "one who walks in high places." An acrophobe may also suffer *gephyrophobia,* the fear of crossing high bridges. Some gephyrophobes are immobilized by terror when faced with driving across soaring spans over precipitous heights.

The fear of being single is *anuptaphobia. Dromophobia* is an aversion to wandering or travel. If you are very superstitious, you may be a *levophobe,* one who fears things on the left, or a *triskaidekaphobe,* who is afraid of the number thirteen. This Greek-based word literally means "fear of three and ten."

Unfortunate *zoophobes* are afraid of animals. Many people cannot tolerate the sight of blood; they suffer from *hemophobia. Homophobes* fear gays, and *heterophobes* have an aversion to straights.

PHOBIAS II

Phobia words have proliferated dramatically in recent decades. Anne Soukhanov, editor of the column "Word Watch" in the *Atlantic Monthly,* writes that the *phobia* suffix "is extraordinarily productive in the formation of other terms....the productivity of [this suffix] is...an exemplar of...people's creativity in coining new words."

So, any identifiable debilitating fear can become a phobia. I was somewhat relieved to learn that a lifelong aversion of mine has a name: *brontophobia,* fear of thunder. The *bronto* here is the same root word that appears in *brontosaurus,* the "thunder-lizard."

Another fairly common psychological malady is *arachnophobia,* the abnormal fear of spiders. But who knew there were clinical terms for aversion to one's stepmother and stepfather—*novercaphobia* and *vitricophobia?* Many of us have feared the wrath of God for our sinful behavior. This too has a name: *theophobia.*

Do you suffer from the fear of peanut butter sticking to the roof of your mouth? No worries: you too are a legitimate phobiac, for you have been diagnosed with *arachibutyrophobia.*

PIE IN THE SKY

The rhyming expression *pie in the sky* refers to anything that never can, never will, materialize. While many English language clichés are centuries old and of obscure origin, *pie in the sky* is a relative youngster with a clearly traceable history.

This expression originally belonged to the lyrics of a song written for the Industrial Workers of the World, popularly known as the Wobblies. This pro-union song, called "The Preacher and the Slave," was penned in 1911 by famous IWW organizer Joe Hill, who had composed several satirical songs for the movement.

"The Preacher and the Slave" was a lyrical jab at the Salvation Army, an organization seen as misguided in their zeal to save the souls of the working class Wobblies who, for their part, simply wanted jobs to feed themselves, not platitudes of eternal rewards for earthly suffering. Sung to the tune of "In the Sweet Bye and Bye," Joe Hill's song went:

> You will eat, bye and bye,
> In that glorious land above the sky;
> Work and pray, live on hay,
> You'll get pie in the sky when you die.

The rhyme *pie in the sky* caught the popular imagination as a cliché symbol for unattainable comfort and wealth and is now used to speak of anything that is a hopeless fancy.

Many cultures have tales of "little people." In Britain, there are fairies, leprechauns, elves, and brownies—diminutive spirits who are sometimes helpful and sometimes mischievous—or even malevolent.

Another tribe of little people is the pixies. Folklore places pixies in the Cornwall region of southwestern England, where locals have described them as small red-haired creatures with pointed ears and almond-shaped eyes. Pixies clothe themselves in garments made of moss, grass, and lichen.

There are several legends attached to the origin of these tiny folk. In one tradition, pixies are miniature vestiges of Celtic gods who lost their powers after the arrival of Christianity. Another story suggests that they are the embodiment of the souls of babies who died before being baptized.

Pixies are pranksters who steal horses and ride them through the night. Though they are not considered powerful or dangerous, pixies can confuse and bedazzle travelers, causing them to become disoriented and hopelessly lost.

And it's this pixie trait that inspired the thoroughly charming but sadly underused term *pixilated,* which began appearing in print in the mid-1800s. Pixilated means bewildered, confused, tipsy, whimsical, intoxicated, as if one had been led astray and confused by the little people. The word appears to be a blend of *pixie* and *titillated.*

A common phrase we use to express delight or smug satisfaction is *pleased as punch*.

The punch in this phrase isn't the one that is quaffed, nor is it the one delivered in a fight. This is the name of the lead character in a puppet show called "Punch and Judy," popular in England since the 1600s. The puppet Punch is quite grotesque in appearance, with his hunched back, long hooked nose, and bulging eyes. Possessed of an evil heart, Punch spends most of the plot stirring up mischief and injury.

The traditional puppet drama depicts Punch murdering his own wife, Judy, and their infant son. After escaping jail, the malicious character goes on to kill a policeman, a lawyer, the devil, and even Death itself. Eliminating his victims with great glee, Punch repeatedly chortles his signature catchphrase, "That's the way to do it!"

The macabre satisfaction this character derives from his evil deeds inspired the expression *pleased as punch* and its variant, *proud as punch*.

This phrase is alliterative, featuring the repetition of the consonant *p*. Alliterative clichés like this one tend to remain popular among English speakers.

Any small, unremarkable town of the American hinterlands can go by the catch-all moniker *Podunk*. Podunk, USA, is imagined to be populated by insignificant people going about their ordinary lives.

Though we speak of Podunk as a fictive burg, there are several geographically fixed Podunks throughout this country. Connecticut, New York, and Michigan all have towns with this name, and sprinkled about the map are Podunk Creeks, Lakes, Ponds, and Schools.

The original Podunk is situated in the general vicinity of Hartford, Connecticut, where the name was historically associated with a subgroup of the East Coast family of Algonquin. In the local dialect of this group, *podunk* meant "place where you sink in mire," or "boggy place," and came to designate both the traditional territory and its people.

The name became associated with any remote backward locale in 1846, when a series of anonymous letters was published in the Buffalo, New York, *Daily National Pilot*. In these so-called "Letters From Podunk," the writer poked fun at small town life and eccentric local characters. The popular letters established the name firmly in American parlance as the generic title of any insignificant, out-of-the-way town.

The fiery poinsettia, a favorite emblem of the winter holidays, is a native of the tropics that grows wild in the highlands of Central America and southern Mexico. Long before Spanish contact, the Aztecs had put the plant to practical use, extracting dye from its leaves and incorporating the milky sap of the stem in an elixir for reducing fever.

Because the poinsettia blooms in winter, 17th century Franciscan friars incorporated the crimson plants in their nativity processions. This association with Yuletide inspired the local name *flor de nochebuena*, "Flower of the Blessed Night."

On Christmas day in 1825, an American ambassador to Mexico, Joel R. Poinsette, visited one of the Franciscan churches that had been lavishly bedecked with the radiant flower. The ambassador, an amateur botanist, was captivated by its unusual shape and color and sent samples to his home in South Carolina. He later propagated the plant, sharing it with friends and botanical gardens around the country.

By the 1850s, Americans had embraced the ambassador's scarlet flower as a lasting Christmas symbol. It was named the *poinsettia,* after its most ardent promoter, Joel Poinsette.

Poinsettia is an example of an eponym—a proper name that's become a common noun.

POLKA

In the 1960s, it was the twist. Back in the '20s, the Charleston. But these fads were mere blips on the dance radar compared to the polka craze that endured for sixty years, holding dancers and musicians in its thrall from 1840 to the turn of the 20th century.

Developing out of a Bohemian folk tradition, polka music and dance were introduced in Prague in 1837. This dance of face-to-face couples in lively 2/4 time proved delightfully risqué to the Praguites, who were accustomed to the more formal waltz and minuet. Ditto the Viennese and Parisians, who wholeheartedly embraced the trend in 1839 and 1844. Then European immigrants imported the polka to the Americas, where its various adaptations are still danced everywhere from Cleveland to Rio de Janeiro.

The polka's early popularity ignited parallel marketing fads for such items as polka hats, polka gauze, and, of all things, polka curtain ties. These have all faded, but the polka dot fabric pattern, developed during the polkamania era, remains a perennial favorite.

The origin of the word *polka* is disputed. It may derive from the Czech word *pulka,* meaning "half," referring to the short, half-time steps of the dance. Another theory has its source lying in the Polish word *Polka,* meaning "Polish woman."

A person gifted with an irrepressibly sunny, optimistic nature is often called a *pollyanna*. The origin of this moniker is a fictional heroine created by American writer Eleanor Hodgman Porter, a New England native who published her sweetly sentimental novel *Pollyanna* in 1913.

The novel tells the story of a girl from a very poor family who compensates for life's difficulties by playing the "glad game," a diversion that looks for any shred of hope during the darkest times. Pollyanna teaches her "glad game" to other needy people, thus changing her little village of Beldingsville for the good.

Pollyanna was an American bestseller from 1913 to 1915. Helen Hays played the lead role in the 1916 Broadway adaptation of the novel, Mary Pickford starred in the 1920 motion picture version, and Hayley Mills revived the movie role in 1960.

The name *Pollyanna* has since entered the language as a synonym for an unflappable and sometimes syrupy and unrealistic optimist.

The Greek-based element *poly-* means "many," and it appears in a large roster of English words. Consider, for example, three terms that refer to specific types of plural relationships: *polygamy, polygyny,* and *polyandry.*

The first, *polygamy,* is the practice of having more than one spouse at a time. The word is a combination of *poly,* the "many" element, and *gamy,* from the Greek word for "marriage."

Polygyny is the custom of having many wives at once, and the practice of a woman having multiple husbands is *polyandry.*

The word for a solid figure with four or more faces is *polyhedron,* which literally means "many sides." A scholar of much or varied learning is a *polymath.* This excellent word means "person who studies many things." The *math* portion comes from a Greek verb meaning "to learn."

The instrument used for lie detector tests is a *polygraph,* or "many writings," so called because it records on paper several small physiological changes at once. Another, more obscure definition of *polygraph* is "prolific or versatile writer."

Someone who worships more than one god is a *polytheist,* and a word divided into three or more segments is a *polysyllable.*

There are dozens more words containing this Greek element that means "many": *polyester, polyphagia, polyp, polychromatic.* They're just a dictionary away.

Despite their reputation as pampered lap dogs, poodles come from a line of hard-working sport animals.

No one knows the poodle's true origins, but one theory holds that its early ancestor was an Asian herding dog that traveled west with tribes of Goths to eventually become a German hunting animal. Others believe the dog found its way from Asia to Portugal in the 8th century with the Moors.

Frescoes and drawings depicting curly haired dogs that resemble contemporary poodles suggest that the breed's ancestors have lived in Europe for many centuries. German artist Albrecht Dürer depicted poodle-like dogs in his 15th century paintings.

Though we often call the dogs "French poodles," the breed was probably developed by the Germans as a hunting dog for retrieving waterfowl in ponds and marshes. A look at the etymology of the name reveals the dogs' original purpose: *poodle* comes from the German name *Pudelhund,* or "puddle dog," from the verb *puddeln,* "to splash."

The diminutive toy and teacup versions of the more robust standard poodle have been favorite lapdogs for centuries. Early in the 1900s, the British slang term *poodle-faker* found its way into print. A man who insinuated himself into the company of affluent women for social or financial advantage, the poodle-faker fawned and clung to the ladies as would an adoring pet.

The source of the word *posh,* meaning "elegant, smart, and fashionable," has never been identified with certainty. But that doesn't mean people haven't spun stories about its origin.

One tale about the genesis of *posh* involves the travels of the Peninsular and Oriental Steam Navigation Company, which, from 1842 to 1970, carried passengers between England and India. It's said that the port-side cabins were the most desirable for the voyage to India because they were sheltered from the sweltering summer sun. On the return trip to England, the opposite was true, of course, with the starboard cabins on the shady side of the ship.

This special port/starboard arrangement was reserved for wealthy and important voyagers, who allegedly received tickets stamped with the word POSH, the acronym of Port Out, Starboard Home, the most expensive and luxurious travel accommodations on the Peninsular and Oriental.

The tale of this acronym is appealing but, unfortunately, has no legs. The editors of the respectable *Webster's Word Histories* write, "As late as 1962 the librarian of the Peninsular and Oriental was unable to find any evidence that POSH was actually stamped on anything."

In fact, no one has been able to identify an etymological source for this word. It may have come from the turn-of-the-20th-century slang term *posh,* meaning "dandy or stylishly dressed man."

Proverb: a short pithy saying that expresses a practical precept or basic truth. Each culture has its coffer of proverbs, common-sense guidelines that are bequeathed from one generation to the next. We've all heard them from a parent or a grandparent, or from someone old enough to have experienced the wisdom encoded in these timeless phrases.

Beauty is skin deep. A friend in need is a friend indeed. All that glitters is not gold. One good turn deserves another. Give him an inch and he'll take a mile.

In 1692, an Englishman, Robert South, wrote, "What is a proverb, but the experience and observation of several ages, gathered and summed up into one expression?" The author of *Don Quixote,* Cervantes, wrote in 1605, "Proverbs are short sentences drawn from long experience." And one Moses Ebn Ezra deftly summed up the qualities of the proverb. It has, he wrote in 1924, "three characteristics: few words, good sense, and a fine image."

Too many cooks spoil the broth. Easier said than done. A little learning is a dangerous thing. Don't put all your eggs in one basket. Two wrongs don't make a right.

Our language has at least three distinct meanings for the word *punt*. The oldest is a term referring to a flat-bottomed, square-ended boat. This term hails ultimately from the Latin *ponto,* which also gives us the word *pontoon.*

Punt is also a sports term. Kicking a ball after it has been dropped from the hands is called *punting.* The origin of this sense of the word is unclear, but it could be a variant of *bunt,* meaning "bump, raise, or lift up."

Oenophiles, or wine-lovers, know *punt* as that indentation in the bottom of a bottle. The derivation of this term has been much disputed, with some claiming a connection to the sports word, since the indentation makes it appear as if the bottle had been kicked, or punted.

But glassblowers might cry foul on this theory, because in their world a *punt* or *punty-rod* is a tool used in bottle crafting. When it's broken off the end of the bottle, it leaves a mark, which, according to this account, is called the *punt,* after the tool itself.

PUSHING THE ENVELOPE

When the *Detroit News* published an article in 1997 about Dr. Jack Kevorkian, the controversial advocate of doctor-assisted suicide, part of the text read, "Dr. Kevorkian has always shown the desire to push the envelope if he doesn't get the proper media attention." Why an envelope, and why would someone push such a thing?

This phrase began appearing in the popular media in the early 1980s. *Pushing the envelope* is something done by athlete, politician, rebellious child, or "Dr. Death" to test the limits of accomplishment, safety, morality, or propriety.

Author Tom Wolfe is responsible for popularizing the expression in his 1979 bestseller *The Right Stuff,* a story about the valor of early test pilots and the first seven American astronauts. In this context, the "envelope" refers to the mathematically calculated parameters in which the mechanisms of an aircraft can perform safely. The term has become a metaphor for the reasonable limits of safety and the boundaries of civility and protocol.

Pretenders to medical knowledge, *quacks,* have been practicing their deceptions for centuries. In the 1500s, for example, quack physicians prescribed "philosopher's egg," an egg pricked and blown out, then refilled with saffron, as a cure for the bubonic plague.

Early American history is full of stories of traveling medicine salesmen who advertised nostrums, concoctions, and ointments "guaranteed" to cure every physical complaint.

Quackery follows us into the digital age with spam-offered cures for obesity, wrinkles, and undersized body parts.

How did the dispensers of useless ointments and treatments come to be called *quacks,* and their pseudo-science *quackery?*

These words derive from the 16th century Dutch term *kwakzalver,* which referred to a medical charlatan. This word, in turn, is a combination of the verb *kwakken,* to make the noise of a duck, and *zalf,* meaning ointment or salve. The *kwakzalver,* or *quacksalver,* was literally one who "quacked" or boasted about his salves. This term is an apt verbal portrait of the American snake oil merchant who hawked his cures with evangelical zeal, then moved on to the next town before his imposture could be discovered.

The derived abbreviation *quack* is still used to refer to unqualified medical practitioners, and *quackery* describes their unscrupulous methods.

RACCOON

Raccoons inhabit all but the coldest and hottest regions of North America. This bandit-faced, ring-tailed creature thrives in both urban and rural environments across the continent. One of the raccoon's favorite meals consists of small aquatic animals such as crayfish, frogs, and crabs, which it appears to "wash" in ponds and rivers with its agile forepaws. This behavior inspired its biological designation, *Procyon lotor,* Latin for "doglike one that washes."

But what about its common name, *raccoon?* Where did it originate, and what does it mean?

English colonists, new to North America's shores in the first decades of the 17th century, found a land teeming with strange new creatures. One of these was the raccoon, which early diarists compared to the fox, badger, and bear. Since the colonists could find no satisfactory European designation for the animal, they adopted the native Algonquin name.

Twenty-seven-year-old John Smith, an English soldier, adventurer, and a significant player in the establishment of Jamestown Colony, wrote in 1624, "There is a beast they call *arocoughn,* much like a badger." Smith spelled the word *arocoughn* in this document, but he subjected it to more tortured renderings in others writings, with additional *g's, h's,* and *u's.* By 1672 the spelling had been simplified to *raccoon,* an Algonquin-derived word meaning "they scrub with their hands."

The Bible's Old Testament opens with the story of God creating Adam from the dust of the earth, and Eve from the rib of Adam. The world's first couple lived in Paradise until they disobeyed God by eating of the fruit of the Tree of Knowledge. After they were expelled from the Garden, Eve gave birth to two sons, Cain and Abel.

Cain grew to be a farmer. His younger brother Abel tended the flocks. When it came time to offer sacrifices to God, Cain the farmer brought some of his produce to the Lord, while Abel offered God the fat portions of the first-born of his flock. Because God favored Abel's animal sacri-fice over Cain's, the jealous older brother slew the younger. Thus Cain became the world's first murderer, and all the more wicked because of his fratricide.

There was a joke circulating in the mid-20th century that went like this: "How do we know that Adam and Eve were troublemakers? Because they both raised Cain!" This joke was inspired by a cliché predicated on the biblical story of the perfidious brother. To *raise Cain* is to cause a disturbance, be rowdy, unruly. When you cause trouble by *raising Cain,* you etymologically summon the spirit of dis-cord, especially that of the jealous, murdering Cain.

READ MY LIPS

On August 18, 1988, George Herbert Walker Bush gave his nomination acceptance address to the Republican National Convention in New Orleans. One of his more memorable statements on that day involved his philosophy on taxation. He proclaimed, "And the Congress will push me to raise taxes, and I'll say no, and they'll push, and I'll say no, and they'll push again, and I'll say to them, 'read my lips: no new taxes.'"

George Bush the elder did not invent the phrase *read my lips*. The expression popped up in a Gary Trudeau *Doonsbury* cartoon in 1987, a year prior to Bush's speech. And there's evidence that *read my lips* has been lurking in the American English slang vocabulary since the 1970s.

But George Bush ignited a fad for the expression, and though it has become a bit tarnished it will forever remain a linguistic marker of the first Bush administration.

Read my lips means, of course, "You can trust me, I assure you that I am telling the truth; you should not only hear my words but watch my lips speaking them." But within two years of Bush's speech, someone fashioned a neologism around the incident: *bushlips,* meaning, ironically, "insincere political rhetoric." The new word caught the attention of the American Dialect Society, a panel of linguistic scholars, which named *bushlips* the Word of the Year for 1990.

Will the real Real McCoy please stand up? For over a century now, Americans have been employing the expression *the Real McCoy* as a synonym for "the real thing, the genuine article." Though millions immediately recognize the phrase, none of us, word historians included, can point to the origin of this expression with absolute certainty. All we can do is take our pick from a variety of possibilities.

Some say it's a mispronunciation of McKay, the name of an importer of a fine grade of whiskey from Scotland at the turn of the 20th century. This theory rests on the notion that one could drink many brands of whisky, but there was only one "real McKay."

Another mispronunciation theory has the word coming from the pure heroin imported from the island of Macao. Again, many products may imitate the best, but there's only one "real Macao."

The most plausible suggestion, though, is inspired by the name of a young American boxer who called himself Kid McCoy. Born Norman Selby in 1873, Kid McCoy became the most celebrated welterweight of his day, with many impersonators appropriating the McCoy name. He reached the pinnacle of fame in 1899 when he knocked out a respected heavyweight fighter. National newspaper headlines the next day proclaimed, "NOW YOU'VE SEEN THE REAL MCCOY!"

Rhinestone

An easy way to add a little low-cost bling to your attire is with rhinestones. Cut to resemble diamonds, glass rhinestones glitter brightly under stage lighting, making them the performer's favorite accessory. The pianist Liberace once owned the world's largest collection of these ersatz diamonds. He had them mounted on his Baldwin piano and even on his roadster. Tens of thousands of them were sewn onto his opulent costumes—even his shoes glimmered with rhinestones.

These clear gems became popular in the mid-1700s after a French goldsmith named Georges Stras began fashioning striking jewelry out of high-quality cut glass. Like diamonds but far more abundant and affordable, the stones were set into intricate pins, buckles, hair combs, brooches, and buttons.

In Europe the clear jewels were sometimes called *strass,* after their maker, or *caillou du Rhin.* The latter came from the name of a gemstone cut from rock crystal found on the banks of the Rhine River throughout Germany and France. Stras's gems, thought to resemble this natural stone, were named *caillou du Rhin,* which translates to the English *rhine-stone.*

RITZY

It was the talk of Europe from the day it opened its doors in 1898. The Hotel Ritz in Paris, named for its founder Cesar Ritz, offered unparalleled service and opulence. With elegant restaurants and bars, gardens, greenhouse bouquets, and 210 guest rooms, each with its own bathroom and fireplace, the Hotel Ritz attracted the most prominent personalities of the day: Ernest Hemingway, Noel Coward, the Prince of Wales, and Marlene Dietrich.

César Ritz had little formal education. At 16, he was hired as a busboy in a hotel dining room but was quickly discharged for lack of aptitude for service. Undeterred, Ritz went on to other restaurant and resort work in France and Germany. After several year's experience, he eventually became manager of London's Savoy Hotel, which he transformed into the city's premier lodging.

After his success with the Hotel Ritz of Paris, he opened the Ritz Hotel London in 1906—just as elegant and just as popular. A home away from home for the wealthy, Ritz Hotels inspired the adjective *ritzy*, meaning "exclusive, sophisticated, luxurious." This word began showing up in print in 1920. Songwriter Irving Berlin invoked the name of the hotels in his 1929 "Puttin' on the Ritz."

César Ritz influenced our vocabulary not only with his surname but with a catch phrase. By anticipating and fulfilling his client's every need, Ritz kept his influential guests returning year after year. He was the first to declare "Le client n'a jamais tort"—"The client is never wrong." This sentiment inspired the later English version: *The customer is always right.*

ROBIN

Though it's the state bird of Connecticut, Michigan, and Wisconsin, the robin is at home everywhere in North America. From the open plains to suburban lawns, these familiar birds enjoy a diet of beetles, cutworms, and earthworms as well as seasonally available berries.

Robins are migratory, and their arrival is a welcome sign of spring. Pairs of the birds nest in trees and buildings and will generally raise two or three broods each summer.

Early American settlers named the North American robin after a common European species, the *robin redbreast,* a small bird with vivid scarlet breast plumage. Europeans had long regarded their robin with affection, citing an old legend that the flames of hell had scorched the bird's breast when it brought humans the gift of fire. Since the bird also appears quite tame and friendly around people, its reputation earned it the moniker *Robin,* an affectionate form of the popular masculine name Robert.

The name seemed appropriate enough for the red-breasted bird of the New World, though the European and American creatures are in fact unrelated. The scientific name of the North American bird is *Turdus migratorius*—*migratorius* because it's a seasonal inhabitant, and *turdus,* despite what the word may sound like, from the Latin word for "thrush."

The familiar aphorism *a rolling stone gathers no moss* has an engaging life history, from its Roman origins to its modern-day American variations.

A Roman actor and writer named Publilius Syrus is credited with originating this expression in the first century B.C. At the time of its coining, and for many centuries thereafter, *a rolling stone gathers no moss* was a proverbial way to say "wanderers can never expect to amass wealth, property, or a good reputation."

By the 20th century, an increasingly restless American society began to prize mobility. Striking out on one's own became an act of bravery and ambition, rendering our rolling stone proverb a bit conservative. In 1914, George Bernard Shaw wrote, "We keep repeating the silly phrase that rolling stones gather no moss, as if moss were a desirable parasite." Turning the expression on its head, some translated the expression as "the sedentary become stale and moss-covered."

This 2,000-year-old Latin proverb has had considerable influence on American popular culture. In 1950, singer Muddy Waters recorded a blues number called "Rollin' Stone," a title that, in 1962, was adopted as a name by a certain British pop combo. Bob Dylan's signature tune, "Like a Rolling Stone," was released on July 20, 1965, and in 1967 the music magazine *Rolling Stone* was first published in San Francisco.

Rule of Thumb

A *rule of thumb* is an approximate measurement, or some general standard that we can go by. Where did this folksy-sounding expression come from?

One theory that's been circulating in recent years posits a 17th century British law that purported to restrict the size of a stick with which a man could legally beat his wife: the instrument of chastisement could be no thicker than the man's thumb—hence *rule of thumb*. But legal scholars and word watchers have yet to locate any record of such a code, making a folk tale—some might say a hoax—of this theory.

Another account attaches the expression to brewers who were said to have gauged the temperature of fermenting beer by plunging a thumb into the brew.

But the most logical origin of this phrase makes the thumb a crude measuring device, since the first joint of the digit is an inch or so in length. So, the *rule of thumb* is a crude but handy ruler for the carpenter or woodworker.

The use of body parts as calibrating devices dates to antiquity. Pacing out dimensions on the ground gave us foot lengths; a yard is the approximate distance between an extended fingertip and the tip of the nose; and horse height is still measured in hands. So the rule of thumb might very well come from this tradition.

Sam Hill

Someone outrageously confounded by a situation might demand "what the Sam Hill is going on here?" or "who the Sam Hill did this?" That Sam Hill—his name certainly loans satisfying emphasis to such outraged inquiries. Who is the real Mr. Hill behind this oath?

Apparently there was a notable Sam Hill, an American politician who may be obliquely attached to this expression. An unsubstantiated story has it that one Colonel Samuel Hill of Guilford, Connecticut, ran for political office many times in the early 19th century. He failed at each election, so to "Run like Sam Hill" or to "Give 'em Sam Hill" is to strive for success regardless of the potential consequences. But this tale is just that: a tale. It's dismissed by most lexicographers for lack of written evidence.

The name has been in use as a convenient euphemism for a stronger oath since at least 1839. The similarity between *hill* and *hell* is obvious to any English speaker. We see the same linguistic pattern in the euphemistic pairing of *cripes* and *Christ, goldang* and *goddamn, heck* and *hell*. Such euphemisms are common and enable the speaker to swear without "really" swearing or offending.

SAMSONITE

Every culture has its "strong man" legend. In the Greek tradition it was the saga of Hercules; in the American Southwest, the tale of Pecos Bill.

Samson is the "muscle man" of ancient Israel. Stronger than a dozen men, Samson killed lions with his bare hands and slew a thousand of his Philistine enemies—armed only with the jawbone of an ass.

Samson was a Nazerite, one dedicated to God from birth to death. Nazerites wore long hair bundled into seven braids, believing that was the source of their prodigious strength.

Samson's treacherous wife Delilah, however, shaved his head, then sold her enervated husband to his enemies, the Philistines, who blinded and imprisoned him.

Over time, Samson's hair—and with it his strength—returned, and the hero waited for the right moment to avenge himself. Finally, shackled in a temple before three thousand jeering Philistines, Samson thrust the pillars of the temple apart, destroying the building and everyone in it, including himself.

The saga of this Old Testament Nazerite is evoked in a most unlikely 20th century word—*Samsonite,* the name of a line of luggage introduced by a Denver trunk maker named Jesse Shwayder in 1910, who, through the name, associated his luggage to the strength and durability of the long-haired champion of the Old Testament.

Word lover John Ayto, in *A Gourment's Guide, Food and Drink from A to Z,* writes that the sausage was one of the first convenience foods. A conglomeration of minced meat and spices stuffed into the membrane of an animal intestine, the sausage has been a source of portable nutrition for millennia. Homer mentions a type of blood sausage in the Greek epic the *Odyssey.* The history of the word reveals the most important preservative ingredient of the sausage: it comes from the Latin term *salsus,* meaning "salted."

Europeans put their own signature on the Roman sausage, stuffing the casings with locally available ingredients. A traditional sausage made in the city of Vienna, for example, became the famous *Wienerwurst,* literally, "sausage of Vienna." The German term for sausage, *Wurst,* evolved from the Latin verb *vertere,* meaning "to roll or turn," a reference to the cylindrical shape of the sausage casing. The *Wiener* of *Wienerwurst* ultimately became the American *wiener* or *weenie.*

SCALAWAG

Nowadays, a *scalawag* is little more than a rascal or scamp. This seemingly innocuous word, however, was once a grave insult.

In the post–Civil War South, a scalawag was a local who supported reconstructionist measures, hoping to profit from cooperating with the Republican administration in the North. In some documents from the era, scalawags were compared to "foul lepers" and deemed "low persons of the baser sort." Considered more vile than Northern carpetbaggers, Southern scalawags were looked upon as traitors.

But the North had its scalawags too, and they showed up decades before their Dixieland counterparts. The *Dictionary of Americanisms,* published in 1848, referred to *scalawag* as "a favorite epithet in Western New York for a mean fellow, a scapegrace." In Trade Union slang, a scalawag was a recalcitrant man who would not work.

Yet another definition of the word, and probably its original sense, was "a lean, scrawny, undersized horse or cow." This leads some etymologists to speculate that *scalawag* derives from the isle of Scalloway in Scotland's Shetland Islands, known for its populations of small ponies, which are of little value as work animals. From this, *scalawag* may have evolved to mean "morally stunted person, one who will not work." But this is only an educated guess offered by word watchers. Every dictionary admits that the origin of the word *scalawag* is either uncertain or unknown.

SCUTTLEBUTT

Synonyms for gossip: *rumor, buzz, chatter, hearsay, scuttle-butt.* How did the last word make it into this family of tat-tletale terms?

A look at *scuttlebutt's* literary history can give us some help here. In 1850, Herman Melville published a seafaring adventure story called *White-Jacket: or, The World in a Man-of-War.* Melville wrote, "There is no part of a frigate where you will see more going and coming of strangers, and overhear more greetings and gossipings of acquaintances, than in the immediate vicinity of the scuttle-butt, just forward of the main-hatchway, on the gun-deck." Melville describes the scuttle-butt as an object placed in a specific area on the gun-deck of a frigate.

When we dissect the word, we get an idea of what a 19th century scuttle-butt looked like. *Butt* is an obsolete term meaning small wooden cask or keg. The verb *scuttle* means "cut a hole in." So, etymologically, Melville's scuttle-butt was a wooden cask with a hole or hatchway. The cask contained fresh drinking water, which was scooped out of the opening with a tin cup or dipper.

So, as Melville suggests, sailors routinely gathered around the cask, greeting cohorts and swapping gossip, a scene strik-ingly similar to modern office conversations around the water cooler. By the early 20th century, the word for the water cask, *scuttlebutt,* was transferred to the gossip generated around it.

SCYLLA AND CHARYBDIS

Singer-songwriter Sting, in 1983, wrote a song called "Wrapped around Your Finger" for his band the Police. It weaves a tale of psychological control, perhaps that of a married woman over her younger lover. The opening lyrics read, "You consider me your young apprentice/Caught between the Scylla and Charybdis."

Sting's *Scylla and Charybdis* alludes to the ancient Greek tale that accounts for the maritime hazards at the Strait of Messina between the island of Sicily and the Italian mainland. With a rugged promontory on one side and a violent whirlpool on the other, the strait has always been dangerous for mariners.

The ancients personified these hazards: Scylla was a six-headed, man-eating monster living in a cave on the promontory; the goddess Charybdis agitated the waters by drinking in and belching out the sea.

The hero Odysseus and his crew found themselves sailing between Scylla and Charybdis during their epic voyage. As captain, Odysseus was forced to decide which monster was least dangerous to his crew. He decided to sail nearer Scylla, who devoured only six of his men, leaving the vessel and most of the crew unharmed.

The legend of Scylla and Charybdis, which inspired an expression meaning " two equally hazardous options," has provided metaphor for many a poet and writer throughout the ages.

The secretary bird, native to South Africa, looks like the hatchling of a midnight rendezvous between an eagle, a cockatoo, a vulture, and an ostrich.

Like the eagle, the secretary bird is a raptor that soars on a seven-foot wingspan and sports an aquiline beak for tearing at its prey. Like the vulture, it has patches of bare red skin on its face. And like the ostrich, this bird is a swift runner on its long slender legs.

Though an excellent flyer, the secretary bird prefers a terrestrial lifestyle. It moves through tall savannah grasses in search of lizards, tortoises, insects, and small birds. It's also famous for capturing snakes, which the bird incapacitates with kicks and stomps from its powerful feet.

Attached to the back of the secretary bird's head and neck is a crest of long, black-tipped feathers, which give the creature a cockatoo-like appearance. The spray of feathers at the bird's neck suggested a name to the first English speakers to encounter the bird in the 18th century, evoking the secretaries of the 1700s who stuck an abundance of feathered quill pens behind their ears or in their powdered wigs.

"Last spring, there were more dandelions on my lawn than you could shake a stick at." "He went to the hardware store again? He already has more tools than he can shake a stick at!"

Oddly, things quantified as abundant incline us to shake sticks at them verbally. This could be one of the strangest idioms in our language. Though the origin of this expression is obscure, at least two theories have been advanced to explain its existence.

Number one: The phrase may have its genesis in tribal confrontation or warfare. Shaking a stick at someone is an ancient gesture of threat or defiance. Perhaps the expression originally referred to overwhelming enemy ranks, more than one could successfully threaten, or shake a stick at.

Possibility number two involves tallying livestock, which might have been accomplished by pointing a stick at each animal in turn as it passed from one pen to another. So having more animals than one could tally, or shake a stick at, would imply a huge number.

This expression first appeared in print, according to the *Oxford English Dictionary*, in a document from the *Lancaster* (Pennsylvania) *Journal* in 1818 that read, "We have in Lancaster as many Taverns as you can shake a stick at."

SHIPS PASSING IN THE NIGHT

The expression *ships passing in the night* is a metaphor for people who meet briefly, then go their separate ways. For example, convention attendees may engage for an intense weekend but rarely interact again. Despite their common interest, there is no permanent contact. They're just *ships passing in the night*.

Here we have another common phrase borrowed from the canon of American poetry. The sentiment came from the pen of the celebrated Henry Wadsworth Longfellow, a New Englander born in 1807, author of the *Song of Hiawatha* and *Evangeline*. In his 1863 poem "The Theologian's Tale," he wrote,

> Ships that pass in the night, and speak each
>   other in passing;
> Only a signal shown and a distant voice in
>   the darkness;
> So on the ocean of life we pass and speak
>   one another,
> Only a look and a voice; then darkness again
>   and a silence.

Many formulaic expressions like *ships that pass in the night* trace their origins to poetry from centuries past. We've borrowed the phrase *an albatross around my neck,* meaning "I am burdened by a problem," from Samuel Taylor Coleridge's 1798 poem *Rime of the Ancient Mariner. Every cloud has a silver lining,* which means "No matter how dire the circumstances, there's always hope," comes from the work of John Milton, the 16th century English author of *Paradise Lost.*

SHOULDER TO THE WHEEL

One day, a wagoner was driving his team of horses to market to deliver some goods. Recent rains had made the track muddy, and the wagon became so thoroughly mired that the horses could no longer move it.

Helplessly staring at the sky, the wagoner called out for Hercules to assist him. Soon the god appeared, but in lieu of a mighty push, Hercules lent the wagoner some advice. "Instead of calling for help," he said, "*put your shoulder to the wheel* and whip those horses. If you won't apply yourself to the problem, neither god nor man will come to your aid!"

This fable from 6th century B.C. storyteller Aesop is the inspiration for our modern expression *put your shoulder to the wheel,* or apply yourself to a task, pitch in, and help when you're needed.

In the 16th century, translators attached a moral to this fable: *the gods help those who help themselves.* Benjamin Franklin is responsible for the modern, monotheistic version *God helps them that help themselves.* He recorded it in his almanac in 1736.

In May of 1811, a set of twin boys was born in a small village in the nation of Thailand, known in those days as Siam. Twins are always remarkable, but these baby boys created a regional sensation, because they were born joined at the sternum by a ligament about three and a half inches long and an inch and a half in diameter, through which their circulatory systems communicated. Despite being conjoined, the twins, named Chang and Eng, grew to be active and healthy.

In 1829, the 17-year-old brothers were introduced to a visiting Scottish merchant, who offered the twins' mother a sum of money to take the boys to England. Chang and Eng became celebrities throughout Europe, and in Canada and America as well, as they made sideshow appearances in major cities on both sides of the Atlantic.

The twins contracted with circus impresario P. T. Barnum for seven years until 1839. Then, with their earnings, the brothers retired from public life, became U.S. citizens, and married a pair of sisters in Wilkesboro, North Carolina.

Though Chang and Eng were not the first pair of conjoined twins on medical record, they were the most famous of their time. Because of their birthplace, Siam, they were known worldwide as the *Siamese twins,* a moniker that for many decades has identified siblings whose bodies are joined.

SILVER LINING

In 1915, Ivor Novello and Lena Gilbert Ford composed the wartime song "Keep the Home Fires Burning." One of the tune's verses goes like this: "There's a silver lining/Through the dark clouds shining/Turn the dark clouds inside out/Till the boys come home." Novello and Ford were not the first to use the encouraging reminder to look for silver-lined clouds during times of hardship, but they did set if firmly in the minds of 20th century Americans.

The notion of the silver lining was centuries old by the time this World War I song was composed. The image was introduced by English poet John Milton in his 1634 dramatic poem *Comus*. The first scene depicts an English lady lost in a dark, wild wood. As she prays for rescue, she sees a hopeful sign in the heavens: "Was I deceived," she says, "or did a sable cloud turn forth her silver lining on the night?"

Two centuries after the publication of Milton's poem, Charles Dickens again invoked the image in his 1852 novel *Bleak House,* in which he wrote, "I turn my silver lining outward like Milton's cloud."

Other writers began to follow Dickens's lead. In 1885, W. S. Gilbert wrote in *The Mikado,* "Don't let's be downhearted. There's a silver lining to every cloud."

Other literary and popular offerings of this phrase have made it a proverbial encouragement for finding hope in the face of adversity.

SKUNK

"There is no quadruped on the continent of North America, the approach of which is more generally detested than that of the skunk. Even the bravest of our boasting race is, by this little animal, compelled to…hold his nose and run, as if a lion were at his heels."

Such was John James Audubon's 19th century observation of this hemisphere's most odiferous creature. But were it not for the skunk's distinctive coloration and signature aroma, the animal would differ little from any other North American omnivore.

Dining on a diet of insects, rodents, birds' eggs, fruits, and berries, the skunk has adapted to almost every habitat on the continent. This creature is typically nocturnal and takes its leisure everywhere it goes, since few predators can withstand its noxious brand of chemical warfare.

Imagine the surprise of the first Europeans to encounter the dreaded black and white one! Since there is no cognate creature on the other side of the pond, pioneers simply adopted the indigenous name already in place for the animal: *skunk*…or, at least, that's what it sounded like to European ears. *Skunk* is a corruption of an Algonquin term that early English chroniclers spelled variously *squnck* or *squuncke*.

The translation of the native word is "animal that urinates or sprays," but the species' Latin denomination, *Mephitis mephitis,* is a bit less technical: it means "stinky stinky."

Most people's 21st century visions of a skyscraper would probably include such architectural behemoths as the Sears Building, rising 1,450 feet above the streets of Chicago, or the even taller Petronas Towers in Kuala Lumpur, Malaysia.

An example of a classic older skyscraper is New York City's art deco Chrysler Building, with its emphatic spire pushing slightly past the 1,000-foot mark.

The word *skyscraper,* in its architectural context, was first applied to the Home Insurance Building, completed in Chicago in 1885. Supported by a revolutionary steel skeletal frame, the Home Building was a ten-story giant in a city of squat brick and wooden structures unable to support their own weight beyond a height of four floors.

Skyscraper, though referencing a relatively modern phenomenon, has been present in the English vocabulary since at least the late 1700s. *Skyscraper* was the name of a long-legged race horse that won England's Epsom Derby in 1789.

In a nautical sense, a skyscraper was the topmost sail on a merchant ship. An English slang dictionary from 1857 says a very tall man might have been nicknamed *skyscraper;* ditto for the high-mounted bicycles of the 19th century, or even a tall hat or bonnet from the same era.

But it's likely that the soaring architectural structure, by far dwarfing the race horse, the sail, the bicycle, and top hat, has appropriated the term *skyscraper* for good.

The *Dictionary of American Slang* defines a *smart aleck* as "one who thinks he knows everything; an obnoxious extrovert."

Gerald Cohen, a professor of languages at the University of Missouri–Rolla, thinks he may have identified the clever Aleck for whom all "obnoxious extroverts" are named. In his *Studies in Slang, Part 1,* published in 1985, Professor Cohen recounts the history of Aleck Hoag, a shrewd New York thief plying his trade in the 1840s.

Hoag worked in concert with his wife Melinda, who, posing as a prostitute, stole her client's pocketbooks while deftly distracting them. Melinda then handed the loot off to husband Aleck as he walked by, a strategy that worked well for the pair as long as they bribed police officers to keep them out of jail.

Aleck escaped arrest for years until he tried to cut the police out of the deal. With schemes increasingly elaborate and secretive, Aleck and Melinda continued their spree of robberies while managing to elude the constabulary. Aleck Hoag was eventually jailed, but the clever con man escaped and remained on the lam until the police finally caught up with him.

So, our moniker might very well have been the way the New York City police expressed their grudging admiration for the ingenious thief Aleck Hoag—the original *Smart Aleck*.

Many favorite English language expressions were born of the fables of Aesop, a 6th century B.C. Greek who told animal stories with human morals. Over the centuries, these simple, traditional tales have engendered such verbal formulas as *wolf in sheep's clothing, the lion's share,* and *don't count your chickens before they're hatched.*

The expression *sour grapes,* explaining the behavior of one who pretends to despise that which he can't have, comes from Aesop's fable "The Fox and the Grapes," which goes like this:

> A hungry fox, spying a cluster of grapes hanging high
> on a vine, did her best to leap in the air and snap up
> the fruit. After many failed attempts, the fox was tired
> and panting and still hungry. Collecting her dignity,
> she walked away from the vine, saying, "I thought those
> grapes were ripe and juicy, but now I see they're too
> sour to eat."

What a long, strange trip it's been for the word *spam*. Moving from the trade name of a canned pork product to the derisive moniker for junk e-mail, *spam* has performed some lexical acrobatics in the past few decades.

Its life story began in 1936 when Hormel Foods Corporation offered a $100 prize to name their new canned meat product. Kenneth Diagneau, the brother of Hormel's vice president, suggested the name spam.

But here's where the lexical trail grows a bit faint, because no one is certain if Diagneau formed SPAM from the first and last letters of SPiced hAM, or if the SP part of the name is an abbreviation for Shoulder Pork. Either way, the name is known to linguists as a *blend word,* just as *breakfast* and *lunch* blended make *brunch,* and *motor* and *hotel* equal *motel.* With billions of cans of the stuff sold since 1937, SPAM's blended name enjoys global recognition.

Spam II

Today there are two *spams:* the canned meat variety, and another synonymous with "junk e-mail." It turns out that these two spams are related through an unlikely tangle of events.

First, there was the famous 1970 "Spam" sketch by Monty Python's Flying Circus, the British comedy group. A couple enters a restaurant, where they are told by the waitress that the day's menu consists of "spam egg spam spam bacon and spam" and dozens of other spam specialties. Meanwhile, an inexplicable chorus of helmeted Vikings in the background sings endless praises to "spam, spam, lovely spam." Their operatic crescendos ultimately overwhelm all conversation.

Then, in the 1980s, in an electronic imitation of the repetitive Viking chorus, abusive computer message board users made it a habit to enter the word *spam* over and over into the computer to scroll other users' texts off the screen.

By the mid-1990s, the word *spam* was increasingly employed to refer to any excessive multiple posting on the Internet. The word has now settled into the cover term for the phenomenon of unsolicited e-mail advertisement.

Sparrow

Several species of small, common birds found the world over go by the general name *sparrow*. These hardy little creatures have adapted to almost every type of environment, flourishing in prairie, marsh, and desert. Even one of the New Testament gospels alludes to the ubiquity of the sparrow: in the book of Matthew, Jesus asks, "Are not two sparrows sold for a penny?"

About fifty species of sparrow live in North and South America, taking such names as fox, vesper, black-chinned, and golden crowned sparrow. The most abundant member of this avian family, the house sparrow, originated in the Mediterranean and was introduced to the Americas, South Africa, and New Zealand. The house sparrow began to thrive near human habitations in the 17th and 18th centuries by subsisting on seeds in horse and cattle droppings.

Sparrow is a word of considerable antiquity, first appearing in recorded documents in A.D. 900. It derives from the Old English *spearwa,* which means simply "flutterer" and was applied by speakers of the language to any small, fluttering bird. The French call the bird *moineau,* or "monk," evoking the sparrow's dull, cowl-like coloration.

SPECT

The Latin root *spect* means "look." This element is the foundation for a sizeable family of common English terms. Sporting various prefixes and suffixes, *spect* becomes *respect, expect, spectacle, spectator.*

Let's take a look at the first term on this roster: *respect.* It consists of the *spect* root and the prefix *re-*, meaning "back, again." *Respect* literally means "to look back again at someone" or "to regard someone favorably."

Attaching *ex-*, which means "out," gives us *expect*, meaning "to look out." *Expecting* is etymologically "looking out for something" or "looking forward to something as certain or likely." If you're *circumspect,* you "look at something from all around," or examine each element thoughtfully.

A *spectacle* is something that everyone "looks" at—an unusual sight or grand display. Someone gazing at a spectacle may do so through *spectacles,* things we see by or look through. A *spectator* "looks at" an activity.

It's a big word family. *Spect* is also at the root of *inspect,* literally "to look into"; *suspect,* "to look at from below"; *speculate, perspective,* and even *specimen.*

Spic and Span is the name of a popular household cleaning product. Its advertising slogan is "How America Says Clean."

Indeed, long before the cleaner was developed, the expression *spick and span* meant "completely clean and neat, shiny, brand new." This brisk alliterative cliché sounds fine in its entirety, but it poses problems when its components are isolated. *Spick:* what does this word have to do with clean? *Span:* how is this associated with neatness?

The reason these individual words sound odd to 21st century ears is that they became obsolete centuries ago. The *spick* in today's expression comes from a Germanic word meaning "nail or spike," and *span* hails from an Old Norse term meaning "fresh wood chip."

Centuries ago these words had a nautical association: a sailing vessel "spick and span new" was equipped with freshly forged nails and newly carved timbers. Etymologically, it was new in nail *(spick)* and wood *(span); sound, clean, and sea-worthy.

The expression was first recorded in a 1579 English document, a translation of one of Plutarch's writings by Sir Thomas North, who wrote: "The were all in goodly gilt armours, and brave purple cassocks apon [upon] them, spicke, and spanne newe."

It's quite remarkable how this expression consisting of fossil words has weathered the centuries.

SPILL THE BEANS

To *spill the beans* means to reveal a secret prematurely, or, to define one cliché with another, to let the cat out of the bag. Though this is a common American expression, the debate surrounding its origin has gone on for some time.

One popular (and colorful) etymology sets the story of this phrase in ancient Greece, where secret societies admitted new members by ballot. The existing members dropped either white or dark beans in a jar—white for a positive vote, dark for the opposite. If the jar was overturned before the voting was complete, the "spilled beans" would prematurely reveal the outcome. Though this makes a tidy tale, it's most likely that and nothing more. The exact expression *spill the beans* didn't appear in print until 1919, so an ancient origin is unlikely.

On the other hand, the verb *spill,* in an extended use meaning "divulge," appears as long ago as 1574. It occurs in such expressions as *spill what you know,* or *spill your guts,* or the simple slang command *spill it.*

But the *bean* part remains a mystery. Even so, the expression *spill the beans* is remarkably persistent in our vast stable of clichés.

Instead of *butter and muffins,* how about *mutter and buffins? Pusgetti* for *spaghetti, aminal* for *animal?* All of us, children and adults alike, occasionally make such comical errors in speech. Tongues slip this way for a variety of reasons: perhaps the tongue's owner is tired, tipsy, nervous, or excited. Sometimes it happens for no apparent reason.

Linguists call this type of speech error *metathesis,* which is characterized by the switching of two sounds, each taking the place of the other: *Kass the petchup. Will you loan me a five bollar dill?* The technical term *metathesis* derives from a Greek word meaning "to place differently."

But metathesis is more popularly and colorfully known as the *spoonerism,* a word fashioned from the name of Reverend William Spooner, 19th century warden of New College in Oxford, England. Legend says Spooner was of a nervous disposition and tended to metathesize, or *spoonerize,* profusely. Some famous examples come from his Sunday sermons, such as, "Yes indeed; the Lord is a shoving leopard." Spooner encouraged his parishioners to "pray for Victoria, our queer old dean." He is attributed with the wedding directive, "It is now kisstomary to cuss the bride." On spying a pair of look-alike siblings, Spooner cried, "Those girls are sin twisters!"

Spooner's penchant for somersaulting letters and sounds was blamed on his nervous disposition and even his albinism. Some suspect he was dyslexic. But accidental or cultivated, so many of these verbal gaffes were attributed to the dear man that they're now called *spoonerisms* in his honor.

SQUARE

For decades, the shape of the square has provided a positive metaphor for balance, honesty, and wholesomeness. Consider its role in the expressions *square shooter,* referring to an honest person, and *square deal,* synonymous with a fair bargain. And a substantial, satisfying plate of food is considered a *square meal.* My first exposure to the "square meal" metaphor came from my father, whose favorite World War II memories included getting to know interesting new army cohorts while eating "three squares a day."

Along about the 1920s, American jazz musicians turned the concept of the solid, wholesome square on its head. Its equilateral form suggested conformity and predictability to the hipsters of the 20th century. In jazz slang, a square was someone who couldn't or wouldn't embrace the music and philosophy of the jazz world. What's more, squares lived in *squaresville,* a leaden world of schedules and stultifying daily responsibilities with no avenues of creativity.

The jazz player's *square* was also reinforced by the boring predictability of a 1-2-3-4 musical beat. In hipster sign language, drawing a box in the air, like a band director conducting 4/4 time, indicated squareness. As a 1959 *New York Times Magazine* article put it, "In the late Nineteen Twenties, an old word acquired a new meaning in the American language. The word was 'square,' and the world of jazz blew it into everyday usage....A square was someone who did not understand their style of music...a square peg in their musical circles."

In France, it's called *esprit de l'escalier.* The Germans know it as *Treppenwitz.* But there is no single word in English to quite describe it.

Both *esprit de l'escalier* and *Treppenwitz* can be translated "staircase wit." Originally, these 17th century terms referred to a moment of belated epiphany after a partygoer leaves the second-story drawing room. While descending the stairs, the departing guest suddenly thinks of the brilliant comment that he should—and could—have made.

In a modern context, *staircase wit* is the cleverness that fails you when you need a devastatingly witty comeback. By the time your acumen revives and produces the rejoinder, the moment is gone. It's a classic case of bad timing, and the scenario may torment you the rest of your life.

It's curious that English lacks a term for this phenomenon, because all of us have felt the frustration of the hamstrung wit. We need a word to help us. Should we adopt, wholesale, the French expression *esprit de l'escalier,* or the German *Treppenwitz?* Or would the English translation *staircase wit* be serviceable enough?

The original *Star Trek* TV series was only three years old when it went off the air in 1969. It nevertheless spawned a legacy of catchphrases that resonate with us still, though decades have passed since the termination of the series.

The very introduction of each *Star Trek* episode engendered two familiar phrases: "space—the final frontier," and "to boldly go where no man has gone before." Trekkies noted an amendment in the latter phrase when it was reprised in the introduction of *The Next Generation* TV series. The new, politically correct version stated that the Star Ship *Enterprise*'s mission was "to boldly go where no one has gone before."

Leonard Nimoy's half-human, half-Vulcan Mr. Spock is associated with an expression that has since become a catchphrase. Puzzled by the reactions of his human shipmates, Spock often responded to their emotions with the comment, "most illogical," or "highly illogical."

But "Beam me up, Scotty," the most famous catchphrase associated with this show, is actually a misquote. This command, allegedly spoken to the ship's engineer, Mr. Scott, played by James Doohan, was never a part of a *Star Trek* dialogue. The closest approximations to that expression were, "Two to beam up, Scotty," and "Beam us up, Mr. Scott." Nevertheless, "Beam me up, Scotty," has become a popular formula to express a desire to exit a place or an unpleasant situation.

STENTORIAN

In the *Iliad,* the Greek poet Homer recounts the story of the decade-long Trojan War. The adventure is full of battles, heroes, monsters, lovers, and the whole panoply of Mt. Olympus immortals.

One of the less-familiar names in the *Iliad*'s cast of characters is Stentor, a Greek herald whose voice, according to Homer, sounded like bronze and was louder than the combined shouts of fifty men. It was Stentor with his mighty voice who faced the Trojan enemy to dictate the terms of war. When the Greeks appeared to be losing the battle, Hera, queen of the gods, assumed the guise of Stentor and shouted encouragement to the troops.

This Greek herald inspired the English adjective *stentorian,* meaning "loud, booming, emphatic," especially when applied to someone's voice. In the 1852 novel *Uncle Tom's Cabin,* Harriet Beecher Stowe wrote, "The stentorian tones of the auctioneer, calling out to clear the way, now announced that the sale was about to commence."

Stentor is further linguistically commemorated in the *Stentorphone,* a device invented in 1919 to amplify music from a gramophone. *Stentorphone* is also the name of a class of extremely loud, high-pressure stops found in cathedral organs. And *Stentor* is a genus of protozoa, so named in the 19th century because their shape resembles a speaking-trumpet, the kind used to amplify the voice.

The simple word *stump* is a hard-working member of our English lexicon. The word does double duty as a noun and a verb and is employed in a variety of idioms.

When *stump* began showing up in English documents in the 1300s, it meant "the part remaining of an amputated or severed limb of the body." The term's progenitor is an older German word meaning "blunt or dull."

By the 1400s, *stump* was extended to the "portion of a felled tree that remains fixed in the ground," a tree stump. Soon the word referred to anything blunted or broken: the remains of a ship's mast, a worn pencil, or an animal's docked tail.

People used to make joking reference to the legs as stumps. *Stir your stumps* was a command to get up and move with purpose. Since the 1600s, the verb *stump* has meant to walk heavily or clumsily, as if with wooden legs. Traveling afoot was *stumping it,* and *fight to the stumps* meant to battle bravely on regardless of the severity of injury or discomfort. The dauntless Black Knight of *Monte Python and the Holy Grail* comes to mind.

When *stump* reached the shores of the New World with English-speaking immigrants, it took on some lively new connotations, most notably *to be stumped,* perplexed, brought to a halt. *Stump,* the North American verb, entered our vocabulary in the early 1800s, reflecting the frustrated efforts of settlers in clearing the densely forested frontier for agriculture. The trees could be felled, but their stumps would not surrender without being dug, pulled, or sometimes dynamited out of the ground. What's more, the tree stumps that absolutely refused extraction were vexing obstacles in the field. Farmers wasted valuable time and effort guiding their mules, oxen, and plows around these stubborn obstructions. When we say *I'm stumped,* then, meaning "baffled, nonplussed," we're linguistically recalling the era when stump removal was a perplexing, near impossible task, and having to work around them was thoroughly exasperating.

Some of the metaphors for those confounding tree remnants proved useful and, it turns out, politically and linguistically significant in the American experience. The largest of stumps, notable local landmarks, were often used as impromptu stages for social and political addresses. As early as 1775, politicians were said to *take the stump* when advocating their party's causes.

Often called *stump speakers,* local politicians *stumped,* traveling throughout a district and literally mounting the felled-tree "platforms" to deliver their *stump oratories.*

Today, the word is used metaphorically each campaign season as candidates for every office deliver *stump speeches* and *stump* for votes, though the platforms are now elegant lecterns, and orations are amplified with microphones and loudspeakers.

Swan Song

A *swan song* is the last performance, the closing words, the final opus of a notable person. *Swan song* is certainly a lyrical and evocative phrase, but how does this bird's melody fit into the picture of someone's last great work?

The ancients believed that swans broke into beautiful song as they sensed the moment of their death. Plato, Euripides, and Aristotle referred to this legend in their writings, as did, more recently, Chaucer and Shakespeare. Socrates used the dying swan as metaphor when he said, "For they, when they perceive that they must die...sing...more sweetly than ever, rejoicing in the thought that they are about to go away to Apollo, whose ministers they are. But men, because they fear death, slanderously accuse the swans of singing laments at the last."

So, swans, according to Socrates, sing gloriously in anticipation of at last seeing their beloved master Apollo. Socrates, who was also dedicated to the god, proclaimed that he would embrace death as did the singing swans, for he too knew that Apollo was his blissful destination.

Poets and writers throughout the centuries have been inspired by the swan legend. But it wasn't until 1831 that the precise phrase *swan song* showed up in print, in a piece by Scottish historian and essayist Thomas Carlyle.

Early in the 4th century B.C., Dionysus the Elder ruled Syracuse, a city-state on the eastern coast of Sicily. Dionysus was, by all accounts, a tyrant, and a paranoid one at that. Constantly fearing assassination, he avoided public appearances and slept in a bedchamber surrounded by a trench with a drawbridge.

Wealthy, powerful, and in control of the beautiful city of Syracuse, Dionysus had his loyalists and flatterers, too. The most vocal of these was Damocles, a local aristocrat who proclaimed enviously that no one could be happier than the rich and influential Dionysus.

One day, Dionysus invited his fawning friend to a banquet and sat him under a sword hanging from the ceiling by a single strand of horse hair. Forcing his guest to dine under the suspended sword, Dionysus explained that a ruler was precariously situated. Just as Damocles feared the potential of the falling sword, so did Dionysus constantly dread the looming threat of assassination.

This story has given us the expression *sword of Damocles,* meaning an impending or potential disaster. In September 1963, President John F. Kennedy summoned this ancient allusion. In a speech to the United Nations General Assembly, he said, "Every man, woman and child lives under a nuclear sword of Damocles, hanging by the slenderest of threads, capable of being cut at any moment. The weapons of war must be abolished before they abolish us."

TABOO

In 1777, Captain James Cook, on a scientific voyage from England to the South Pacific, landed on the island of Tonga. One of Cook's diary entries written during his Tongan tenure reads: "Not one of [the islanders] would sit down, or eat...anything. On expressing my surprize at this, they were all taboo, as they said; which...signifies that a thing is forbidden."

This is the first English citation of the word taboo, a term common among Polynesian societies, under a variety of spellings. Cook and his crew could make no sense of what seemed to them countless arbitrary island prohibitions. Certain foods, persons, and places were Tongan taboos; to violate these proscriptions was sometimes punishable by death.

For a half-century after Cook's voyage, the Polynesian term appeared in descriptions and accounts of Island societies. Sometime in the 1830s, though, English speakers adopted the word *taboo* to refer to a practice prohibited by any social custom. In the 1930s, it emerged as a specialized linguistic term to designate socially offensive words or phrases. Profanity, blasphemy, and obscenity are generally classified as taboo utterances.

In 1931, the fragrance designer Dana called its new perfume Tabu, a name chosen to suggest the exotic Polynesian islands and the allure of the forbidden.

When Columbus came ashore on the West Indian islands in October 1492, he and his crew encountered the Taino people, native inhabitants of modern-day Cuba, Puerto Rico, Jamaica, and the Bahamas. The Taino subsisted on fish, lobster, turtle, and mollusks. They also grew potatoes, cassava, beans, pumpkins, and maize. Expert mariners, the Taino traveled from island to island in large, dugout canoes. It was the Taino and their island neighbors who introduced Columbus and his companions to tobacco, a crop that was taken from the West Indies and imported to Europe.

Within a few decades of Columbus's landfall on these islands of the New World, the native populations had become victims of the disease, genocide, and assimilation imposed by the European incursion. Though the Taino are not extinct, they have never recovered their pre-contact numbers—estimated by historians at about a million.

The Spanish adopted several native Caribbean words and dispersed them throughout the world. One such Taino word is *tobacco*. So is *barbeque,* the name for a wooden lattice on which meat was roasted over a fire. Also from the Taino language, through intermediary Spanish, comes the word *canoe,* the native term for the dugout watercraft. *Hurricane* is also an indigenous Caribbean word, and one that Columbus himself adopted after experiencing such a storm in 1495.

Take to the Cleaners

When cheated, robbed, duped, or defrauded financially, American English speakers might say they've been *taken to the cleaners.*

The phrase seems to be the linguistic offspring of the 19th century expression *cleaned out,* meaning stripped of everything of value, as if one had had his pockets, house, and bank account thoroughly purged or "cleaned" of their contents.

The derived cliché *taken to the cleaners* began appearing in print early in the 20th century, coming into its own in the 1930s. The *Random House Historical Dictionary of American Slang* lists a citation from 1933 that mentions a "wily old gambler" who "takes them one and all to the cleaners." In 1934, Raymond Chandler wrote in his story *Finger Man,* "I'm in a jam. But I'm not going to the cleaners....Half of this money is mine."

The general consensus among phrase watchers is that this cliché was inspired by the advent of commercial American dry-cleaning establishments, which proliferated after World War I. The expression is most likely a variation on a linguistic theme: from *cleaning up* and *cleaning out* comes the modern approach to monetary loss: being *taken to the cleaners.*

It was once quaintly called the "kid-glove orange" because it was so easy to peel. The tangerine, like its cousin the orange, is believed to be indigenous to Southeast Asia. First cultivated in China and Japan some 2,000 years ago, the tangerine spread westward along trade routes to the Mediterranean.

In the 1840s, the British got their first taste of this delicate citrus fruit when it was brought to Britain from the Moroccan port of Tangiers, situated directly south of Spain on the Strait of Gibraltar. The British called the fruit the "Tangerine orange," literally, the "orange from Tangiers."

For decades prior to the 1840s, the word *Tangerine* with an upper-case "T" had been a fairly common English adjective. It meant simply "of or from Tangiers," just as the adjective *American* means "of America." The *Oxford English Dictionary* provides a citation from 1718 that speaks of "an old Tangereen captain with a wooden leg."

There is evidence of the word becoming a color word in 1899, joining its citrus cousins *orange* and *lemon* in designating shades of color.

Tangerine is one of the many words in the English lexicon with an exotic life history, which you will find in a dictionary of word origins. Take a few minutes to browse through some delicious etymologies.

In the 15th century, a curious epidemic swept southern Italy. The symptoms included frenzied, uncontrolled whirling and thrashing of the body. The cause, allegedly, was the bite of an indigenous spider.

In keeping with a folk remedy, bite victims were encouraged to continue their frantic dancing until the spider's venom was purged from the body. In some accounts of this epidemic, musicians were recruited to accompany the victims until they collapsed, exhausted but cured.

The condition was called *tarantism,* because it was believed to be initiated by the bite of the tarantula, a large hairy arachnid of southern Europe. The spider, in turn, was named after the seaport town of Tarento, situated in southern Italy, in the "arch" of the Italian "boot." In the 18th century, Europeans encountering the great hairy arachnids of the Americas christened them *tarantulas,* literally "spiders of Tarento."

The frenzied whirling of the victims of 16th century tarantism became the basis for the *tarentella,* a lively folk dance in 6/8 time, traditionally performed in southern Italian and Sicily. Some elements of the dance were introduced to the ballet in the 18th century. The formal, musical structure of the tarentella was established by such composers as Franz Liszt, Frederic Chopin, and Sergei Rachmaninov.

The *Guinness Book of World Records* lists Teflon as the world's slipperiest substance, noting that it has "the lowest coefficient of static and dynamic friction of any known solids."

The slick substance was developed by serendipitous accident in April 1938 by a DuPont chemist. Working with coolant materials one day, the chemist noticed that the gas in one of his experimental containers unexpectedly congealed, forming a waxy substance that clung to the sides of the container. Refined, the new matter was trademarked in 1945 by DuPont as *Teflon,* an abbreviated version of its chemical name, tetrafluorethylene.

Teflon has since found hundreds of applications—everything from insulation and lubricant to artificial arteries for the heart, with perhaps its best-known use being a coating for the famous Teflon non-stick cookware.

But in 1983, Colorado congresswoman Pat Schroeder came up with a novel political application for this chemical term. Assessing then-president Ronald Reagan's uncanny ability to deflect criticism and judgment, Schroeder dubbed him the "Teflon president." "He sees to it that nothing sticks to him," Schroeder said, in allusion to the slippery surface of the famous cookware.

The development of this American English word from chemical label to wry political moniker is another example of language changing before our very eyes.

TEMPEST IN A TEAPOT

A *tempest in a teapot* is a big fuss over a small matter, an uproar about a trivial thing. *Tempest in a teapot* was seen in print in various American publications in the mid-1800s, but it was probably well established long before then. The expression was recorded in the *Colombia Spy* of Colombia, Pennsylvania, in 1879. The article accused some Colombia citizens of creating a "tempest in a teapot" over one Katie Patterson, the first African American girl to graduate from the local public high school.

Margaret Mitchell had her Southern heroine utter the phrase in the 1936 novel *Gone with the Wind*. "I consider the whole affair a tempest in a teapot," said Scarlett coldly.

English speakers on both sides of the Atlantic have used other, similar phrases to express the same sentiment. In the 1600s, it was *storm in a cream bowl,* or *storm in a wash basin.* The current British equivalent is *storm in a teacup.*

The Spanish version is *drown in a glass of water.* In French it's a *storm in a glass of water.*

All these expressions were likely inspired by a phrase taken from the writings of Cicero, a Roman lawyer and philosopher who lived from 106 to 43 B.C., but his version was *make waves in a ladle.*

Something inconsequential, trifling, or of poor quality is said by some to be *not worth a tinker's damn*. This somewhat old-fashioned phrase has many synonyms: *not worth a plug nickel, …a red cent, …the paper it's written on, …a hill of beans,* and the like. But *tinker's damn* is especially interesting because of its disputed origin.

In Britain, tinkers were itinerate tradesman who mended pots and pans. The word *tinker* derives either from the tinking sound of their metalworking or simply from the word *tin*.

Locals viewed the traveling tinkers with suspicion. For hundreds of years, *tinker* was a name for a thief, rogue, or vagrant. It's said that tinkers were an earthy crowd, swearing so freely that their profanities had lost potency. So, a mere *tinker's damn* would be fairly worthless.

Another suggestion for the origin of the phrase has the *damn* spelled *dam*. Here, a *tinker's dam* is a small retaining wall of clay or dough fashioned around the hole in the pot to hold the solder as it was being applied. The clay, worthless after the repair, was discarded as the useless *tinker's dam*.

Most word watchers agree the cursing theory is the winning contender, with the "retaining wall" account simply a prudish attempt to sanitize the word *damn*.

TIP

American English is awash in acronyms—words formed from the initial letters of a string of words. You can find examples of acronyms every day in the newspaper: FEMA from Federal Emergency Management Agency; NASCAR from National Association for Stock Car Auto Racing.

Occasionally, stories circulate about acronyms that actually never were—we might call them "folk acronyms." *Tip,* the word for the gratuity left for a server, is one interesting example. Stories persist that *tip* is the acronym for "to insure promptness" and that the acronym came out of 18th century London coffeehouses, where customers dropped a few coins in a box when they entered the establishment. The box was allegedly printed with the letters TIP, "to insure promptness," and the monetary offering was said to encourage the shop owner to take good care of the customer.

Although this story provides a neat etymological history for the origin of the modern restaurant *tip,* no documentation exists to verify the coffeehouse boxes marked TIP. The more prosaic account of this word is that it first appeared early in the 17th century as a thief's slang for "giving a small present of money." Another theory has the term coming from *tipple,* "to drink," which could have developed into giving the bartender a "tip."

Humans have been smoking tobacco in one form or another for thousands of years. The Spanish, who borrowed tobacco from the Caribbean natives, imported the leaf to Europe, and through European cultivation and trade, tobacco is now a global commodity.

The word *tobacco* probably comes from the Taino, a Caribbean people whom 15th century Spaniards discovered rolling dried leaves of the plant, burning the ends, and inhaling the smoke.

Before too many decades had passed, Europeans were smoking tobacco in pipes and as cigars. The origin of the word *cigar* has been disputed. One theory has the term coming from *cigarra,* the Spanish name for the cicada, an insect whose leaflike wings are said to resemble a rolled cigar leaf. Others favor the notion that the word comes from the Mayan verb *sicar,* meaning, "to smoke."

In any case, the French turned the word into a diminutive in the early 1800s: *cigar-ette,* or "little cigar." Throughout the 1800s, Americans rolled their own cigarettes, but by the 1880s machine-rolled smokes were becoming available. These were subjected to a variety of 20th century slang terms. Cigar smokers, considering them effeminate, called factory cigarettes *pimp sticks.* Other monikers for boxed cigarettes included *skags, weeds, butts,* and *fags,* from the older British word meaning "burning ember." As concerns arose about the health effects of tobacco consumption, cigarettes acquired the moniker *coffin nails.*

TOBOGGAN

If you grew up in the snowy northern tier of North America, you've probably ridden a toboggan, the long, flat runnerless sled with its characteristic curled wooden nose.

Invented by north woodland natives, the toboggan was traditionally made of two planed boards of birch or tamarack joined with wooden cleats. The front of the boards were curled backward to prevent the sledge from plowing into the snow, and the arcing wood was then tied in place with sinew. Drawn by dogs or humans, the toboggan was an excellent conveyance in heavy snow for meat, hides, and household belongings.

Though most subarctic North Americans crafted their own variations of the snow sledge, it was the Micmac people of the eastern maritime region who gave the world the familiar long, birch toboggan. The Micmac, a subgroup of the large Algonquin family, traditionally inhabited Nova Scotia, Cape Breton Island, Newfoundland, Massachusetts, and Maine.

From the Micmac language comes the noun *toboggan*. The word was first appropriated by French missionaries and traders who contacted the Micmac in the 1600s. American English speakers borrowed it from the French in the 1700s.

Have you ever wondered why an athletically inclined girl is sometimes called a *tomboy?*

Let's break this word down, starting with the last syllable first. *Boy* has been a term for "young male" or "lad" since the 1300s. And *Tom,* short for *Thomas,* has a 500-year history as a generic name for a male of any species; he's the common man in *every Tom, Dick and Harry;* he's the Tom in *tomcat, tom turkey,* even the derogatory *tomfool.*

So, when *tomboy* appeared in print in the mid-1500s, it referred not to a girl but to a rude, rough, aggressive young man, a "boy's boy," a *tom-boy.* Decades later, the word began to be referred disparagingly to girls who acted like independent, forward boys, or to young women with questionable moral behavior. Protestant reformer John Calvin wrote in 1579, "Women must not be impudent, they must not be tom boys, they must not bee unchast." So, from the late 1500s, the word was synonymous with "strumpet" and "harlot."

But in 1876, English novelist Charlotte Yonge wrote, "What I mean by 'tomboyism' is a wholesome delight in rushing about at full speed, playing at active games, climbing trees, rowing boats...and the like." Now we consider tomboys to be active, sporty, and healthy. They're most assuredly no longer strumpets or harlots.

TREE HUGGER

People who embrace the environmentalist ethic, especially those supporting the preservation of forested land and the restriction of logging, are sometimes called *tree huggers.* Environmental activists, while they don't literally embrace redwoods and ponderosa pines to save them from destruction, were given their nickname after a "tree-hugging" movement that started high in the mountains of India.

In 1972, in a northern Indian village, the locals decided to protest commercial logging of the native ash trees that the villagers depended on for firewood and animal fodder. The people considered several protest strategies, including burning the trees scheduled for removal and lying down in front of the logging trucks. They ultimately resolved to clasp the trunks of the trees, using their bodies to thwart the logger's axes.

The locals were successful in their protest. No ash trees were felled that particular day, and the incident ignited several identical protests in nearby villages. Speakers of the Hindi language called this strategy *Chipko Andolan,* which means "Adhere-to-the-Trees Movement." Translated into English, *Chipko Andolan* became "Tree Hugger Movement."

The incident became a touchstone for discussions related to environmental issues, first in India, then around the world, and *tree hugger* entered the folk lexicon as a synonym for a forest conservationist.

In 1894, a songwriter named Charles B. Lawler crafted the words to a tune called "The Sidewalks of New York." Part of the chorus reads: "Boys and girls together/me and Mamie O'Rourke/tripped the light fantastic/on the sidewalks of New York."

The expression *trip the light fantastic* is a rather elaborate way of saying "dance." Songwriter Lawler borrowed this phrase from a bard of yesteryear, John Milton, who in 1632 wrote a poem called *L'Allegro*. Milton's verse invokes the spirits of mirth and laughter throughout: "Haste thee, Nymph, and bring with thee/Jest, and youghtful Jollity,.../Sport that wrinkled Care derides/And Laughter holding both his sides./Come, and trip it as you go,/On the light fantastick toe."

Milton's verb *trip* does not mean stumble but rather move gracefully, and *the light fantastic toe* is an allusion to the nimble, fancy footwork of a skilled dancer. When later writers reprised Milton's line, they excised the word toe from the formula, so now the expression is rendered simply *trip the light fantastic*.

But that's not the end of the tale. In 1967, the band Procul Harum recorded the rock ballad "Whiter Shade of Pale." Songwriter Keith Reid put a new spin on Milton's ancient phrase with the opening line: "We skipped the light fandango/Turned cartwheels 'cross the floor."

TUPPERWARE

They were touted as "the most sensational products in modern plastics." They were available in "frosted pastel shades of lime, crystal, raspberry, lemon." Best of all, they were indestructible. The 7-ounce polyethylene bathroom tumblers were the brainchild of chemist and entrepreneur Earl Silas Tupper. In the mid-1940s, most household vessels were glass, but Tupper's simple plastic tumbler was on the first wave of a sea change in domestic containers.

Earl Silas Tupper, born on a New Hampshire farm in 1907, became convinced that plastic was the material of the future when he was hired as a polymer expert for DuPont in the 1930s. After he left the conglomerate, the chemist established the Tupper Plastics Company in 1938. He developed the world's first unbreakable plastic, which he fashioned first into tumblers, then, in 1947, into kitchen bowls with fitted lids, which that year's October issue of *House Beautiful* called "Fine Art for 39 cents."

Earl Tupper offered his polyethylene wares exclusively through home parties, where American housewives could sample and buy the amazing, indestructible storage containers.

The New Hampshire chemist changed the way America served and stored food. He also added a new lexical item to the American wordscape: *Tupperware,* a proprietary name registered in 1956, and now a common word for an even wider range of plastic products.

Have you ever wondered why the baked bird on your Thanksgiving table shares the name of a country situated half a world away? This is the story of a native New World bird that's called a *turkey*.

The tale of this shared name begins in 1519 when explorer Hernando Cortez and his Spanish company arrived in the heart of the Aztec empire and found the people raising and eating a large bird they called *huexolotlin,* a name imitating its gobbling call. When Cortez returned to Spain, several *huexolotlin* were in his ship's hold.

The Spaniards, who found the meat of the bird agreeable indeed, dropped the exotic native name of the creature and re-christened it "el Pavo" and the "Indian fowl."

By about 1530, the descendants of Cortez's imported "Indian fowl" arrived in England. But because the first specimens were transported to the British Isles on Levantine merchant ships originating in Turkish territory, the British assumed the exotic birds were natives of Turkey. By the 1600s, *turkey cocks* and *turkeys* were common in the farmyards and on the tables of the English people.

Imagine the surprise of the first European immigrants to this continent when they discovered all the "turkeys" on the shores of the New World.

Most of us have an umbrella on hand for practical, inexpensive protection against the rain, but this simple device has a richer and more interesting history than you might think.

In the Middle East of thousands of years ago, for example, umbrellas were emblems of rank and royalty. In Egypt, parasols of papyrus and palm fronds represented the sky goddess Nut, who arched her body over the earth like an umbrella over the head of a king. Greek and Roman women of high status carried umbrellas as sunshades, and they were sometimes even used to protect the effigies of the gods during their celebrations.

There is evidence that the Spanish and Portuguese were fashioning umbrellas for use against the scorching Mediterranean sun as early as the 15th century. The English considered them effeminate, even superfluous, since excess exposure to solar radiation was not a concern on the British Isles. By the mid-1700s, however, Londoners began carrying modified umbrellas for protection against precipitation, though the originators of that practice were jeered at and ridiculed. The French, who were not so averse to the device, called it a *parapluie,* "against the rain."

Today, of course, most Britons and North Americans carry umbrellas. Whether it is used as sunshade or rain guard, the umbrella's ancient history is revealed in the etymology of the word. First appearing in English in the 17th century, *umbrella* is Italian in origin and means "little shadow."

The proverbial expressions *practice what you preach* and *look before you leap* are of considerable antiquity, both having been traced to writings from ancient Greece.

A proverb of very recent vintage is *the opera ain't over until the fat lady sings,* meaning "don't concede defeat prematurely; don't give up too soon."

A mere linguistic infant, this expression gained national attention in 1978 when the San Antonio Spurs battled the Washington Bullets in the National Basketball Association playoffs. San Antonio sportswriter Dan Cook used the expression *the opera ain't over until the fat lady sings* to encourage Spurs fans to hope for a victory. Some accounts say Cook coined the phrase as a parody of the cowboy proverb *the rodeo ain't over till the bull riders ride.*

Even though the Spurs lost, when the playoffs came to a close that year, the "opera" phrase was familiar to millions of American sports fans. The expression suggests, of course, the iconic image of a heroically proportioned soprano with a horned helmet, singing the final aria of an opera.

The opera ain't over until the fat lady sings has several corollary expressions: *Church ain't out until the fat lady sings. Once the giant is dead, the pantomime is over. Don't count your chickens before they're hatched.* And of course Yogi Berra's famous reminder, *It ain't over till it's over.*

Vertere Words

The Latin verb *vertere,* meaning "to turn," is the progenitor of a large clan of modern English words. *Vertere* is represented in such words as *divert, vertigo, revert, vertebra.*

The word *revert* is composed of the prefix *re-,* meaning "back," and the root of *vertere.* To *revert* is to turn back to a former place or condition, and to *reverse* is to turn backwards, inside out, or to overturn. For example, the reverse drive in your car "turns you back" in the opposite direction.

Let's take a look at *vertebra,* the word for a bone in the spinal column. The notion of "turning" is encoded in the word because a vertebra is a bony pivot of sorts; the individual members of the vertebral column literally and etymologically "turn" one on the other.

One who makes a wholesale turn toward a new philosophy or religion is a *convert.* The verb form, *convert,* means to "turn completely."

To *divert* someone is to turn that one aside from his intended course of action. Sometimes this is done with a *diversion,* or distraction.

Vertigo, another member of the *vertere* family, is a condition in which the external world seems to be "turning" about one's head.

A *pervert* also "turns"—that is, away from what is considered right, proper, or good. The prefix *per-* in this word means "wrongly," so etymologically, a pervert makes "wrong turns."

In the pantheon of ancient Roman gods, Vulcan was the mighty blacksmith to the deities. Deep in the bowels of Mt. Etna, on the island of Sicily, Vulcan built a great forge where he created armor for the warrior gods, fashioned a golden throne for Juno, hammered out Jupiter's thunderbolts, and crafted Cupid's delicate love arrows.

Sometimes Vulcan's fires would blaze above the rim of Mt. Etna, throwing smoke, flame, and rock into the Mediterranean skies. In the early 1600s, Vulcan loaned his name to English speakers in *volcano,* the word for a mountain that belches gas, fire, and lava, evoking an image of the divine blacksmith working overtime in his forge below.

The term *vulcanize* was also inspired by the Roman fire god. Vulcanization is a process that fortifies rubber with sulphur and heat, two significant components of volcanic activity. In the *Dictionary of Word Origins,* etymologist John Ayto comments that *vulcanize* "appears to have been coined around 1845 by a certain Mr. Brockedon, a friend of the English chemist Thomas Hancock, an early pioneer of the process."

Vulcan is not the only ancient deity whose name is associated with the world of science. The Greek god Atlas shows up in the name for a collection of maps, and the goddess of the rainbow, Iris, has given her name to the colored portion of the eye.

Wet behind the Ears

If someone tells you you're *wet behind the ears,* it means you may have to grow up a bit, or perhaps you are too callow and inexperienced for the situation at hand. One-word synonyms for this expression are "naïve," "untrained," "innocent," and "unsophisticated."

Wet behind the ears is an American idiom of uncertain vintage. It alludes to the indentation behind the ear of any newborn creature—the last spot on the body to dry after birth. By extension, someone *wet behind the ears* has figuratively just been born and lacks the maturity or sophistication or experience to navigate life's complexity.

Wet behind the ears is just one of the hundreds of idioms in American English. Other examples include such admonitions as *go fly a kite* and *don't beat a dead horse* or fanciful notions like *hauling someone over the coals* or wearing a *birthday suit.* Idioms like these are nonsensical when literally interpreted. You aren't literally whipping a lifeless equine when you *beat a dead horse;* instead you're belaboring a point for no good reason. Idioms are colorful allusions to other technologies, circumstances, or activities.

In the 6th century B.C., Old Testament prophet Ezekiel and his Israelite kinsmen were forced out of Jerusalem by Nebuchadnezzar, the powerful king of Babylon. While living in exile in Babylonia with his fellow Israelites, Ezekiel began to have strange and foreboding dreams: images of howling windstorms out of the north, and skies filled with lightning. One of Ezekiel's most mystifying prophetic visions revealed a bizarre quartet of winged beasts with calves' legs and human faces. The creatures were accompanied by four moving wheels made of gemstone. The Old Testament account reads: "As for the...wheels and their construction: their appearance was like the gleaming of a chrysolite; and the four had the same likeness, their construction being as it were a wheel within a wheel."

Ezekiel's description of this portion of his dream inspired our expression *wheels within wheels,* referring to an interconnected arrangement of circumstances. The cliché implies a complexity of motives and dependencies that may not be readily apparent. Oscar Wilde used this biblically derived expression in his 1895 play *An Ideal Husband,* in which he wrote, "Politics is a very complex business. There are wheels within wheels. One may be under certain obligations to people that one must pay."

Proverbs are snippets of wisdom and advice transferred from one generation to the next. One fine example of compact proverbial wisdom is *when in Rome, do as the Romans do.* This pithy admonition to travelers to observe local custom is generally believed to have originated in a letter written by St. Ambrose, a 4th century bishop of Milan.

Translated from Latin, St. Ambrose's advice reads: "When you are at Rome live in the Roman style; when you are elsewhere live as they live elsewhere."

These words were part of a letter written in about A.D. 387 to St. Augustine, who was confused about the proper day for fasting. St. Augustine knew that the Roman Church had decreed that Saturday was the day set aside for abstinence from food. Yet, in Milan, where St. Augustine resided, the Church had no such requirement.

Wondering which practice to follow, St. Augustine consulted the wise St. Ambrose, who replied with some advice that has since become enshrined in our treasury of proverbs.

WIN HANDS DOWN

Mike Duffy, TV critic for the *Detroit Free Press*, wrote a review of the Warner Brothers series *Jack and Bobby*, the story of two young small-town brothers and their history professor mom. In his September 2004 review, Duffy called the series witty, fun, and honestly emotional; *"Jack and Bobby,"* he wrote, "wins hands down" in the fall television contest.

Hands down. We find this expression anywhere there's a competition to be won and lost, in sports, chess matches, or spelling bees. The *hands-down winner* prevails with seemingly little effort, and usually by a significant margin.

This expression may logically suggest a card-playing origin. In reality, though, the sport that inspired this cliché is much more animated than cards: it's horse racing.

To *win hands down* is an allusion to the custom of jockeys to relax their grip on the reins when victory is certain. The winning horse gallops easily to the finish line with its jockey relaxed and riding with his "hands down." This term began appearing in print around the turn of the 20th century.

Most eponyms, or proper names that have become general terms, are attached to men: Rudolf Diesel of the diesel engine, Daniel Fahrenheit of the thermometer scale, and Louis Braille, the namesake of raised letter writing for the blind. The profusion of male eponyms for scientific and engineering inventions is predictable in a culture where such products have tended to come from men.

With regard to other cultural arenas, however, a roster of eponyms based on women has emerged. Women's eponyms have been historically associated with such things as questionable morals, food, and anemic character.

Take, for example, Jezebel, the nickname of a loose, shrewish woman. Jezebel was an Old Testament queen, married to Ahab, the king of Israel. Jezebel was famous in the scriptures for painting her face with cosmetics and worshipping foreign gods.

St. Audrey was an English abbess who founded a religious sanctuary near London in the 7th century. St. Audrey (traditionally pronounced *Sint Audrey*) is the eponym of *tawdry,* which originally referred to the cheap trinkets bought and sold on her feast day.

Dame Nellie Melba was a 20th century Australian opera diva with a prodigious appetite. She is the eponym of both *Melba toast,* her diet food, and the more decadent *peaches Melba.*

And the adjective *maudlin,* meaning mawkishly sentimental, comes from the New Testament's Mary Magdalene (pronounced *Mogdlin* in Britain), who is often depicted as the weeping and repentant—or maudlin—sinner.

In the fashion category, we find a word inspired by the

19th century American feminist Amelia Jenks Bloomer, a champion of women's dress reform. In the days of huge hoop skirts, Amelia Bloomer advocated simple pantaloons for women. The fashion and her surname generated the word *bloomer,* used in wry reference to women's underwear.

A *delilah* is a seductive, treacherous woman. The eponym of this nickname is the Old Testament Delilah, who betrayed her husband Samson by delivering him, through trickery, into the hands of his Philistine enemies.

A *bloody mary* is a drink, of course, but its eponym is Queen Mary I of England, who, in an effort to restore Roman Catholicism to her homeland, had nearly 300 Protestants executed. Her deeds are reflected in the name of the red cocktail.

To be accused of *woolgathering* is to be chided for day-dreaming or inattention. *Woolgatherers* may also engage in unprofitable employment or trivial hobbies. What exactly is woolgathering, and why does the word carry such a negative connotation?

Wherever sheep are kept, tufts of their wool inevitably become snagged on branches, bushes, thorns, and fenceposts. In centuries past, children were sent out to the pasture to collect scattered bits of wool for the spinning pile.

Meandering from tuft to tuft, and often stopping to play, the young woolgatherers moved aimlessly across the landscape, not accomplishing much of value.

Those who wander and daydream today are metaphorical woolgatherers, chasing tufts of fantasies with no real plan to make much of them. The concept is many centuries old; the *Oxford English Dictionary* lists a citation that appeared in 1553.

When a linguist defines *slang,* she might say that it is informal, nonstandard vocabulary, consisting of words and expressions used to indicate membership in a particular social group. Slang is characterized by how quickly it changes over time.

Writers, philosophers, word lovers, and poets who have used and observed slang throughout the centuries have voiced strong opinions about this casual communication. Some find it creative and invigorating, while others consider it linguistically degenerative.

Among the detractors of slang we find A. P. Herbert, a British politician and writer who said, "American slang is…a nervous disorder. It is St. Vitus's talk. I think of it, reluctantly, as a language which is always taking its trousers off." Ambrose Bierce, in his infamous, stinging lexicon *The Devil's Dictionary,* wrote that slang is "the grunt of the human hog with an audible memory. A means of setting up as a wit without a capital of sense."

But British playwright John Galsworthy was a defender of slang. In 1927 he wrote, "Slang is vigorous and apt. Probably most of our vital words were once slang." In 1959 poet Carl Sandburg wrote admiringly, "Slang is a language that rolls up its sleeves, spits on its hands and goes to work." G. K. Chesterton, a 20th century British novelist, said, "All slang is metaphor, and all metaphor is poetry."

Language has always been a source of wonder for philosophers, scientists, and writers who have mused on its complexities, mysteries, and endless uses. Some consider it a gift or an instinct; others actually view it as an impediment to thought.

In the 4th century B.C., Athenian philosopher Aristotle wrote, "Nature...does nothing without some purpose; and for the purpose of making man a political animal she has endowed him...with the power of reasoned speech."

In a similar vein, Dante wrote in 1304, "To man alone of all existing beings was speech given, because for him alone was it necessary."

In 1871, Charles Darwin, maintained in *The Descent of Man* that "language is an art like brewing or baking....It differs, however, widely from all ordinary arts, for man has an instinctive tendency to speak...whilst no child has an instinctive tendency to brew, bake, or write."

Others have written on the flaws of human language. In 1964, British journalist Arthur Koestler wrote in his book *The Act of Creation,* "Words are a blessing which can turn into a curse. They crystallize thought....they give articulation to vague images....But a crystal is no longer a fluid."

Kahlil Gibran, in the section "On Talking," from *The Prophet,* offers this perspective: "And in much of your talking, thinking is half murdered./For thought is a bird of space, that in a cage of words may indeed unfold its wings but cannot fly."

When Wyoming was admitted into the Union in 1890 as the forty-fourth state, it wasn't the only Wyoming on the map. There were towns called Wyoming in Kentucky, Michigan, and Nebraska, and the name also adorned valleys, streams, and peaks throughout the countryside.

All these uses of the name derived from the original Wyoming in northeastern Pennsylvania. Situated in the traditional homeland of the Delaware Indians, the Wyoming Valley of Pennsylvania borrowed its name from the vocabulary of these indigenous people; it's an anglicization of a Delaware word meaning "at the big plains."

In 1778, Wyoming Valley was the site of a massacre of two hundred American colonists by Tory rangers and their Native American allies. In 1809, British poet Thomas Campbell crafted a long dramatic poem about the Wyoming Valley massacre. Called *Gertrude of Wyoming,* the poem became quite popular with 19th century American readers—so much so that the epic inspired settlers to situate the name *Wyoming* in various places on the American map.

The western Territory of Wyoming was organized in 1869. Its name was suggested to Congress by representative J. M. Ashby of Ohio, who, like many Americans of the day, was acquainted with the famous poem *Gertrude of Wyoming.* Named for a valley over 2,000 miles to the east, Wyoming became a state on July 10, 1890.

You've Come a Long Way, Baby

In 1968, the Philip Morris tobacco company launched a campaign for Virginia Slims, the first cigarette designed for women. Magazine ads for the product, contrived to appeal to young, independent-minded females, featured re-created scenes of women engaged in arduous, early 20th century tasks such as feeding livestock or hanging out the wash, all the while clad in long dresses and tight corsets.

Juxtaposed against each scene of sepia drudgery was a svelte, fashionably dressed model holding a slender Virginia Slims cigarette. Each ad featured the statement, *You've come a long way, baby,* implying that womankind had traveled far on the road to equality and independence.

This is another example of an advertising slogan that achieved catchphrase status. The phrase enjoyed considerable currency in the 1960s and '70s, having successfully "caught" the people's attention through repeated usage. *You've come a long way, baby* was, for several years, a popular way of saying, "You've got a lot of options now, you're free and independent."

The catchphrase even inspired a song and the name of an album collection. In 1979, Loretta Lynn recorded "We've Come a Long Way, Baby," a musical demand for equality and satisfaction in a relationship, and British musician Fatboy Slim released a techno-dance album called *You've Come a Long Way, Baby* in 1998.

ZEPHYR

In the world of the ancient Greeks, the four winds were governed by the gods. Boreas sent icy blasts from the skies of the north. Notus of the south wind swept hot breezes and fog over the Grecian landscape. The god of the east wind was Eurus, whose home was near the palace of the sun.

But the fairest of the wind gods was Zephyr. His mild western breezes always announced fine weather and clear skies. Throughout the ages, poets and writers have invoked Zephyr's name as a metaphor for any soft, gentle breeze. Shakespeare used the word in his 1611 play *Cymbeline,* and in 1807 American writer Washington Irving wrote this about the passing of winter: "The flowers, the zephyrs, and the warblers of spring, return…after their tedious absence."

This wind god's name has also been attached to types of light, soft yarns, fabrics, and garments. In the 19th century, *zephyr shawls* of delicate embroidered cotton were worn in warm weather, and athletes of earlier years donned lightweight *zephyr shirts.*

In March 1949, the god of the west wind was commemorated afresh with the christening of the *California Zephyr,* the ultramodern passenger train that sped between San Francisco and Chicago. Zephyr's divine image was emblemized on the train's promotional materials as a winged figure, streaking through the skies with the west wind behind him.

Zip, Zipper

Though prototypes of the zipper existed in the late 19th century, it wasn't until the early 1920s that the average American had a chance to see and operate one.

Originally known as "hookless fasteners," zippers were introduced to the public by the B. F. Goodrich Company, which used them as a closure device for the 1923 design of their rubber galoshes. A Goodrich executive came up with a new name for the hookless fastener after the *zzzip* sound it made when opening and closing the boot flap. Goodrich, capitalizing on this clever onomatopoeia, marketed the galoshes as "Zipper Boots." The company failed to patent the name, though, so *zipper* remains a generic rather than a trade name for this type of fastener.

The word *zip* has been around a bit longer than *zipper*. It was recorded as early as 1875 as a syllabic imitation of the sound of a bullet passing through the air, or the tearing of cloth.

Then, in about 1900, the word appeared as a slang synonym for vitality, force, or pep, so Americans could talk, for example, about the *zip* in the tempo of a song. About the same time, *zip* turned up as another word for a grade of zero. Some sources speculate that the *z* in both *zip* and *zero* is responsible for the synonymy, but that's only conjecture.

In June 1962, the president appointed an advisory board of the Post Office Department to discuss strategies for remodeling the nation's mail delivery system. In the preceding decades, the country had moved from an agricultural to an industrial economy, and the volume of business mail had increased radically.

By 1963, business correspondence accounted for 80 percent of U.S. mail circulation. Coincidentally, the network of railways, the traditional mail carrying system, was shrinking. There was a need for new postal transportation routes and a strategy to monitor them all. The solution, as outlined by the advisory board, was to assign a five-digit postal code to every address in the country, with each succeeding numeral denoting an increasingly specific area.

The zip code plan was instituted on July 1, 1963—ZIP being the acronym of Zoning Improvement Plan. The architects of this new routing arrangement appropriated the word *zip,* a 19th century verb meaning "to move briskly," and fashioned an acronym out of it. It was cleverly designed to suggest that mail travels quickly from sender to recipient when the new five-digit code was included in the address. The apt acronym was important to the success of the new postal plan; today there is 95 percent compliance with the zip code program.

Bibliography

BOOKS

Ammer, Christine
1989   *Fighting Words.* NTC Publishing Group, Chicago.
1993   *Have A Nice Day—No Problem!: A Dictionary of Clichés.*
        Plume Books, New York.

Ayto, John
1991   *Dictionary of Word Origins.* Arcade, New York.
1994   *A Gourmet's Guide: Food and Drink from A to Z.*
        Oxford University Press, Oxford.
1999   *20th Century Words.* Oxford University Press, Oxford.

Barnhart, Robert K., and Sol Steinmetz, editors
1988   *The Barnhart Dictionary of Etymology.* H. W. Wilson,
        New York.

Bryson, Bill
1995   *Made in America: An Informal History of the English
        Language in the United States,* Vol. 1. William Morrow,
        New York.

Byrne, Josefa Heifetz
1974   *Mrs. Byrne's Dictionary of Unusual, Obscure, and
        Preposterous Words.* University Books, Secaucus, NJ.

Cassidy, Frederick S., Joan H. Hall, et al., editors
1985–   *Dictionary of American Regional English.* 4 vols.,
        continuing. Harvard University Press, Cambridge, MA.

Ciardi, John
1987   *Good Words to You: An All New Dictionary and Native's
        Guide to the Unknown.* HarperCollins, New York.

Claiborne, Robert
1983   *Our Marvelous Native Tongue: The Life and Times of the
        English Language.* Times Books, New York.
1989   *The Roots of English.* Crown Publishing, New York.

Collings, Rex
1993   *A Crash of Rhinoceroses: A Dictionary of Collective Nouns.*
Asphodel Press, Kingston, RI.

Crystal, David
1995   *The Cambridge Encyclopedia of the English Language.*
Cambridge University Press, Oxford.
1993   *An Encyclopedic Dictionary of Language and Languages.*
Blackwell Publishers, Oxford.

Dalzell, Tom
1996   *Flappers 2 Rappers: American Youth Slang.* Merriam-
Webster, Springfield, MA.

Davies, Peter, editor
1983   *Success with Words: A Guide to the American Language.*
Random House, New York.

Dickson, Paul, with Paul McCarthy and Julie Rubenstein, editors
1994   *War Slang: American Fighting Words and Phrases from the
Civil War to the Gulf War.* Simon and Schuster, New
York.

Dunn, Mark
2005   *Zounds! A Browsers Dictionary of Interjections.* St. Martin's
Press, New York.

Farkas, Anna
2002   *The Oxford Dictionary of Catchphrases.* Oxford
University Press, New York.

Flavell, Linda and Roger
2000   *The Chronology of Words and Phrases: A Thousand Years in
the History of English.* Kyle Cathie, London.

Flexner, Stuart Berg
1982   *Listening to America.* Simon and Schuster, New York.

Flexner, Stuart Berg, and Anne H. Soukhanov
1997   *Speaking Freely: A Guided Tour of American English from
Plymouth Rock to Silicon Valley.* Oxford University Press,
New York.

Freeman, Morton S., and Edwin Newman
1993   *Hue and Cry and Humble Pie: The Stories Behind the Words.*
        Plume Books, New York.

Funk, Charles Earle
1985   *A Hog on Ice and Other Curious Expressions.*
        HarperColllins, New York.
1985   *Thereby Hangs a Tale: Stories of Curious Word Origins.*
        HarperCollins, New York.
1986   *Heavens to Betsy! and Other Curious Sayings.* Perennial
        Library, New York.

Funk, Wilfred
1978   *Word Origins and Their Romantic Stories.* Bell Publishing,
        New York.

Gelbert, Doug
1996   *So Who the Heck Was Oscar Mayer? The Real People Behind
        Those Brand Names.* Barricade Books, New York.

Goldin, Hyman E., editor
1950   *Dictionary of American Underground Lingo.* Twayne, New
        York.

Grimal, Pierre, and Stephen Kershaw
1991   *The Penguin Dictionary of Classical Mythology.* Penguin
        Books, London.

Hanks, Patrick, and Flavia Hodges
1989   *A Dictionary of Surnames.* Oxford University Press,
        Oxford.

Hendrickson, Robert
1987   *The Facts on File Encyclopedia of Word and Phrase Origins.*
        Facts on File, New York. Republished as *Henry
        Encyclopedia of Word and Phrase Origins.* Holt, New York,
        1990.

Hirsch, E. D., Jr., Joseph F. Kett, and James Trefil
1988   *The Dictionary of Cultural Literacy.* Houghton Mifflin,
        Boston.

Kacirk, Jeffrey
2000   *The Word Museum: The Most Remarkable English Words Ever Forgotten.* Touchstone Books, New York.

Kohl, Herbert
1992   *From Archetype to Zeitgeist: An Essential Guide to Powerful Ideas.* Little, Brown, Boston.

Landau, Sidney I.
2001   *Dictionaries: The Art and Craft of Lexicography.* Cambridge University Press, New York.

Lighter, Jonathan E., J. Ball, J. O'Connor, and Jesse Sheidlower, editors
1994-97 *Random House Historical Dictionary of American Slang.* 2 vols. Random House, New York.

McCrum, Robert, Robert MacNeil, and William Cran
1986   *The Story of English.* Viking, New York.

McQuain, Jeffrey
1999   *Never Enough Words: How Americans Invented a Language as Ingenious, Ornery and Resourceful as Themselves.* Random House, New York.

McQuain, Jeffery, and Stanley Malless
1998   *Coined by Shakespeare: Words and Meanings First Penned by the Bard.* Merriam-Webster, Springfield, MA.

Merriam-Webster
1989   *Webster's Word Histories.* Merriam-Webster, Springfield, MA.

Mills, Jane
1992   *Womanwords: A Dictionary of Words About Women.* Free Press, New York.

Morris, Evan
2000   *The Word Detective: Solving the Mysteries behind those Pesky Words and Phrases.* Algonquin Books. Chapel Hill, NC.

Morris, William, and Mary D. Morris

1988   *Morris Dictionary of Word and Phrase Origins,* 2d edition. HarperInformation, New York.

Palmatier, Robert A., and Harold L. Ray, editors

1989   *Sports Talk: A Dictionary of Sports Metaphors.* Greenwood, Westport, CT.

Panati, Charles

1989   *Panati's Extraordianry Origins of Everyday Things.* HarperCollins, New York.

Randall, Bernice

1991   *When Is a Pig a Hog? A Guide to Confoundingly Related English Words.* Prentice Hall, New York.

Rawson, Hugh

1981   *A Dictionary of Euphemisms and Other Double Talk.* Crown Publishing Group, New York.

1989   *Wicked Words.* Crown Publishing Group, New York.

Rees, Nigel

1999   *The Cassell Dictionary of Word and Phrase Origins.* Cassell, London.

Rheingold, Howard

1988   *They Have a Word for It: A Lighthearted Lexicon of Untranslatable Words and Phrases.* Jeremy P. Tarcher, Los Angeles.

Rogers, James

1985   *The Dictionary of Cliches.* Facts on File, New York.

Simpson, John, and Edmund Weiner, editors

1989   *The Oxford English Dictionary,* 2d edition. Oxford University Press, Oxford.

Sorel, Nancy Caldwell

1970   *Word People.* American Heritage Press, New York.

Soukhanov, Anne H.

1995   *Word Watch: The Stories Behind the Words of Our Lives.* Henry Holt, New York.

Sperling, Susan Kelz
1982   *Tenderfeet and Ladyfingers.* Penguin Books, New York.

Tuleja, Tad
1990   *Marvelous Monikers: The People Behind More Than 400 Words and Expressions.* Harmony Books, New York.

Urdang, Laurence
1989   *The Dictionary of Confusable Words.* Ballantine Books, New York.

Webber, Elizabeth, and Mike Feinsilber
1999   *Merriam-Webster's Dictionary of Allusions.* Merriam-Webster, Springfield, MA.

Wells, Diana
2001   *100 Birds and How They Got Their Names.* Algonquin Books, Chapel Hill, NC.

Wentworth, Harold, and S. B. Flexner, editors
1960   *Dictionary of American Slang.* Thomas Y. Crowell, New York.

White, Robert J.
1994   *An Avalanche of Anoraks: For People Who Speak Foreign Languages Every Day—Whether They Know It Or Not.* Crown Publishing, New York.

Winchester, Simon
1998   *The Professor and the Madman: A Tale of Murder, Insanity, and the Making of the Oxford English Dictionary.* HarperCollins, New York.

INTERNET RESOURCES

Chiasmus.com. www.chiasmus.com
Double-Tongued Word Wrester. www.doubletongued.org
Native Word of the Day. www.knba.org
The Phrase Finder. www.phrases.org.uk
The Word Detective. www.word-detective.com
Wordspy. www.wordspy.com
World Wide Words. www.worldwidewords.org

Index